One Life, Mine

Emma S. Garrod

Emma S. Garrod

One Life, Mine

Emma S. Garrod

ILLUSTRATIONS

ANCESTORS

Writing the story of one's life, no matter how unimportant that life has been, seems to be the thing to do when you become a senior citizen. So that is what I am setting out to do. Someday my grandchildren or great-grandchildren may find pleasure or amusement in reading this.

My birth date is November 23, 1882. As far as I know, my birthplace was a flat at Fourth and Brannen streets in San Francisco, California, upstairs over a saloon.

My parents were both German. Father was Ferdinand Stolte, a native of Bremen, born November 13, 1847. He had two more names, August and Otto, but used only the initial *F*. His father was Wilhelm Stolte, and his mother's maiden name was Charlotte Muller. Wilhelm Stolte was a cigar manufacturer with a factory in Bremen; later, the factory and family were moved to Bremen Haven. There were six children, five boys and one girl. Of these, Ferdinand was the eldest. At about fourteen years of age, having finished grammar school, he left home to become a cabin boy on a sailing ship. *Tales of the Sea* by F. Stolte tells about his life as a sailor.

The second son was Carl, of whom I know nothing except that he and Ferdinand did not get along together.

Next was Louis, apparently the favorite of the brothers. Perhaps the fact that he died in his twenty-first year while serving his time in the newly established military service had something to do with the kindly recollections. Anyway, it was in memory of him that I was given my second name, Louisa.

After Louis came Eugene. He went into the cigar business with his father, married a girl named Minna, and had three children: Lotte, Louis, and Emilia. Louis died after the end of World War I; he accidently shot himself with an American gun he was examining. Lotte married (the husband's name I do not know), and she died leaving one or two children. What became of Emilia, I do not know.

The last son was Wilhelm. He as a youth went to an uncle, Eugene Stolte, whose wife was named Josephine. This uncle owned a silk dyeing works in the city of Creffield. There Wilhelm learned the silk dyeing trade. They handled the raw silk as it came from China or Japan in the skeins made as the floss was unwound from the cocoons. When Wilhelm came to America, there was no work for him in that line, so he became a bartender. He never married.

The last of the children was a little girl, Emilia. She lived at home until she became engaged to marry Henry Spiering.

Mother, Anna Franziska Peters, was a native of a small city in northern Germany, Uekermunde. Her birth date is May 16, 1858. She was a kind and gentle person, tall and slender with blue eyes and beautiful brown hair.

Her father was Christian Friedrick Peters, born on November 1, 1812, a native of Wolin, an island in the Baltic Sea just off the coast of Poland. Her mother, also a native of Wolin, was Friederika Johanna Weichbrod, born May 29, 1813.

The story—as I learned it from my second cousin Ingaborg Hempel, who lives and is a high school supervisor in West Berlin, Germany, and with whom I correspond—is this: a widow in Ueckermunde had inherited a coppersmith shop from her late husband. My grandfather C. F. Peters was engaged to manage this shop. After some time, he married the widow; and a daughter, Paulena, was born.

Now this I believe but have no proof of that the widow's name was Dettmann and that she had a son, Louis. There is no other way to account for Uncle Louie Dettmann. Mother always spoke of him as her brother. Paulena's mother died while she was still a baby, and C. F. Peters married Johanna Weichbrod.

There were five children from this marriage, three girls and two boys. The first child, Emma, for whom I am named, was handicapped—whether from birth or illness I do not know. She was unable to walk but became an excellent needlewoman and supported herself that way.

Eda, the second child, married Fritz Hempel. They had one child, a son named Fritz after his father. This Fritz was a flutist in Kaiser Wilhelm's Orchestra at the time of World War I. His wife was Helena. They had one child, the teacher in West Berlin, Ingaberg.

Then there were two sons, Albert, who became a sailor and was lost in the Arctic waters, and Julius, a coppersmith like his father. Both were bachelors.

The third girl, Anna, was my mother. Her mother died when she was seventeen; soon after her mother's death, she and Julius set out for San Francisco by way of Panama, I think; they traveled by steamer. I know they crossed the Isthmus of Panama by train. I remember her telling how she was surprised when a very black porter on the train spoke to her in German.

To return to the story of Johanna Weichbrod as told by Eda Peters Hempel to her granddaughter Ingaborg:

The Weichbrod family came from the Estate Wartow, Wartoff on the Baltic Sea Island, Wolin. They go back many generations to somewhere in the fifteenth century. The Weichbrods are descendants of Polish Woiwods. The title Woiwod is equivalent to a German duke or Heroz.

In Poland, these Woiwods were electoral dukes, "princely electors," who became commanders of the army during the fifteenth century. The former kingdom of Poland was divided into districts or Woiwodships, of which the Woiwods or dukes were governors. One can also say that the Woiwods were senators, for they had seats and the right to vote in the senate. The term "Woiwod" was also used in Russian Poland until the Revolution, World War II. Then it became "government" or district.

When Johanna Weichbrod informed her people of her marriage intentions, a pear tree growing on the Estate Wartow was felled and rafted or floated across an arm of the Baltic Sea to Ueckermunde; there it was made into a beautiful Biedermeir (English, Victorian style) wardrobe or hope chest for the bride's trousseau. Her granddaughter, Ingaborg Hempel, still has this chest in everyday use.

The home in Ueckermunde has long since passed into the hands of the Russians.

To balance the history of Mother's ancestors, Father often stated that his mother could claim relationship to the family of Queen Victoria, that her father's mother was Victoria Mary Louisa, daughter of Francis, Duke of Saxe-Coburg Saalfeld.

COMING TO AMERICA

Anna and Julius Peters came to San Francisco because Louis Dettmann and Paulena Peters had made the venture some years earlier and were established there. Louis was partner in Henry Sanders's coppersmith shop at First and Mission and Paulena married a seafaring man, August Juds, also German. Julius was immediately given employment in Sanders's shop. Anna worked as maid in several different households. I remember her speaking of the Spinneys. They lived on Larkin, near Washington, which was way out with no paved streets nor sidewalks and sand dunes all around. The Sanders family also lived in this neighborhood. Anna and the Sanders's daughter Johanna, later Mrs. Adolph Blaich, became lifelong friends.

At this time, Ferdinand Stolte decided to give up the long sea voyages he had been making and go into the lumber and produce-hauling business on the Pacific Coast with headquarters in San Francisco. When he made this decision, he also decided to apply for citizenship in the United States of America. So on August 28, 1876, he appeared before Judge Lonzo Sawyer in the Circuit Court of the United States, for the District of California; there he renounced his allegiance to the Emperor of Germany and by order of the court was declared to be a citizen of the United States of America.

Among his San Francisco acquaintances was August Juds. While visiting in the Juds's home, he met Paulena's newly arrived sister, Anna. They were married on August 12, 1879, by the Lutheran minister, Pastor Fuendeling.

About this time, the West Coast suffered a depression. Shipping and all other businesses suffered hard times, so Ferdinand sold his interest in the schooner and invested his money in a saloon at Fourth and Townsend. Just before their marriage, he sent money home to bring his brother Eugene and his wife to America. Imagine his surprise when upon arrival, they turned out to be his youngest brother Wilhelm, his sister Emilia, and her fiancé, Henry Spiering. He wasn't pleased, but there they were, and he could not send them back. Henry and Emilia soon married; the two men found employment and took care of themselves from then on; following the line of least resistance, they both worked as bartenders. Wilhelm, whose name was soon Americanized to William and was usually called Billy, died a bachelor.

After some years, Henry owned his own business. He called the place "The Odeon Brother in Law." It was in the Wholesale District on Front Street. The Spierings had two sons, Henry Emile and Fredrick August. Henry became a druggist, married, and had one son, James. I believe James and his family are somewhere in the Bay Region. Henry died during the 1918 flu epidemic, a few days after being drafted. Fred was a salesman and a very fine amateur photographer. He too married but had no children. He died some years ago.

Paulena Peters Juds died about 1881, leaving a son, Gus, a daughter, Pauline, and a baby boy who soon followed his mother. Uncle Gus, like F. Stolte, left the sea and for many years was a warehouse man for one of the railroads. He placed his little daughter in care of a group of nuns; the boy stayed with his father. As Pauline grew up and needed to support herself, she did dressmaking for some very wealthy ladies, so much of her work was with silks, satins, and velvets. When her father reached retirement age, he whiled away the time piecing quilts from the odds and bits of material his daughter had accumulated. Uncle Gus was a big man, six feet plus and big in all proportions. How he set those tiny stitches or managed that little bit of a needle with his outsized fingers was always a mystery to me. I learned of Pauline's death many years ago. Whether her brother Gus is still living, I doubt.

Uncle Louis Dettmann married a girl named Meta from Santa Rosa or near there. I think the family was Swiss, and the name was Sutter. They had a son, Fritz, who for many years was in the lumber business in San Francisco. Fritz had an only daughter, who, by last report, was married and lived in Santa Rosa.

My sister Charlotte Johanna joined the family on June 16, 1880, and I came along on November 23, 1882. At that time, the family lived in a flat over a saloon at Fourth and Brannen. At about three months, I caught the whooping cough and for months on end that's all I did, whoop. I must have been a sorry little specimen.

A Home In The Mountains

Sometime during those years, Uncle Julius had left the city and for a time worked in the Napa County wineries, going there, I think, to set up stills which had been built in the Sanders and Dettman shop. How he found his way into the Santa Cruz Mountains, I don't know, but knowing that part of the country through him my father purchased 160 acres of land from a Mr. Birce in 1881. At first, he did nothing with this place. It was leased or rented or maybe the Averys just lived there. There wasn't much farming done. For that matter, there wasn't much to do. There was some orchard and a tiny, mixed-up vineyard.

As I visualize the old orchard now, (which was then a new orchard just coming into bearing), there were 25 cherries, 2 Royal Annes, 2 pie cherries, and the rest Black Tartarians; 3 figs, a white Smyrna, and 2 that bore delicious brown fruit, sometimes almost as big as teacups; 10 or 12 Bartlett pears, 2 Winter Nellis, and 2 Easter Bury, a late winter pear; 2 English walnuts and 2 California walnuts; 1 Royal Apricot and a variety of plums, 1 egg plum, 2 greengage, 2 Equit, 6 damsons; a dozen peaches, of which a few were early strawberry and the rest Crawfords. There were at least 40 almonds and 60 or more apples. Among the apples were Skinner Seedling, Newton Pippens, Belle Flowers, Spitzenburg, Pearmaine, and Greening and also 150 or so French prunes. As these trees were all set 20 feet apart or 100 to an acre, it comes out about 3 acres of orchard, and about 1/4 acre of vineyard made up of Sweetwater, Muscat, Malvoise, and Rose of Peru.

The summer or fall of 1883 when Mother despaired of getting me over whooping cough and her neighbors told her she might as well stop trying. The folks decided to try a change of climate and came to spend some weeks at the Lexington Hotel located about three miles south of Los Gatos; before the coming of the railroad, it had been a stage stop on the way to Santa Cruz. They rented a horse and buggy and drove about the hills every day. I doubt if Father had ever driven a horse before then.

The story is that the first sign of life or interest I showed was one day when they had stopped at the Rouse place on the Black Road. I raised my head from the pillow on which Mother carried me and smiled at an old hen and her chicks scratching in Mrs. Rouse's flowers. That stay in the mountains ended my whooping cough.

The next summer, we returned to the mountains and spent several weeks in a little house known as Strong's Cabin, in a field near Grizzly Rock, several miles beyond Father's property. Later that year, 1884, Father sold his interest in the saloon and early in December, the Stolte family moved to a house in the Santa Cruz Mountains at the upper end of Black Road.

Of the actual moving, I remember nothing, but have been told that sixteen-year-old Jimmie Newell, with his team and wagon, helped to bring our household goods from the railroad station to the ranch.

I can recall the house and the barn on the western slope somewhat below the road. The house was a small, low building against a dug bank. The roof's edge was so near the top of the bank that some hounds of Avery's would jump onto the roof and sleep there. The yard was a pretty spot with four big black oak trees nicely spaced around the outer edge. To one side of the house was a barrel to which the water was pumped by a ram from a spring farther down the hill. There was a lilac tree beside the barrel, and a pear tree nearby, with many oaks, madrones, and laurels growing wild roundabout. The barn was a short distance south of the house in no better repair.

I have a faint memory of a man Fred Beam and his brother Pete who owned the land just beyond us. Pete had a peg leg and no longer teamed, but Fred hauled wood which had been cut on their place to Mountain View where they lived. Each load meant a two-day trip, so Fred Beam arranged to spend the night at our place.

Early in the morning when he went to the barn to feed and care for his four horses, I would follow him. Then to keep me from under the horses' feet, he would pick me up and put me in the manger in front of a big boy named John. John was a gentle creature, and I grew very fond of him. He had some funny little curls just in front of his ears, and Mr. Beam told me that someday he would grow horns like a cow. After all these years, I have never seen a horse with horns. After his chores were done, Mr. Beam would pick me out of the hay and carry me back to the house for breakfast.

Barns And Animals

During 1885, Father and Uncle Julius tore down the old barn and built a new one all shipshape and foursquare to the wind. Now, in 1963, part of it still stands but looks sadly weather beaten. The barn was a split-level building. The upper part level with the yard was designed to store the year's supply of hay; there were covered hatches in the floor down which the hay was pushed into racks over the mangers. There was also space here for the wagons and storage room for seed grain, chicken feed, etc.

In the lower part, there were planked stalls for four horses, storage room for milled feed, such as crushed barley for the horses, bran for the cows, and middlings for the pigs. Plows, harrows, cultivators, all small horse-drawn tools were housed here during the winter.

At convenient points were hooks for hanging the harnesses and saddles. These hooks were cut from trees where the trunk and branch made a suitable angle. These hooks were spiked securely to the studding and other supporting posts. On the south side but connected to the stable by a covered walkway, they built a cow barn with stalls for eight cows, a pen for the pigs, and two more pens for any calves that happened to be around. The loft for the cow's feed, hay, and some year's cornstalks, also a chopper to cut up those cornstalks was overhead. This could be reached by scrambling up over the cows' heads from the mangers or across the covered walkway from the main barn.

At first, each cow had a tie rope fastened to the manger with a slip loop at the free end to drop over the cows' horns. Later, Father put in toggle chains, Y-shaped affairs with the tail fast to the front of the manger, and the free ends snapped around the cow's neck. These gave the cows more freedom but were more difficult to put in place as you had to put your arms around the cow's neck to do so.

The main barn was built from first-grade redwood lumber. Any usable material from the old barn went into the cow barn; the roofs were covered with split shakes, also redwood, thin sheets 3 ft x 6 in x 1/4 in. When the buildings were finished, they built a corral using the east side of the buildings for one side and redwood pickets for fencing the rest with a gate to the yard, a door into the walkway from which both horse and cow stalls could be reached or straight through to another door which opened into the back pasture known as the gulch. There was also a set of bars leading into the orchard. So they had a secure and sheltered place for the animals when they were not tied in their stalls. They also built a tidy little chicken house off by itself.

A team of horses came with the place, a buckskin called "Jack," gentle, lazy, and sometimes balky and a little gray mare named Mattie, the first horse I ever rode. Next, Father bought a matched pair of bay mares, Emma and Cora. Cora came to grief the first summer. She had been tied out to feed on a hillside, became entangled in the rope, and died of a broken neck. Emma was around for years. Father always specified which when speaking of either Emma, by saying Emma Horse or Emma Girl. An old brown cow also came with the place. She was known as Mother Boss. Father bought some young cows from a neighbor, Ed Richardson, which I remember as Brownie, Paulie, Feddie, and Reddie. These cows were of the Devon breed which had originated in Devonshire, England; a smooth, reddish brown in color with a showing of white on their bellies and udders, and perhaps a white heart or star on their foreheads and horns of medium length. Quiet and easy to handle, of mixed value, they were sought for both meat and milk.

THE HOUSE

With the animals all taken care of, the family spent the winter in the old house. By spring the plans for a new house were in order, and the actual work of building began.

First, the basement or cellar was excavated by hand with picks, shovels, and wheelbarrow. I think both Father's brother William and Mother's brother Julius were there at the time and helped with the work. This cellar extended under the entire front of the house with a smaller section maybe twelve or fifteen feet square to one side under what became the kitchen and back porch. The whole excavation was lined with sandstone, gathered from the place and held in place by a mortar made of lime and sand. A French stone mason living nearby was employed to do the rock work. The open side of this structure was closed with a freestanding stone wall with two doors and two windows and high enough so as to form a level surface all the way round for the sills of the house to set on.

As the house took shape, the front faced the southeast and looked toward the almond and apple orchard. Across the front was an open porch about six feet wide. Here, the front door led directly into the living room about fifteen feet square with a bedroom off either side. The right hand room about fifteen by twelve feet had a window in each outer wall but had no closet. The left-hand bedroom overlooking the yard also had a window in each outer wall and was about the size of the other but lost space because of a stairway to reach the attic. But it did have a fair-sized closet using the space under the stairs. This was always Mother's and Father's bedroom.

Coming into the front room from the porch, you found the door was in the right-hand corner of the room with a window in the center of what was the rest of that wall. In the center of each side wall were the doors to the bedrooms. Diagonally across the room at the left-hand corner of the last wall was the door into the rest of the house. Most of the rest of that wall was taken up by a sandstone fireplace. Three blocks of stone formed an arch over the fireplace with the date 1886 cut into the keystone. There was a wooden mantle and some wood trim on the front and at each side were small closets, the left hand one used to store guns and ammunition, and the other for books.

From the living or front room you entered the kitchen-dining room, perhaps twelve by eighteen feet. At the northeast end of this room was a small bedroom not more than ten by twelve feet with a window and a small corner closet. In the dining room, there were two windows in the outside wall and directly under the windows a bench, a sort of locker-type affair divided into three parts, one used to store newspapers, etc.; the middle one for potatoes, and the last one for toys and most anything you could cram into it. In the corner beyond the windows was a floor-to-ceiling storage place for dishes and supplies. Directly behind the living room fireplace stood the stove with the chimney leading into the stone chimney of the fireplace. The cookstove and the fireplace furnished the heat for the whole house. Sometimes the corners felt pretty cold.

The attic stairway at first was in the dining room, but a wall was moved making the dining room-kitchen a little smaller, while the stairway and the sink located in the opposite corner found themselves in a closed-in portion of the back porch which became a small separate kitchen with water piped in.

The walls of the rooms were nine feet high, the lower half covered with four-inch-wide tongue and groove beaded redwood topped by a neat little molding just wide enough to set small things on; only you weren't supposed to. The ceilings too were covered with the tongue and groove redwood. The upper half of the walls was wallpaper.

The whole house was built of good clear redwood except the floors which were six-inch tongue and groove pine. All this lumber was shipped from San Francisco. This included shingles for the roof. I think the invoice totaled about $400.

The stairs led up to an unfinished attic. Most of it had a good pine floor, and the roof was shaped like a short stemmed *T*. It was under the stem of the *T* with one window facing northwest that the rafters were covered with cloth which in turn was covered with wallpaper. The side walls closing off the last bit of the rafters were only about three feet high, and there was also a closet and a wall closing off the rest of the attic. There we girls had our bedroom. The rest of the attic was used for dry storage. Before winter set in several barrels of flour (four fifty-pound sacks made a barrel), several one-hundred-pound sacks of sugar, pink or bayo beans, some sacks of onions, and home-dried prunes, raisins, apples, and figs were all stored there. Several boxes of yellow laundry soap were also included. Empty fruit jars and cans, in fact anything that needed to be kept dry, went up those stairs.

Once, some friends who were moving from Los Gatos to San Francisco gave us a great collection of *The Youth's Companion* that went back for years. They too were stored near an east window. So when I couldn't be found doing whatever I had been told to do, I was sure to be in the attic lost in a story.

The smaller part of the excavation or cellar became the milk cellar where we set the fresh milk in shallow pans for the cream to rise so it could be skimmed off next day and when enough was collected made into butter. The fresh eggs, as they were brought from the barn, were also kept here as well as anything that was preserved, canned, jellied, or pickled.

Most of the fruit, cherries, peaches, pears, and tomatoes, dozens of quarts of each, were cooked by the open kettle method and then since glass jars, although available were expensive, quart-size tin cans were used for storage. These cans were equipped with a flange into which a neat tin cover fitted; to seal them a resinous red substance known as "sealing wax" was heated to pouring consistency and carefully poured into place, after being sure no moisture remained on the flange to cause air bubbles. When the cans were to be opened, a sharp tool was needed to scrape away the wax. We had a funny old can opener which did the trick nicely. All traces of the wax had to be removed. It didn't taste good before emptying the contents of the can.

Meats, both salted beef and pork as well as smoked hams, bacon, and sausages, also sauerkraut and salt-cured beans, were kept in the darkest, coolest part of the main cellar. To reach these storage places, there was another steep stairway from the back porch to the yard. So there was a continual hurrying either up or down stairs for whatever supplies were needed in the kitchen. The lumber from the old house was used to build a woodshed, a workshop, and a bunk room for any out of the family working man who stayed with us. The workshop was equipped with a bench or counter for woodworking, and another known as the file bench for metalwork with corresponding tools on or near their designated places. There was also a portable forge and anvil.

Beyond the far end of this building was an outhouse or privy. There again, it was a matter of down and up those back stairs.

Altogether, our home was secure and reasonably comfortable, compact, and unhandy as any ship that ever sailed; the only difference was that it was firmly anchored to the mountains. In his youth, my father went "up aloft or below." I spent mine going "up attic or down cellar."

The excavation of the cellars resulted in two bits of level ground confined by stone walls and lath fences; the one in front of the house was Mother's flower garden. There grew a lovely pink duchess rose and a snow-white La Mark, and the lilac tree, and also violets, wallflowers, velvet pinks, etc. The back piece was intended for a vegetable patch, but the shortage of water defeated that.

Along with the other masonry work, they built a reservoir for water well above the house so the water would come to the house and yard by gravity. When finished, it was six by six by six with a nice smooth cement lining and a neat gable roof to cover. The rock and cement work was all underground. There was always water in the spring below the house. Getting it up the hill was the problem. Over the years, Father went from the ram, to a ship pump, to a gas engine. All these devices presented difficulties. Therefore, water was a very precious commodity and never ever wasted. Faucets were not allowed to drip, and two pans of water never used if one could possibly be made do.

For light after night had fallen, there were candles, lamps, and lanterns. The lamps were of various shapes and sizes. All had a bowl for kerosene or "coal oil" as we knew it then. This bowl was topped by a screw-on burner, fitted with a wick to suck the oil up to the flame and a glass chimney to protect it from drafts and also to diffuse the light. There was a hanging lamp in the living room decorated with glass prisms which threw off rainbows when the sun touched them in the daytime. Footed lamps were in the dining room and bedrooms, and one in a bracket with a reflector behind it was on the kitchen wall over the sink. In the milk cellar there was a candle, and candles were used to move about the house; it was considered too dangerous to trot around with an oil lamp.

Lanterns were used outdoors or in the barn. Sometimes one was tied to a vehicle to give light and warning when on the road at night. Lanterns were metal except for the glass chimney which was covered by a metal hood so wind and rain could not put out the flame. They were carried by a wire handle or bail and could easily be hung up. Both lamps and lanterns had to be filled, if not daily, at least often the wicks trimmed and the chimneys washed and polished. Later, when I reached teen age and the responsibility was mine, I got many a scolding for not attending to them in the morning as I should have.

Coal oil was purchased from the grocer in square five-gallon cans with a permanent spout in one corner of the top. Two cans came in a wooden box.

While all this building was going on, the general farmwork was also taken care of. The young trees were just coming into bearing. I learned about prunes the first summer. I can still see us: Mother, Father, sister Lotte, never called by her whole name Charlotte, and myself walking up the lane, the short bit of roadway from the yard to the public road, on our way to the prune orchard; Mother carrying a pillow in a snow-white slip, for me, the baby, to sleep on while the others picked up prunes. At that moment I was not sleepy but told Mother I wanted to find "eine schone grosse" one big one. Later they found me fast asleep on the ground in the sunshine, a prune in each hand. Mother never again carried a pillow to work for me to sleep on, though I've had many a stolen nap cuddled down on the ground out of everybody's way.

The Stolte House, Built in 1886

The cherries and peaches too are good to remember. The first cherries hung high on the supple branches of the young trees. As Father bent the

older than Lotte and I. Our family visited them quite regularly, and Josephine and Emile were the first children I remember playing with.

There were other French, Italian, and Swiss people in that neighborhood. Their plantings were mostly grapes. Each farm had its own wine cellar, and every household its clay or stone oven, in which a fifty-pound sack of flour was turned into round loaves of bread at one baking. It was good bread and never seemed to get dry or stale.

These people brought other old country customs with them, too. For instance, one Sunday afternoon Leon Baile, Mrs. Bernard's handsome young brother who had come to America some years before, came to tell my parents goodbye as he was leaving for France in a day or two, since his father had written that he had found a suitable wife for Leon and he should return home at once and be married. So he did. She was not only suitable but a charming young lady. They spent a long and I think a happy life together and reared two daughters.

The Lottis were from Italy, several families, all cousins. The girls were beautiful with dark eyes, black hair, and olive complexions. Romanizinis were Swiss and Todts from Alsace-Lorraine.

Down the Black Road were the Olaves from Chile and the Beggs from Pennsylvania. Both these families had numerous children. Bill Chilcote, alone, and the Newells, a jolly Irish family with six children were also neighbors. Over the years, the Newells were our closest friends. There were Thomsons, Bakers, Raymonds, Rouses, and others.

Along the summit to the south about two miles away were our nearest neighbors, the Minis, with two sons Joseph and Johnny from Bohemia, and the Gists, Pennsylvanians with two older daughters Lucy and Addie. Nickels and Sharps and an assortment of single men were also in the area. Way over on the Bear Creek Road lived the Van Lones, Hoffmans, String-fellows, and Mallots. On the ridge beyond the Richardsons near Grizzly Rock was the Nickerson family: a son, Stillman, and a daughter, Mandy, whom I loved dearly. Their home was a story and a half house, built entirely of hand split redwood.

It seems the Nickersons were part of a group of Mormons from Utah who had come to California after the Civil War. There were three families which had broken away from the main group and come to the Santa Cruz Mountains intending to raise race horses.

The land between our place and Minis was known as the Senter Place. A little house by a big maple tree near a spring and a few black raspberry bushes were all that remained of their stay. The other family whose name was Brown were said to have been the leaders of the three. They had settled on the Bear Creek Road just inside the Santa Cruz County Line, giving their name to the Brown School district, which functioned for fifty years or more. The Browns had moved away, so we never knew them.

A country road

The Nickersons left the mountains shortly after we came there, but many years later I found Mandy again. She was sister-in-law to my sister-in-law. They had married Pfeffer brothers.

An amazing piece of work done by these early settlers was fence building. A man would locate a corner stake of the piece of land he was taking up and set out to build a fence along the survey line of that forty—or eighty-acre piece. Most of these fences were built of six-foot redwood pickets set on about twelve-inch centers. You could follow these fences by sight on and on, uphill and down. If you lost one because of brush or deep gulches way off in the distance, you could pick it up again where someone else was following the same line. To this day, small sections of these line fences still exist.

WOODCHOPPERS

At this time, there was much wood being cut in the mountains, some to clear the land for farm plantings, some just for the money that might be gained from its sale. This was called stumpage. The roots and small trees were left in place, trusting to nature to grow another crop. It usually did in ten or fifteen years. This cutting was done either by the landowners themselves or by men paid to do so, known as woodchoppers.

There were two types of woodcut, one for household use, known as stovewood, usually hardwood; the various oaks, madrone, laurel, etc., cut into fourteen or sixteen in lengths and split into convenient sizes for the average kitchen cookstove, usually about three by three inches. The other type was cut in four-foot lengths and only split down to a size a man could handle easily. This was fourfoot or cordwood, mostly oak or Douglas fir, known as pine. It was sold to commercial furnaces in the valley. Stovewood was the most expensive to have cut. It was often paid for by the tier and measured three tier to a cord. Cordwood was always cut and sold by the cord with pine the cheapest, being the easiest to work. Tanbark was another money crop, taken from the virgin forest. The tan oaks grew mostly in the deeper canyons, and men would buy just the bark, felling the trees in the spring when the sap was flowing freely, stripping off the bark in four-foot lengths, and leaving cords upon cords of good hardwood to go to waste. The bark was brought up out of the canyons by donkey pack trains, to some roadway where wagons could be loaded to haul it to tanneries.

The woodchoppers were a class by themselves: older men who had seen better days, invariably single or at least alone. A woodchopper with a wife was seldom heard of. Mostly they lived each man by himself, way off in the woods in a carelessly built cabin near water. He might have to climb up and down for a mile or more to the spot where he was working and carry all his groceries and other things in on his shoulders. But there was one thing he did not have to do. He did not have to pack water—that seemed very important, although he certainly used very little of it!

Those who didn't drink to excess when they succeeded in gaining possession of a gallon or two of wine or an occasional bottle of whiskey were most likely somewhat unbalanced mentally.

One that stands out in my memory was Peter O'Shaunessey ("Crazy Pete"), an Irishman, tall and well-built, of amazing strength, with piercing black eyes, a high-bridged nose, and coal black hair and beard—always too long and uncombed. He went unbathed too, his clothing always in rags and oh-so-dirty. The way he lived and what he cooked in his tumble-down shanty was beyond description. And his mind was full of vagaries and fancies.

Pete worked for Father for years clearing land and cutting cordwood. He had two imaginary associates, the Little One who was good and the Big One who was bad. Sometimes he would cut down a big pine, four or five feet in diameter and then go home and not touch it again for weeks. If asked about it, he would explain that the Big One had been there and put knots in it and made it too hard.

Then would come a day when his ax and saw could be heard hard at work. Pete would explain then that last night the Little One had jumped over it, and now it was easy to cut.

In the spring, he would plant little gardens here and there in the woods. When some cow came by and ate his vegetables it was all right; "the good Lord had told her to."

Even though his mind wasn't right, Pete could figure. He always knew how much he owed for supplies and how much he had coming for work done. He also knew how to put short odds and ends and unwieldy chunks of wood at the bottom of his ranks of cordwood or build his wood right over a carefully hidden stump, so it wouldn't show when Father measured the wood to settle accounts.

When he had a few dollars in his pocket, he went to town and gambled at cards, and there were always fellows around ready to draw him into a game and later brag about cheating him.

Finally, he left us to take a job some miles distant. He came to the house to say goodbye, explaining that it was hard to leave your own people, and we were all the family he had, but the good Lord wanted him to, so go he must. Some people at the new location were afraid of him and eventually had him committed to the Agnew Insane Asylum where he met death the morning of the 1906 earthquake.

There were two Germans, Carl Emersleben, the son of a German professor, with a wonderful education, gentlemanly manners, and an unmanageable taste for alcohol. His partner was Wilhelm Freitag ("Friday"), a misplaced weaver, a nice old man, but also given to drink. These two were always together working for a while and drifting off to some other job and drifting back again.

Teamsters

The men who hauled the wood, "Teamsters," were young, just getting out on their own, venturesome, and trying to establish themselves in the world. Mostly they owned their horses and wagons. Some were proud of their teams and treated them well; others, I am sorry to say, underfed, overloaded, and abused their animals and should never have owned them.

Some had just one wagon, others used two. One man even had three, coupled one after the other. These wagons had four wheels, the hind ones somewhat larger than the front ones, perhaps four feet in diameter, made of wood with steel tires and axle boxes. The axles too were steel. Except for bolts and bindings, the rest of the wagon was wood. The beds varied in length from twelve to sixteen feet, maybe more. The first wagon had a seat for the driver and his helper, "Swamper." The seat was three or four feet above the floor of the wagon bed, set on springs to make for easier riding and a footboard to brace his feet against. In the center of the seat was a small covered compartment, the jockey box, to hold a few tools and personal belongings. One man I knew, having no watch, carried an alarm clock there.

There was always a brake which worked only on the hind wheels tightening and releasing wooden blocks against the tires. The brake was connected to the driver's seat by an iron rod bolted to a lever and ratchet which the driver could manipulate either by hand or with his foot.

There was a pole or tongue at the front to which a team of horses was hitched by wiffletree and neck yoke. This formed the steering gear for the whole rig. Sometimes the seat was cantilevered so far forward that the driver saw only the heads and shoulders of his first pair of horses.

The second wagon had no seat as no one rode there. The brake was somehow managed by a rope the length of both wagons, sometimes wrapped around the driver's arm, sometimes attached to the brake lever. The first pair of horses was hitched directly to the wagon and because of extra parts to their harnesses, called "breechings," were responsible for helping to hold the load on steep down grades. They were called wheelers. The next pair was the swing and third pair or sometimes three abreast were leaders. Occasionally, a teamster had a fourth pair strung out ahead, or a man drove only wheelers and one to lead. Then he had a spike team.

Usually the leaders had metal arches on their harness

Wallace Moody hauling cordwood

hames, on which were hung five or seven bells as big as coffee mugs. They made a wonderful jingle-jangle that could be heard a long way. These bells gave warning of a heavy outfit on the road so that other travelers could find a suitable place to stop and wait for the big ones to come by. The loaded wagons going downhill always had the right of way.

These loads of cordwood, sometimes six or more cords at a time, were held in place by stakes which in turn were secured halfway up their length by stay chains across the load from stake to stake, a ring on one end and a hook on the other. These stakes were often purposely allowed to slant outward until the load took on the appearance of an inverted pyramid. Everyone was duly thankful when such a load passed safely on its way.

A light rig like two horses and a spring wagon might be caught in a bad spot. I know this happened to Mother one day. The men on the big rig unhitched her horses, led them past their wagons, set the light wagon off the road into the brush, drove their load past, came back, put Mother's wagon back on the road, hitched up the team, wished Mother a pleasant good day, and proceeded down the road.

Among these men, I remember the Mullens brothers Tom and Billy and the Grant boys John and Joe.

ROADS

The Black Road, at that time called Reservoir Road, was eight miles from Los Gatos to home. The first three miles, from Los Gatos to Lexington, now Highway 17 South, were a narrow, dirt road with a few wide spots where one could wait to let any rig coming the other way pass. This section was known as the Grade. It was deep with dust in the summertime and equally deep with mud in the winter.

About a mile out of town, there was a steep and narrow road which led off to the right and out of sight around a corner. It was closed by a gate on which a sign said, "For Sale, Honey, 80¢ a gallon."

So occasionally, Father would stop by the gate and wait while Lotte and I walked up to the Butler house at the end of the road carrying an empty gallon syrup can to be filled with honey; sometimes we had to wait while Mr. Butler set a five-gallon can in hot water on the kitchen stove to melt the honey to pouring consistency.

Mr. Butler was known to all as Honey Butler. He also manufactured a tonic from local herbs which was called Butler's Linger Longer and which was on sale in local stores.

The first mile of Black Road up the mountain, known as The Dobie, was without shade, unbearably hot in summer and very cold and muddy in winter. Then came the Brush, more sheltered from the elements and on better ground. Next was Raymond's Cut and the Water Trough, Gist's Road, and by Newell's to Begg's Hill, the Gooseberry Patch or Spanish Flat, the "S" Bend, the Madrones, Stolte's Hill and home.

It made the climb up the mountain shorter to have it broken up that way. A light team and wagon could make the trip down to Los Gatos in an hour or an hour and a quarter; the return trip was perhaps two and a half hours, and a team pulling a heavy load needed four hours or more.

Once, coming home from shopping in Los Gatos, Mother had a runaway. As we passed by the Newells, their dogs ran out barking and nipping at the horses' heels. Away they went and were soon out of control. As they turned a very short corner, the wagon upset and we were thrown out, and the horses clattered off up the road.

Mr. Newell and his son John came to our rescue. John picked me out of a hazel bush, set me up on a bank, told me not to cry as I wasn't hurt, and hurried off to catch the horses with which he soon returned. They righted the wagon, fixed what was broken, helped retrieve the scattered groceries, and we were able to go on home, somewhat shaken but otherwise unhurt.

The road along the summit of the mountains, now Skyline Boulevard, was just a road in spots where it had been necessary to dig a passway from point to point. The rest was just a track through open fields, generally along the ridgetops, in and out among trees or rocks. When one track was washed into ruts by the winter storms, the next man along moved over and started a new one.

As this road passed from one man's land to another's, there was sure to be a gate. There were extra gates, in and out, if the road passed through a cultivated field or someone's yard. Gates of various designs and efficiency, some that only an inventive genius could think of, were to be seen. Along the five or six miles of the Summit Road with which I was familiar, from Herrings to Sharps, there were fourteen gates. Despite all these gates, it was a public road and anyone could travel it who wished to. The only requirement: "Shut the gate." There were no gates on the Black Road in my time, but as I recall, it was the responsibility of the people living along it to keep it in passable condition.

The men would gather at Lexington with their teams and tools and work their way up. It was a matter of much criticism that each man and his equipment dropped out upon reaching his own place. So the last miles were left to the few living on the summit. Perhaps they were all working out their road tax. I don't know.

After some years, these roads were taken over by or deeded to the counties—Santa Clara and Santa Cruz—improvements made and their care paid for with tax money. On the Black Road, as far up as water was available, the county had men with tank wagons wet down the road several times a week to keep the dust under control.

The road along the top was never watered, so the dust was always inches deep. People wore dusters, and the ladies wrapped veils or scarfs over their hats and made the best of it. And all the gates were removed which was a great improvement.

SCHOOL BEGINS

Now the question of school came up. There were established schools in the community, but we lived in Santa Cruz County, so that was where we belonged. Castle Rock School was four miles away to the north, but a road went only half the distance. Brown School to the south was five miles the way the crow flies, but nearer ten by the road, and not much road at that. Down the Black Road in Santa Clara County was Lakeside School, five long miles away but at least on a passable road.

Since Lotte was now six years of age, Father arranged for her to attend Lakeside. For transportation, he bought a little cream-colored horse called Joe for her to ride; being afraid she might fall and become entangled in the stirrups if she used a saddle, Father spread a blanket, held in place by a surcingle or belt on the horse's back, for her to sit on, and sent his little daughter off to school with her lunch, slate, and pencil in a bag over her shoulder.

This soon proved too much for her. The horse would not obey her but would turn about and head for home whenever he took the notion. All Lotte could do was get off and lead Joe as far as Newells, where Mollie, about twelve, would take charge and Joe carried both the last several miles to the schoolhouse, which was some distance up the Thomson Road. Just how long Lotte attended Lakeside, I don't know, but she was a brave little six-year-old to attempt it.

Meanwhile, the people along the summit began to think about a school of their own. Mr. Linscott was superintendent of Santa Cruz County schools at that time. With his help, a school district called Central was formed by taking some territory from both Brown and Castle Rock districts. A school board of trustees was elected or perhaps appointed by Mr. Linscott, I'm not sure. I'm sure of Stolte and Nickels and pretty sure Sharp was the third. They chose a spot on the Nickels's place on the edge of a small orchard by the side of the road as the most centrally located place in the district for the schoolhouse. The people gave the lumber and built the house, sixteen-foot-square board and batten, a door at one side opening right onto the road, a window in each of the other walls. The first term they were able to borrow furniture enough from the Browns. The playground was the roadway and the nearby woods. There were two privies across the road screened by the native shrubs.

The first teacher was Miss L. C. White from Santa Cruz. Her salary was fifty dollars a month, and she paid Mother sixteen a month for room and board. Every day we walked to and from school, the mile and a half through the fields and woods. Going to school was a wonderful adventure for me. I loved every minute.

Some of the children who belonged in Lakeside enrolled at Central because it was nearer. Lotte and I, Joe and John Mini, Ada and Willie Nickels, Hattie, Mittie, Wilbur, Winnie, Jamie, and Barney Sharp, Lulu Beggs, Richie, Arthur, and Dolf Olave are all that I can remember. Johnny Mini and I became inseparable friends. We played, studied, and fought the other kids, side by side, until we reached the sixth grade.

Besides the teacher's desk and chair, desks and seats for the children, there was a blackboard on one wall. There were two maps, one of Santa Cruz County, the other of the hemispheres of the world, a shelf which held a few reference and supplementary reading books, and an eight-day clock over the blackboard. There was another shelf for lunch pails and nails under it for hats and coats and a cast-iron box stove in the center of the room with its chimney straight up through the roof. In the corner near the lunch shelf stood an upended box with a division in it. This took care of the water pail and washbasin, and a roller towel was nearby.

The children took turns carrying the water from a spring at least an eighth of a mile down the hill. This pail was filled every morning and sometimes again at noon. The water carrier was supposed to be careful when dipping the water from the spring not to stir up the mud and to avoid bringing too many "wrigglers," mosquito larvae, and pollywogs. A few were acceptable. He or she was not supposed to let any grasshoppers along the way jump into the water either. Everyone drank from the same tin dipper which floated in the pail when not in use. And one basin of water was considered enough for everyone to wash in at noontime.

The school day was from nine a.m. to four p.m. As Santa Cruz County had nine grades at that time, the teacher might have classes if not in every grade, at least scattered through them and often only one or two pupils in a class. The largest class I was ever in numbered five. All textbooks were purchased by the parents. Every youngster had a slate and slate pencil, a slate rag, and water bottle for cleaning the slate between lessons. It was not considered nice to spit on your slate for moisture to erase the preceding lesson.

At the teacher's desk, among other things, was a handbell with which we were called from our play at noon and recess time and to tap, tap us into the schoolroom and back to our desks. She also had extra slate and lead pencils, a box of steel pens, a bottle of ink for filling the little inkwells set into the tops of the upper-grade desks, and chalk for the blackboard which incidentally was a nice smooth piece of slate about six feet long and three feet wide. Foolscap, paper for the older children to write on with lead pencils or ink, and drawing paper for Wednesday's art classes were both passed out one sheet at a time.

The prize of the whole room was a Webster's Dictionary, a great big beautiful book at least six inches thick, bound in tan calfskin, with little niches on the front with the letters of the alphabet, each in its proper place. This book had many illustrations, and when we littlest pupils were very, very good, we were allowed to turn the pages and look at the pictures.

Miss Lucy Osborn, from Watsonville, followed Miss White. Her term was not a happy one. My guess is that she was lonely and homesick; she was also given to fainting spells which frightened all the children out of their wits. After some unpleasant occurrences in the household where she boarded (not Mother's), she returned to her home and never came back.

LITTLE SISTER

The school year was from July 1 to June 30 of the following year, with eight months of classes. Because of roads and weather, a long winter vacation was considered advisable. So the school terms were from the Monday after July 4 to Thanksgiving, with a week of vacation in October for Teachers' Institute. Then December, January, February, and part of March were vacation. The spring term was from the middle of March to sometime in June.

On December 6, 1888, a wonderful thing happened in our house: My sister Josephine Anna was born. First thing that morning, Father called Lotte and me to Mother's room. There was our neighbor, Mrs. Herring, holding this tiny baby in her lap. I looked at her very carefully and said, "She has lanterns in her eyes." From that moment, I felt she was mine, more mine than anyone else's.

When she was old enough to be fed with a spoon, she was given something called Millen's Food. It looked just like browned flour mixed with warm milk. The responsibility of feeding her in the morning while Mother went to the barn to milk the cows was given to Lotte. I had the job of making the cocoa for breakfast. Mother would have put the milk in a copper pot on the stove to heat; I was to stir in the measure of powdered cocoa when the milk was hot and move it off the fire. That milk invariably boiled over, while I watched Lotte feed the baby. I can still hear the sizzle when it hit the hot stove.

Even though I couldn't feed her, Little Sister was my main concern. As soon as she could walk, we went exploring just around the garden, and in the yard we found endless things to entertain us: flowers to find, wild pansies, shooting stars, baby blue eyes, forget-me-nots; or we could watch bugs, all kinds of ladybugs and ants, red, black, big, small, and in-between, butterflies, moths, and beetles. The opportunities were endless; all we had to do was look.

The barnyard animals were our most intimate friends: old hens and baby chicks; calves were fun. They would suck on our fingers or sleeves or the corners of our aprons. Baby pigs were a never-ending joy. The only drawback to school was not being able to take Little Sister with me.

PLANTINGS AND FIRST HARVESTS

While Father was helping to organize the school district, the work of improving the farm was also going forward. Two blocks of Jonathan apples were planted, one below the road beyond the other apple trees, the other one on the hill above the road between the prunes and peaches.

As the land was cleared by Pete and others, vineyards were also planted: Shabeneau, Matereau, Zinfandel, all black wine grapes for making claret or similar wine, and Tokay, Chassler, and white Verdel, table grapes for city markets. These grapes would also make white wine. These plantings were made from cuttings from the vineyards of our French and Italian neighbors, carried home on Father's shoulders in bundles of four or five hundred at a time. When they were being planted, one of my uncles, usually Billy Stolte, would punch a suitable hole in the ground at the proper spot, as the planting ground had all been surveyed and marked into eight-foot squares. He used a crowbar to make these holes. Mother would set a cutting in place, then tamp fine soil around it and move on to the next one. Later when some which hadn't rooted had to be replaced, Lotte and I could do it, but we used a hoe and the layering method. After some years when the peach trees died, for various reasons, that flat and the hill above were planted with Sauvignon Vert, a heavy-bearing white wine grape.

The first small crops of prunes Father took to town and, I believe, sold them fresh to Alexander Hildebrand. Mrs. Hildebrand was a longtime friend of Mother's. They owned land at the eastern end of Main Street in Los Gatos, I think, from about where the Christian Science Church is now, to Alpine Avenue and back to the top of the hill. Part of their place became the Oak Hill subdivision. Their orchard came to the edge of Main Street. The buildings were back at the foot of the hill. A sign over the driveway on Main Street said, "Alexander Hildebrand, Fruit Dryer."

When the Hildebrands sold out and returned to San Francisco, Father must have decided to go into the fruit business himself. By then he had built, with the help of Fritz Wherner—an excellent carpenter who lived nearby—a big building for fruit storage and general use. It had a stone walled wine cellar under it. In this building, he installed a prune grader which was motivated by a crank on a large cogwheel which moved a small cogwheel on the end of an axle and was turned by hand. A flywheel on the other end of the axle helped a little. The grader divided the prunes into four sizes.

Out in the yard he set up a dipper, a round-bottomed cauldron which held about fifty gallons of water. This was heated with a wood fire. When ready to use, that is at the boiling point, a pound or two of Babbit's lye was added.

With a supply of three-by-six trays on hand, he next took out the almond trees since they were not good bearers. This plot of ground became the dry lot. He also built a dryer, to be used in case of rain before the harvest was finished. This was a small square building just big enough to take three stacks of trays; each tray slid on its own track, thus leaving space between for air circulation. There were about fifteen trays to a stack. There was a cellar-like space underneath where a wood-burning furnace was put in place and a ventilator in the peak of the pyramid-like roof. The dryer was not successful; after catching on fire several times the first season, it became a storage place for odds and ends.

With all this preparation accomplished, Father was ready for business. Besides his own prunes, he bought from Minis', Sharps', and a new neighbor, L. N. Sabin. It seems impossible now, but after grading all this fruit by man and woman power, Father patiently dipped it all through the boiling lye water, then through clean water to wash off the lye, pailful by pailful. The pails held about three gallons, with many holes cut into the entire surface to allow drainage before the fruit was dumped on to the trays, where it was carefully spread one prune deep. About eight trays at a time were hauled to the dry lot on a horse-drawn sled.

Some years when the rains came early, getting those prunes dry was a long and tedious job. In case of a shower or even the threat of one, everyone hurried out to stack those trays. When the sun came out again, the job was reversed and the trays set out again. I distinctly remember one afternoon late in November hastily clearing the fruit on the last stack of trays into boxes and carrying them into the house, one by one upstairs and then spreading those prunes on the attic floor where they finally dried.

As the young orchard came into bearing, there were pears and apples to dry. When the pears were ripe and yellow, each pear was cut in half, the blossom, stem, and core removed and the halves placed face up on trays, then left in the sulfur box overnight to be bleached and put out in the sun to dry next morning.

When the pears reached this point, there were the yellow jackets to contend with. I learned to trap them by filling a large shallow pan, probably a discarded milk pan with water, placing it near their line of flight, and for bait suspending over it, in a horizontal position a defeathered blue jay, which someone had shot for me. This bait was about one-half inch above the surface of water upon which I had poured a covering of kerosene. When the unsuspecting "jackets" gathered to devour the bait (they preferred meat to fruit), each one would gnaw off a small bit and start for home. But before becoming airborne, they made a downward curve, which was sure to land them in the oil. When that happened, their flying days were over.

We also dried apples, which were peeled, cored, and sliced on small, hand-operated machines. These too were sulfured before being set in the sun. Figs and grapes were dried for home use—good nibbling material. After a few years, the neighbors put in their own equipment, and Father handled only his own fruit and no longer graded it.

On my sixth birthday, I was allowed to go to town with Father all by myself. He had a load of dried prunes all sacked on one-hundred-pound burlap bags ready to be delivered somewhere in or near Los Gatos. The seat of that big wagon seemed awfully high up in the air to me. It was a cold day so someone wrapped a blanket tight around me and told me to "hang on good." As my feet could not reach the footboard, it really took some holding on to keep me up there.

Father had borrowed an extra team to use as leaders from Mr. Sabin, "Dan and Venture." The road was so muddy in spots; the horses had to pull even though we were going downhill.

From Lexington into town, the mud was thinner, and the horses traveled along nicely splash, splash, splash! That was a wonderful day, but I was a cold and tired little girl when we got home that evening after dark.

The Sabin Family

The Sabin family must have come into the community about a year after Central School was established. They lived on a place between the Gists' and Sharps's and joining the Nickels's place. They called it Tip Top Rancho.

There was a little girl, Frankie, younger than I. We became very good friends. As she was not in my grade, she didn't interfere with my friendship with Johnny. They were Easterners but had lived in Alameda before coming to the mountains. Who owned the place before them, I don't know. It was planted with prunes, pears, and grapes. They also had a fine patch of red currants and another of blackberries.

Mrs. Sabin took little interest in the farming activities and not much in the housekeeping either. I guess she shouldn't be blamed for that. It was a very tumbled-down sort of a house of four rooms. The living room had been built over and around a pile of native sandstone boulders, the place for the fire roughly chopped into the center boulder and a makeshift chimney pushed up through the roof. Frankie and I would climb up and slide down those rocks by the hour. The rest of the house was dark and gloomy. During the winter, she moved to Los Gatos, saying the winter storms frightened her, and she wished to be near a doctor in case of need.

Mr. Sabin ("Lute") probably had more formal education than most of the men we knew but somehow lacked practical know-how. He worked so hard and accomplished so little. They were frequent visitors at our house, and we often went to theirs. Lute was a great talker and storyteller. His name was really Lucian Norris Sabin.

He always had time for us children. Though just a little girl, I was always Miss Emma to him. When I tried to tell him something, he always had time to listen; most grown-ups didn't. I thought he was wonderful. One of his troubles—he had many—was a mortgage. He always had that mortgage to pay off. One of my dreams at that time was to grow up, earn lots of money, and give it to Mr. Sabin to pay off that mortgage.

His orchards weren't so extensive. I think the whole place was forty acres, and part of that was woodland and pasture, but he had more equipment than anyone else. Every newfangled riding plow, cultivator, or what have you that was invented, Sabin got, because, as the salesmen said, "Every up-to-date farmer should have one." These fancy contrivances were soon added to the junk pile. He also liked to work a big crew; one harvest season, he established a Chinese camp. There seemed to be strange men all over the place, even one in Mrs. Sabin's kitchen.

There were numerous horses, too. Where every other man used two on a mower, plow, or other piece of equipment, Lute hitched on four. With all his equipment, he was a great hand to borrow. One member of the family was Mrs. Sabin's mentally retarded brother, Frank. He would arrive at our house driving a horse hitched to an old Petaluma cart with a note from Lute, whose writing was completely illegible. Father would quiz Frank as to what was being done on the Sabin place that day, make a guess, and send Frank home with whatever he thought was needed.

One year as the grapes in the Tip Top Rancho vineyards ripened, they were crushed and pressed and the juice boiled in great kettles, put into fifty-gallon barrels, and then shipped to Alameda to Mr. Sabin Sr., a great advocate of prohibition. He in turn intended to bottle and market it as a nonalcoholic wine. This was a failure because despite being boiled, that juice would ferment and become alcoholic anyway.

In the course of time, Emma, Florence, Lute, and Omega were added to the family. Frankie died of typhoid fever in her tenth year. When Omega was three, her mother was committed to Agnews State Hospital and died there. She and Frankie are buried on the ranch. In the end, that mortgage took the place, and Mrs. Sabin Sr., step grandmother to the children, undertook their care with the stipulation that Omega's name be changed to Sylvia. Lute died when about grown up. Emma married someone named Umberto, whose last name I never knew. Mr. Sabin and the two younger girls met death in an auto-railroad train accident.

Lute's story about the Indiana farmer still lingers in my mind. This farmer, tired of shoveling snow all winter long, in his effort to clear a path in the snow to his barns so his animals could be taken care of, finally built one big barn to house them all under one roof. In the barn, everything was automatic, so feed and water were always available to his animals, and he would only have to shovel those paths once when the storm was over or could even wait until the sun melted the snow. One dark wintry day, all the animals were brought in, just in case a storm did break; the automatic feeders and water supply set in motion, the farmer went to bed that night, content and satisfied.

During the night, the granddaddy of all blizzards struck; for six days and nights, it continued, and the farmer stayed safe and snug by his fire, confident that his animals were safe. When the storm ended, he dug a tunnel to the barn door. When he got the door open, he found the whole place packed solid with snow; all his animals were smothered and dead. Well, he puzzled his head about it for a long time. How did the snow get into his beautiful barn? At last he remembered; while nailing the shingles on the very peak of the roof, one nail went wrong. So he pulled it out and reset it but did nothing to close the hole it had made. There was his answer: the wind had blown all that snow through that nail hole. I puzzled over that story longer than the mythical farmer did about the snow, finally deciding it wasn't true.

After caring for an out-of-work brother-in-law, wife, and young son all one winter, and the next year, for another destitute relative with wife and three children, he said, "You can't catch a fox in the same trap twice, but you can catch him in another just like it but worse." Poor Lute—always optimistic but never winning.

MISS DORA ZMUDOWSKI

After Miss Osborne, Miss Dora Zmudowski came to teach and live with us. She too was a native of Watsonville where her parents had extensive farming interests. Miss Dora taught at Central for three or four terms until she was called home because of her mother's illness.

Everyone was sorry to see her go; as I think back, I am sure she was the favorite, not only my own but for all the other kids as well. She understood our country ways and, even more important, she understood children. Knowing her taught us much that wasn't in our books. She would use part of the lunch hour to read aloud to all who would gather in the shelter of the big pine tree and listen. I especially remember James Fennimore Cooper's *Leatherstocking Tales*, which inspired all the children to play "Indians" instead of Drop the Handkerchief, Pom-Pom Pull-Away, Crack the Whip, Blind Man's Bluff, etc. Jumping rope was a good pastime for the older ones, best when Richie Olave brought his father's braided rawhide reata to swing for us.

Miss Dora was a big girl, blue eyed and redheaded, with the fair skin and freckles so often found with red hair. She had a brother, but he died a very young man, unmarried. There were also two sisters. All three remained spinsters and lived well past the eighty-year mark.

The youngest, Mary, was a high school teacher in Watsonville for many years. At the time of her death, we learned that the last of the family property was willed to the State of California. This included a half mile or so of beach along the Monterey Bay, which is now designated Zmudowski Beach under the State Division of Parks and Beaches.

While Miss Dora was with us, her sister Mary, then in high school, like students now, was studying biology and always in search of specimens. One of our after-school duties was bringing in the cows. This particular afternoon, the cows had wandered way down the canyon below the big pine. After we got them started toward home along a brushy trail that followed the windings of the creek, we spotted a tarantula, a great big one; we promptly decided to take him home for Miss Dora's sister.

Lotte was carrying a hazel stick about four feet long and three-quarters of an inch thick. By putting the end of the stick just in front of the tarantula, he climbed on and started slowly up the stick. When he got too far up the stick and too near the hand holding it, I took the free end. By reversing the slant, turn, and turnabout, we kept that poor spider crawling up that stick all the way home, put him in a jar, and he finally reached Watsonville High.

I have in my garden today two roses, the Ragged Robin and a sweet pink rose, started from plants Miss Dora brought Mother over seventy years ago.

Once she brought us three young geese. Mine was Kate, Lotte's Grace, and Josie's Hans. They lived with the chickens, and I watched over them like a mother goose myself. The following spring, Kate and Grace both chose nesting places. It was fun to watch them carefully cover their eggs with leaves and twigs whenever they left their nests. The incubation time for goose eggs is thirty-two days. Every morning, the goose leaves her nest for a short time to forage for food and water. On returning, she gently rolls the eggs about with her beak, changing the position of each egg before settling down on her nest for the next twenty-four-hour stint.

When the goslings hatched, they were the cutest little creatures I had ever seen. They grew at a surprising rate. By late summer, they were fully feathered and almost as big as their parents. Every day the whole flock would sweep back and forth the full length of the yard, making a great commotion of flapping wings and gabbling voices, until one fine day those flapping wings carried them right off the yard over the nearby trees, on down the canyon as though they were heading for the ocean twenty air miles away. Maybe they reached it; I never saw track or trace of my beloved geese after that day.

SHOPPING

San Francisco and Los Gatos

Ever since we had moved to the ranch, each summer we looked forward to a visit from the Spiering family. I was very fond of my cousin Henry, but we did have some lively disagreements, which sometimes ended in fisticuffs. Almost every winter, we made a return visit to San Francisco, staying with the Spierings.

The noises and smells of the city, plus the lights at night, always confused me. There were too many people, and I couldn't understand why there were so many houses.

I enjoyed riding on the cable cars, when we could ride outside on the "dummy." There was also a wonderful steam train with open cars which I looked forward to. This railroad crept along the edge of the ocean cliffs from the far end of either Sutter or California Streets past Land's End to Sutro Heights and the Cliff House with its Seal Rocks. It really crept—teenage boys would amuse themselves by jumping off and running alongside awhile, then jumping on again.

Besides calling on relatives and old friends, there was a place known as Woodward's Garden which we visited, sort of a carnival and Gay Way. I remember going to the theater, either the Tivoli or the Orpheum, where ladies danced in rows with almost no clothes and blue hair. And I remember walking in Chinatown where the men wore strange, loose black or dark-blue clothes, their hair in long pigtails made longer with colored silk and on their feet they wore very queer-looking shoes.

While in the city, Father would purchase supplies for the ranch from various wholesale merchants he had known while living there. One was the grocery firm of McElroy and Magner. From them, he would order such staples as five-pound cans of ground cocoa, wooden boxes of soda crackers, wooden tubs of salted herrings and salmon bellies, and always coffee. At first it was green coffee beans which Mother would roast in the oven, and every morning the proper amount was ground in a special mill, fastened on the kitchen wall. Soon roasted coffee was available, but it still had to be ground. There was also a supply of ground chicory root, of which a small quantity was always added to the pot for better flavor.

The folks soon learned that it was wise to deal with the local merchants in Los Gatos. There they followed the established barter system. The grocer would take any surplus, butter or eggs, and credit them against your order. The feed and grain man would take wood in exchange, etc. Butter was shaped into two-pound rolls by packing it firmly into wet wooden molds, then wrapping it in something called "butter-cloth," as flimsy as modern cheese cloth but stiffer. The box in which it was carried to town was covered with a wet blanket or canvas to keep it cool and firm enough to handle. At the store, it would be set on the open counter, sometimes covered with a cloth or paper, more often not. What price the butter brought, I can't say. I do know there were dozens of eggs that went for ten cents a dozen.

Grocery stores were different then. They carried very little canned goods and almost no paper packaged foods. There was usually a big yellow cheese on the counter beside the butter. The customers indicated the size piece, and the clerk cut it for him. There were crackers in an open barrel, also sugar, rice, beans, rolled oats in open sacks with scoops in them, arranged against the wall of the counter. Whatever quantity was ordered was scooped from the sack into a paper bag, folded shut, and tied with a string. Tea came in tin boxes—you chose the mixture you wanted. We always used oolong and uncolored Jasmine in equal proportions. Incidentally, the string came in balls which were put into a fancy cast-iron container with the free-end threaded through a hole in the bottom. Then the whole thing was suspended from the ceiling over the counter, so the free end was always dangling handy for the grocer.

My earliest recollection of a grocery store was one on East Main Street in Los Gatos, about a block beyond the bridge on the west side of the street. There was a big oak tree in front of the store with a railing around it, where people tied their horses. I think there was a plank walk in front of the building. Inside it was dark and crowded, the merchandise piled on counters and stacked in boxes and sacks on the floor. Who owned the place, I can't say.

On one trip to town, a shaggy brown dog, which had stayed at our place after the Averys had left, followed us. While the folks were shopping, the dog came in. He was probably hungry after his long walk. Anyway, Mother saw him trot out the door with a side of bacon he had helped himself to. With an exclamation of dismay, she called Father's attention. He gruffly told her to be quiet and instantly denied knowing the dog.

It seems to me there was a fire on the east side of town. That and the railroad being on the upper west end of Main Street caused businessmen to establish themselves along West Main and the first block of Santa Cruz Avenue. There Harry Edwards, an Englishman, and Curt Roemer, a German, were partners in a grocery. A Mr. Malloy had a fruit stand where he bought and sold and traded fresh vegetables and fruit. The grocer, as I remember, sold only potatoes and onions.

When meat was wanted you went to the butcher shop. I think Bill Pepper had the only shop in town. It was on the south side of West Main Street almost on the corner of Monte Bello Way. Everything was in the open, sides or quarters of beef hanging on hooks along the walls, also a dressed hog or two, a veal if available, perhaps still unskinned, a few spring lambs, or something simply called mutton. According to the piece ordered, the butcher would put a quarter or whatever size piece he needed on the chopping block and with knife and hand saw cut it, wrap it, in heavy brown straw paper, tie it with string, and that was it. The floor was always covered with sawdust which took care of any drip of blood from the meat. Usually there were some quarters of beef and an unskinned veal outside by the door until needed in the shop. Soup bones, liver, hearts, and such, were mostly giveaway material. The butcher would buy or take in trade a well-dressed beef or veal. Sometimes he would go out to the farms and do the butchering himself.

There was a place on the creek north of the Main Street bridge which had been a flour mill, but in my time, it was an ice factory. Great blocks of ice were made there, which were sawed to usable chunks and delivered to housewives' kitchens by the ice man.

Mr. Brunaugh sold dry goods, yard goods: ginghams, lawns, fine woolens, velvets, and linings, also all the little things like needles, pins, thread, buttons, and hooks and eyes. That store was a wonderful place to see.

Although some men's clothing could be bought ready-made, most men had a navy blue or black serge suit for special occasions which probably cost ten or fifteen dollars, while work shirts and denim pants could be had for fifty or seventy-five cents. The women and children's clothing was either made by the mother or a dressmaker who was hired to come to the house and do it.

There was a drugstore, and the names Watkins and Skinkle come to my mind, but I think there was someone else before them. E. E. Place followed his father selling furniture and coffins and was the only undertaker in Los Gatos.

Two young doctors came to town about now, Frank Knowles and Robert Gober. They always drove well-kept, fast horses and would go to anyone in need day or night. Dr. Knowles had most of the mountain people. I think this came about because he was single and perhaps naturally more venturesome than his colleague. It was an accepted fact that in the wintertime when many roads were impassable, either of these men would drive as far as possible, then leave their rigs and walk the last miles to reach their patients and often carry both medicine and food to the distressed families.

The Lyndon Hotel was on South Santa Cruz Avenue and Main Street, and R. R. Bell's feed barn and woodlot was just beyond at the corner of Broadway and South Santa Cruz Avenue. There were also blacksmith shops, a livery stable, several saloons, a harness shop, and the United States Post Office, and not to be forgotten, two laundries, one French, the other Chinese.

Once we watched a Fourth of July parade: people riding in buggies and surries, all trimmed with flowers and tissue paper streamers. The Grand Army Veterans in their blue uniforms marching in true soldier fashion; lodge and school groups also marching. The music was furnished by groups with fifes and drums. Horseback riders also took part, some in the line of march in groups and others dashing hither and yon all over the place. Some of the stores had special representation. One I admired very much was a young lady marching for Brunaugh's Dry Goods Store. She was wondrously bedecked with chains of ONT thread, safety pins, and all sorts of notions. I believe the young lady was Miss Louise Van Meter, for many years first-grade teacher in Los Gatos Primary School. Besides all this organized activity, there were many small boys and numerous men, shooting firecrackers, all sorts and sizes from giants which were set off one at a time to little ones braided by the dozens into packs. These packs were often unrolled and tied to a stick and the bottom one lit. They would then ignite each other making a glorious sputter and bang. The whole town seemed covered by the smell of burnt gunpowder.

I remember the Grocery Wagon Man. I think he came from the store of Edwards and Roemer. His call was designed to be a midweek supplement to the Saturday shopping trip so many farmers made. He was a very young man, perhaps eighteen. His name was Fred Suydam, and he was very tall, very thin, always full of fun and jokes. He would come clattering into the yard with a spring wagon and a fast-stepping team, deliver whatever Mother had ordered the time before, and take eggs, packed in bran for safety, also butter if Mother had it ready, write down her next order and be off again. He always carried a box of white clay pipes, his giveaway item for children to blow soap bubbles with. If you dropped one, it was sure to break, but the next week he gave you a new one. Some men really used these clay pipes for tobacco smoking.

After a year or two, the Grocery Wagon no longer came, but the butcher shop sent out a wagon once a week; this was an enclosed, somewhat insulated vehicle and always carried a big chunk of ice in an effort to prevent meat spoilage. Elmer Dakin drove such a wagon when Mr. Ed Yocco owned the shop on Santa Cruz Avenue. After "Duck" Shirley had bought this shop, Jack Purviance drove the wagon for him.

BEYOND LOS GATOS

Beyond Los Gatos was the open valley. I remember beautiful, far-reaching hay and grain fields. Beyond seeing the fields and in the late summer the great stacks of baled hay, I knew little except that our young neighbor Bill Van Lone spent his winters in the valley plowing for hay.

The baling was done with Petaluma presses, unwieldy pieces of equipment. Where the loose hay was pitched by hand with long-handled pitchforks, into an upright chute just the width of the finished bales, the loose hay had to be packed into rough cakes in order to be passed along to become segments of the finished bale. To accomplish this required firmness, an agile man, very often a Chinese, was detailed to climb into the chute and jump up and down on the loose hay to pack it—a far-from-easy job. To this day, the mechanical gadget which does the same job on the modern balers is spoken of as The Chinaman.

Great horse-drawn thrashing machines also worked in the fields, but I never saw them. The finished bales tied with light three-strand rope weighed from two to three hundred pounds. The salvaged rope was useful for any number of things, from a little girl's jump rope to horse halters. As we used very little baled hay, our supply of rope was limited. As Father in his young years had often to trust his life to the holding power of a length of rope, we learned early to treat rope of any degree of usefulness with respect.

Many men at this time kept greyhounds. It was a common sight to see a half a dozen or more of these very slim, fast-moving dogs following their master along the street as he attended to his errands.

The reason for them was the sport of hunting jackrabbits. The men, each with his pack of hounds, would meet at a given spot in the open fields; at which point many a bet was made as to whose dog would win; this meant which dog would catch and kill the first unfortunate rabbit.

The ambition of every youth in the community then as now was to own his own transportation. The first step was usually a saddle horse; the later possession of a four-wheeled buggy and a fast-stepping horse put him high in the social life of the neighborhood. Once they were so established, they could travel far and wide over the valley. One young man, a Los Gaton—suffering a slight speech difficulty but otherwise very much one of the boys—often explained his horse "Could wun like a wabbit on the Alum wock woad."

Miss Wadworth's Term

In July 1892, Miss Mary Wadsworth of Aptos came to the school, a very young, agreeable person.

At that time, anyone having graduated from high school could take the county examinations; if their marks were passing, they became bona fide school teachers and received credentials to that effect. Then these fledgling teachers applied for positions with the far-out country schools, because the town and city schools would not employ inexperienced teachers. At times this was very unfair to the country children. Some, of course, were natural-born teachers doing a great deal for their young charges, besides giving them so many paragraphs from the various textbooks to memorize.

That's what school mostly amounted to—memory work. Every Friday, we all recited a "piece." I usually selected mine at Friday noon, stood up at one thirty and glibly reeled it off and forgot it just as quickly. I remember one I learned for Miss White, the first year of school. It was her selection:

> Little drops of water,
> Little grains of sand,
> Make the mighty ocean
> And the pleasant land.

The highlight of Miss Wadsworth's term was Columbus Day, October 12, 1892, the four-hundredth anniversary of the discovery of America. It must have been a national thing, for the entire program came in printed form, with speeches, recitations, and songs all taken care of. It was the teacher's job to assign them to the various pupils. The children and Miss March, the teacher of Castle Rock School, were invited to join Central and share the program. The trustees of Central erected a flag pole, and Central's first flag was raised and saluted. After the program, which began about ten in the morning, everyone came to our place and shared picnic lunches under the cherry trees. Somewhere I have a Columbus Day badge, a bit of green satin ribbon with gold printing on it, given me by Fred Herring, one of the big boys from Castle Rock.

Miss Wadsworth stayed only the one term. The one personal thing I remember about her is that when she did her laundry on Saturday, she always starched her handkerchiefs so they would be like new.

LEARNING TO WORK

By this time, I was big enough to help with many things; Lotte was without doubt of most help in the house, as I always preferred being outdoors. There were many things I could do, like dishes before school. I would pin my list of spelling words above the sink. By the time the breakfast dishes were washed, I also knew my spelling for that day.

The dusting on Saturday seemed useless to me, all those chair rungs! Whoever looked at them? And besides that, they just got dusty again. I could peel potatoes, shell peas, or string beans, as well as go into the garden, which was now located in a good loamy piece of ground way over beyond the vineyard and dig or pick them. I could run all sorts of errands and bring in wood and kindling for the kitchen stove; not having a great surplus of paper to burn, there was always a supply of pitch pine kept by the stove. The older pine trees, as they were cut for cordwood, would sometimes produce sections of dead wood in which the sap gathered until the wood became a soft brown color and the sap didn't drip. This wood cut into six-inch lengths and then split up very small made excellent lighters; one little piece lit by the match was enough. The matches, of course, were the old phosphorous and sulfur variety. I had also learned to crochet lace, to trim our canton flannel panties, muslin petticoats, and white aprons, to do simple hand sewing and darn the holes in my stockings.

The churning seemed always to be waiting for me. From the light, oarlike stick passed through the hole in the lid of the four-gallon cream crock which went round and round; to the dasher, a round wooden plate with many holes bored in it, fastened on the end of a handle which was passed through the same hole in the lid and worked up and down, to a wooden churn with a windmill-like arrangement inside, which was turned by a crank, to a barrel churn on a sort of axis, so the whole thing flipped over and over, no mechanism inside; but woe betide you if the lid wasn't clamped on tight. I knew them all intimately.

Mother tried her best to teach us to read and write German, and a little of her teaching stayed with me over the years. Her efforts to teach us German were made more difficult by the fact that Father, proud of his birth in the Free City of Bremen, where Low German was the folk language, liked to declare that "Platt Duetsch is de veldt Sproke" (Low German is the world's tongue), and to please him Mother had learned Low German. Now they usually conversed in its guttural syllables. She wanted us to know the school or printed High German. As we grew older, and in school, when spoken to in German, we quite naturally answered in English. Despite Mother's efforts, the der, die und das, and all the shadings of German grammar are still beyond me; although I can understand German when spoken to in that tongue and make myself understood if the need arises.

I must have learned English by osmosis. Until my fourth year, no one had ever heard me speak anything but German. Mother was very surprised one day when a stranger came to the door and asked directions to a neighbor's home to hear me give the answers he needed in English. Miss White, my first teacher, was equally surprised when she heard me chattering in German.

Father would often say, when anyone complimented Mother on having three nice little girls, that he would gladly trade the lot of us for one boy. I must have more or less believed him, for I certainly worked hard at doing all that a son might have done for him. I am sure now no son would have. There were the night and morning chores, which had to be done during schooltime as well as vacations. That meant helping with the milking and feeding everything—cows, horses, calves, pigs, and chickens—as well as cleaning up the stables, all before breakfast.

By this time, the band of cows had changed and grown in numbers. As each calf was born, it was given a name, so we had Dolly, May, Queenie, Jane, Bess, Nell, Trina, Gescha, Muggins, Daisy and others, and always a Prince, King, Jim, or Bud. As one was sold or otherwise disposed of, the next calf fell heir to the name. These animals all had distinct and individual personalities. Just because Queenie was a cow didn't mean that she behaved or responded to a situation just as Daisy or Dolly would, even though they too were cows. As the pastures over which the cows could roam were not fenced and covered any uncultivated land, they could reach, most cows wore bells on leather straps around their throats, all sizes, big bells that went "bong, bong" down to little tinkling bells on the calves. Eight or ten cows being driven home at dusk along some wooded trail or road made the most beautiful music imaginable. Of course, these bells weren't put on the cows for their aesthetic value, but to make it possible for little girls to find them when they had strayed a mile or two down some unfamiliar canyon.

Daisy, a big black cow, would let you ride her, if you were big enough and quick enough to get on her back when she wasn't looking. I was neither big enough nor quick enough for her. But any of the older cows would let you hold on to their tails and get yourself towed up the steepest parts of the trail.

We also had two young horses, Dick and Tom. Dick was born on the place March 17, 1889. Tom was purchased from Mr. Baker. They were black as colts, then became dapple grays, and finally white. White horses are hard to keep clean, so every now and then they got a soap and water bath which was quite a job. Dick would snort and prance and be as difficult as possible. Tom would stand and take it with a "What can't be cured must be endured" expression in his eyes. Dick would reach into the pigs' trough, push the pigs aside, and eat or drink whatever he could reach; but put even a very little pig in the wagon behind him, and you had trouble on your hands. Tom objected to bicycles. Men and boys would come up beside a team bent low over the handlebars of their wheels and pedaling furiously. This pace was known as scorching as they came alongside. Tom would give a quick sidewise kick, always missed. Then he would try to bite them as they whizzed past his head. He never got one, but would go on his way shaking his head as if he enjoyed a good joke. There also was Birdie, a chunky, gentle bay mare. We could ride her, drive her single or with one of the grays, or work with her on the farm.

All the horses knew how to open the stable doors. The doors were fastened with sliding bars with pegs for pushing the slides back and forth. They could move the slides by grasping the pegs with their teeth. The gate at the top of the lane had a rope loop, dropped over the upright poles that came together as both sides of the gate met; they could all lift that rope off neat as you please, but Dick was the only one who tried to close the gate again. He could hang the loop of rope back on one upright without trouble, but the two swinging in opposite directions proved too much for him. The back stable door couldn't be opened so easily, so the two grays would team up against Birdie and push and nip at her until she went to the door and banged on it with her front hooves. This trick brought someone from the house to scold them and let them in, or enough banging shook the fastener loose, and they let themselves in.

As the animals seemed almost like people to us, we knew our neighbors' horses too. Ed Richardson's saddle horse was Hoodlum, Fred Herring drove

Mollie and Stella, Nickels had Bum and Dapple, Newells had Julie and Fanny, John rode Sister, and his brother's horse was Sancho, Nick's little bay was Nettie, Sam Beggs called his riding mule Quito.

Father always aimed to get the seed for hay into the ground by New Year's. After he plowed the ground, he seeded it by hand. While he was doing that, I would drive Birdie hitched to a harrow and round the field all day to cover the seed.

I learned to prune the young grapevines, and it needed no great amount of brains to pick up the prunings in the orchard and pile them for burning or to set gopher traps.

Wet weather was a fine time to wash and oil all the harnesses. Father always moved into the kitchen with this job. How Mother put up with it, I don't know. It certainly made a mess of her nice clean kitchen. Every strap and buckle was undone and scrubbed with warm water and plenty of soap, then hung up to dry, and the next day oiled with warm Neatsfoot oil. Sometimes we spent the day in the workshop, perhaps mending harnesses, with linen thread well waxed with beeswax or a black substance called "pick." Instead of needles, he used very straight and stiff hog bristles, which were twirled and waxed into each end of the thread so the two ends passed each other in and out for every stitch, and there was a hole punched through the leather with an awl for every stitch.

I became expert at sorting nails, screws, and bolts, then putting each size into its proper container. Sometimes he made new ax or hand tool handles or a plow beam of wood or sharpened the plowshares, mattocks, and picks. Using the forge and anvil, I could work the bellows for him. When he did the axes, brush hooks, scythes, and pruning shears on the grindstone, I could turn it.

The most unpleasant job that came up at this time of year was getting the year's meat supply in order. That meant that several pigs were slaughtered, also cows. The coldest weather was always chosen for this. I hated to have any of the animals killed, but after someone had done that part of the job, I could help skin and dress the beef. Then the carcass was hung high in a tree with the help of a block and tackle and left there for a day or two until it was thoroughly chilled. Then Father took over the job of cutting it up and all, but what Mother knew could be used fresh was salted and packed in barrels, covered with salt brine, strong enough to float an egg or potato, and stored in the cellar for future use.

As the pigs, besides giving us hams, bacon, fresh and salt pork, also furnished sausage, head cheese, and lard, doing them was a bigger job.

First thing the blood was saved and had to be stirred or beaten until cold to keep it from coagulating. Next the whole pig was dumped in a barrel of scalding water and all the bristles and the thin outer cuticle scraped off with knives or iron bands shaped especially for that purpose. Particular care was needed to get the head and feet clean. The surplus fat from the entrails was removed and saved, the intestines cleaned and washed, the inner lining was carefully removed, and they were washed again for sausage casings. The stomach was turned inside out and the inner lining removed so as to use the remainder for head cheese that could be smoked. These carcasses too were hung high in the cold night air. The next day these were cut up and except for that on the hams and bacon, all the fat and skin or rind were removed and taken to the kitchen to be cut into strips and the fat parted from the rinds, which were put with the cut-up heads and feet and cooked. For this, the dipping kettle had been scoured until it shone, and all this collection cooked out there.

By the time I was helping with all this, we had an enterprise, Food Chopper, which helped a great deal. Before then, this material was all done by hand, the fat carefully cut into tiny cubes and other things, either cut fine or put into wooden bowls and chopped. Now the fat and cooked meat went through the "grinder," as we called it. When the fat had all been ground, it was tried out or rendered in large pans on the cookstove. The end result? Gallons of good sweet lard and plenty of cracklings.

While the meat was cooking, there was pepper to grind in a special pepper mill, onions to peel and grind, as well as the raw liver. Then all the cooked material, except that reserved for head cheese, all went through the food chopper. A certain amount of rye flour was added to both the liver and blood sausage mixture which was then filled into the casings; short sections of cow horn made it possible by inserting it in one end of a casing, to get a firm grip and, at the same time, worked like a funnel, leaving enough room for the flour to expand. The ends were tied and the sausages cooked in the wash boiler. The third kind of sausage was raw meat, ground very fine, well-seasoned with salt and pepper, and stuffed into casings as tight as possible and smoked. It was called "metwurst." The other sausage and some head cheese could also be smoked. Doing so added to both taste and keeping quality.

The hams, bacon, and other meat cuts were also well salted, packed in barrels, and covered with brine to which brown sugar had been added. After ten days, the bacon was ready to be smoked. I think the hams were left in the brine for a month. To smoke the bacon and hams, they were washed in cold water to remove the salt and left in freshwater for a day. Each piece was equipped with a cord with which to hang it. They were all hung in the open overnight to air dry and ready for the smokehouse in the morning.

The smokehouse was a small building about four-feet square and eight-feet high with a tight door and screened ventilating holes near the top with crossbars up high to hang the meat on and a place at the bottom where a slow-burning oak sawdust fire was kept burning. It was really a freestanding chimney. The meat was kept in this place a week or longer until it had taken on the proper smoky color and texture. The finished product was hung away in the darkest, coolest corner of the cellar.

Before the salted meat—either beef or pork—was cooked, it had to be freshened, first by washing and then left in the fresh cold water for a day at least. These cold winter days were great for slow-cooked dinners like a chunk of salt pork simmered all morning with dried prunes and fresh or dried apples, seasoned with cinnamon, cloves, and orange peel, sweetened with brown sugar and topped with beautiful fluffy dumplings. Or a thick bean soup made with salt beef, potatoes, onions, carrots and white navy beans—the whole lot cooked for hours. Raw potato pancakes with applesauce made a fine supper. Breakfast was no dry toast and black coffee affair; there was coffee, of course, and hot chocolate for us children, with perhaps pork chops or veal cutlets, oatmeal mush, and fried potatoes, or generous helpings of brown beans cooked with a meaty ham bone. Some mornings there were eggs with ham or bacon, and always homemade bread and butter.

When there was nothing else to do, there was Little Sister to play with. Mostly we stayed outdoors, taking longer walks, looking for ferns and wildflowers. Josie could now go almost anywhere I could, so a trip through the gulch and home by the road was just a pleasant stroll of several miles.

Lotte and I had one Christmas where each of us was given a beautiful big doll. As Lotte no longer played with hers, it went to Josie. I have never again seen dolls just like them. Their features were made of paraffin wax. If left too near the fire or out in the sun, this consistency wax would become soft and the faces blurred. So we would try to remodel them, but they never looked the same, poor dollies. But we could spend rainy hours sewing for them and playing house with them. Later, we had some other more durable china-headed dolls but really never played with them much. When we tired of play, I could read, sometimes aloud to Josie but more often to myself. There were books from the school library available, of which *Five Little Peppers* and *Little Women* were good for rereading again and again.

Father subscribed to two weekly papers, the *San Francisco Chronicle*, which didn't interest me much, and the *Santa Cruz Surf*, which I watched for because it had a comic strip about a lion. *The Youth's Companion* came every week, so there was the new one, as well as the stack of old ones up in the attic. I continued to subscribe to *The Youth's Companion* until it went out of publication during the 1920s.

The mail had to be picked up at the post office in Los Gatos. Any passing neighbor would willingly carry letters to the post office for mailing and on his return trip bring back whatever had accumulated there.

MISS SOBEY AT CENTRAL AND JOHNNIE'S DEATH

When Miss Ellen Sobey came to teach, spring of 1893, school was different. Miss Sobey was older, perhaps fifty, with snow-white hair, strange hazel eyes with a white band just inside the edge of the iris, a native of England, not long in America, with no experience of country living nor country children. We had been accustomed to starting the school day by joyfully singing "My Country 'Tis of Thee," and perhaps "Marching Through Georgia," etc. Now we folded our hands and very quietly recited the Lord's Prayer. That was fine until someone in the community reminded the trustees that the California State School Book of Laws did not allow it.

Many others of her teaching methods were strange to us, but we adjusted. I never heard her join in the singing, but she taught us several songs by using a pitch pipe. First we learned to sing the musical scale; after that, we worked on a lullaby that went like this:

> "Sol la sol me do me re do
> re me re sol sol re me re do (repeat)
> Baby is going to bye lowland,
> Going to see the sights so grand.
> Out of the sky the wee stars peep,
> Watching to see her fast asleep."

We also learned the "Canadian Boat Song" that way.

She was very strict about no nibbling during school hours, but midafternoon she often took an apple or pear and her pearl-handled fruit knife and would either walk about the room or sit at her desk and eat it. We kids thought that very unfair.

Miss Sobey lived at our house, there too she was different from the teachers we had known, more demanding and difficult, which made it hard for Mother.

It was during her stay that a man named Harry Winchell, one of the neighborhood's drinking bachelors, gained title to the part of the Nickels's property that the schoolhouse stood on and promptly objected to its being there. So Mr. Mini said, "There is room on my land," and a new schoolhouse was built a few hundred feet from where the first one stood. This was a bigger and better building, eighteen by twenty-four feet, the outer walls covered with redwood rustic. The same furnishings were used inside. There was a space about five by six feet closed off from the rest of the room and equipped with shelves to hold supplies and the library books of which the school now owned about two hundred all numbered. Each was stamped with a rubber stamp stating they were the property of Central School District of Santa Cruz County. A winter or two before several school districts had all their books stolen. As the books had no identification, they were never recovered.

The new house had native trees surrounding it: oaks, laurels, and pines. The boys found they could climb some of the younger trees and enough boys could bend the tree near enough to the ground so the first boy could slide off, run to the base of the tree, start climbing, and become the last one. When tired of the game, or when the bell rang for school, the tree was supposed to be held down by the boys already off so that the last one could get down safely. One day they all forgot or didn't notice that Johnnie had not reached the ground; the tree snapped back and acting like a catapult, threw him, hurting him more than anyone realized. This happened shortly before school closed for the winter. During vacation, we learned that Johnnie was ill with brain fever. Just before Christmas, Mr. Withrow—a new neighbor—came to tell us that Johnnie was dead and the funeral would be day after tomorrow.

I remember that funeral as plainly as though it had taken place yesterday. It was raining that morning when the neighbors gathered in the Minis's yard. The coffin was carried from the house by six young men and placed in Mr. Thomson's spring wagon and covered with an oilcloth. Then this sad little procession, people from the neighborhood, perhaps a dozen open vehicles and half a dozen saddle horses, everyone wrapped in waterproofs or other winter gear, fell in line and followed Mr. Thomson slowly down the road, eight miles to the Catholic Church, then on Santa Cruz Avenue in Los Gatos.

The mass was completely beyond me, but when the priest spoke a few words in English, I was shocked and still am, because all he did was scold the parents for not attending church regularly.

When we left the church, the rain had stopped. We went on to the cemetery in Union District on Almaden Road which had only just been opened. The cemetery before this one was at the corner of Santa Cruz and Saratoga Avenues. In those years, there was a redwood box placed in the grave to receive the coffin which was lowered into its resting place by long leather straps passed under the coffin and the ends given into the hands of the pallbearers by the undertaker. The lid of the redwood box put

Central School—1893
Miss Sobey, Johnny Mini, Lotte Stolte, Ada Nickels, and Emma Stolte

Josie and Shep ready for school

in place, the priest or minister offered the last prayer and the final words of "ashes to ashes and dust to dust." The mourners still waited until the grave was closed, a shallow mount built over it, and the flowers lay in place.

This last task was sometimes done by men employed by the cemetery, sometimes by friends and neighbors. There is no sound more heart-wrenching or so final as that of the first clods of earth thudding on the lid of a coffin box.

At the closing of Miss Sobey's stay, June 1894, there was the usual Last Day Program and gathering of neighbors for the school picnic. Joseph Mini graduated from the ninth grade that day, thus becoming the first alumnus of Central. He went on to high school in Los Gatos that September. Mr. Charles Gertridge was managing the Lyndon Hotel at that time. Joseph secured room and board at the hotel by taking over the dishwashing job. After three years of high school, he enrolled at Stanford University, again working at various jobs for his room and board. Graduating with a degree in engineering, he secured employment with the Pacific Gas and Electric Company and remained with them until he retired. From the beginning his work took him to the PG&E installations in the Sierra Nevada. I understand he took an important part in the location and building of the dam which forms Buck's Lake.

Miss Sobey comes to my mind whenever I happen to pass the spot where the schoolhouse stood. Returning from a weekend, which she had spent with another English lady who lived at Skyline near Loma Prieta, she brought with her a small bit of English ivy which she had the boys plant at the southwest corner of the house, with appropriate ceremonies during which the history of the ivy plant was told, and the little eight-inch slip, named for her friend Mrs. Crane. We all took our turns carrying water for it, and it took root and grew. Now though Miss Sobey has been dead these many years, the schoolhouse dismantled and moved to another location over half a century ago, that little plant has grown and grown until it covers the entire hillside, climbing over sticks and stones, even up into the forest trees, more at home than the native plants that were there before it.

WATER COMPANY LAKES

As I stir up memories and try to put them down in consecutive order, I find myself uncertain as to what happened when. Changes, of course, had been going on all the time, but I, just a child, had gone along my own little paths, unconcerned with the neighborhood beyond, home, school, and the few people I knew best.

But these things happened or were there during my school years, of that I am certain. For all I knew, the lakes in Lakeside District and from which the school and community took their names had been there always, made by nature. But I was mistaken; the lakes were man-made for the San Jose Water Company and were officially the Howell Reservoirs.

When Mr. Dresser and his family (there were two daughters June and Carrie, both in their late teens) came to live at the lakes, Mr. Dresser was overseer of the Water Company's properties. They had a telephone installed, the first one on the Black Road. This proved a great boon to everyone, for in any emergency, if a doctor or other help was needed or an important message had to be sent, that telephone saved hours of travel in all sorts of weather and brought help ever so much sooner.

People roundabout could go boating on the larger lake, in flat-bottomed rowboats. They could also fish there; it was well stocked with black bass and catfish. One could watch schools of catfish from the banks at most any time. I think to fish there a permit from the Company office was required, or you'd better be sure that Mr. Dresser liked you.

One year about 1896 or '97 the whole country suffered a drought, and the lakes were dry. Johnny Newell grew hay in the bottom of the big lake and also tried to burn out the tulies along the edges. That fire smoked all summer, but by the next spring when the lake was full again, there were the tulies as thick and green as ever. The lakes being dry caused the water for the trough at the Raymonds's to stop flowing, which proved that the nice little stream by the roadside with its ferns, watercress, and thimble berries was really seepage from the lake. That trough being dry was hard on both animals and humans. It was a great comfort that water, sweet and cool, beside the dusty road on a hot summer day.

There was a third Water Company Lake farther up the road and some distance from it. A mile or so of private road was built before the work on the lake began. I remember this well because both the road and the lake lay within our walking range. The land was purchased from the Bernards. We had often enjoyed Sunday picnics beside the little stream flowing along the bottom. They built dirt dams at both ends of this piece of land, thus causing two streams from the nearby hills to flow into it. The winter rains always filled it to the brim. It formed a very pretty lake just at the edge of the Bernards's barnyard; the horses and cows waded and drank from the edges, so did all the neighbors' animals if they happened to stray that way. A fine flock of ducks and geese swam on it. At first it was stocked with freshwater perch. But these grew to tremendous size and rooted along the bottom and the dirt banks keeping the water muddy, so the Company had the lake drained, hired men with teams and fresno scrapers, dredged the poor fish out of the mud and dumped them overboard. Next the lake was stocked with black bass which were very good fried.

It was here one afternoon, as I climbed up on a stump which stood half in the water, that I heard a splash. Looking to see the cause, I saw a rattlesnake swimming toward the opposite bank, climb out of the water, and disappear into the weeds. Grass and ribbon snakes, water dogs or salamanders, and turtles were always along the water's edge.

After a while, the Bernards sold the rest of their land to the Water Company and moved to Mountain View. The Water Company now owns extensive acreage adjoining this lake. In the summer the, water gate is opened and the water runs down Lydon Gulch where it is again confined in other facilities as needed. At all three lakes, the gates are now locked—no fishing, no boating, no picnics anymore.

Lake Ranch

ROAD IMPROVEMENT

During these years, the travel paths were slowly being turned into county roads. Santa Cruz County took the lead in this. Almost every spring, there was a piece of road being built on the west side of the county line. The watershed was accepted as the official dividing line between Santa Clara and Santa Cruz counties. Mr. Nickels built the piece from the Lake Ranch trail to the corner where the gate closed the way down the Stoltes's ridge. Someone else took it around to the Monroes's gate, and then Mr. Herring and his sons built the last west side piece to their place.

The sections of road on the east or Santa Clara County side of the line remained the same old tracks through woods and along the ridges for some time. Finally, something began to be done about it: the first piece north of our place was built by a little Mexican named Amagonda (probably misspelled) and his helper, One-Arm John. John's one hand had been destroyed while he was employed mining at New Almaden. He wore a heavy steel hook strapped to his forearm, and with the help of this hook, he could handle many tools and lift heavy weights with surprising ease. Eventually the road was built all the way to where the Saratoga Turnpike crossed the summit.

The same thing was happening toward the south. Nearly all the work needed lie on the Santa Cruz side. Ed Cushing and his sons did most of that; now one could drive comfortably the whole distance along the summit.

As far as I knew, the County Supervisor's reason for being elected to office was so they could look after the roads and keep them in order. Anyone signifying a willingness to do the work himself or see that it was done could be appointed Road Master. This man kept records of work done, sent reports of same to the Supervisor who in turn issued warrants on tax funds for this work. The compensation was considered good. I think it was $2 per day.

My father took over the piece from our place to the Monroes's gate about a mile. Every fall ditches were dug across the road to lead off the winter rains, and culverts were repaired and opened. Always when a storm was bad, he would put on his rain clothes, "oil skins and Sou-wester"; these garments had been made by Mother of heavy unbleached muslin and consisted of a pair of pants legs attached to a belt and a double-breasted coat which reached to the knees and a hat with a brim narrow in front widening to the sides and back so water couldn't run down inside his collar. The finished articles were given several coats of linseed oil. When dry, they were both light and waterproof. With these, he wore knee-high, well-oiled leather boots, the soles studded with hobnails to make for more secure footing. The hobnails were often placed in patterns. Father's boots printed the letters ABC every step he took. So well protected from the weather, he patrolled the road. If the banks slid in or out it often took days, sometimes weeks, to repair the damages. In the spring, the cross ditches were filled and the whole road smoothed up and put in order.

The Black Road, having the most traffic and nearly all of it from the Summit to Lexington either uphill or down grade, according to which way one happened to be traveling, was always in bad shape by spring, no matter how hard the local man had worked to save it. So Charlie Reynolds, a young Los Gatos man who did teaming and general contracting, would take the job of repairing it. He would plow up the whole roadbed, with a heavy gangplow and four horses, then smooth the whole thing with an equally heavy V drag, a triangular contrivance built of planks shod with iron and hitched in such a way that the loosened dirt was spread evenly over the roadway. If it rained hard right after the job was done, most of its value was lost; if there happened to be a dry spell before the newly stirred earth was packed hard again, it made for more dust; but if nature cooperated nicely, we had a good road.

Reynolds always drove handsome, well-kept horses, dapple grays which wore the best harness and bells available. It was a pretty sight to see them come snorting up the road. He was the only man to take three wagons loaded with cordwood, all hitched together, drawn by six horses, down that road. How he managed I'll never know, for he controlled his team with a jerk line, which somehow was threaded from the leaders to the driver, just one continuous strip of leather, and he, instead of being perched on the high seat of the first wagon, was riding on the back of the near wheeler.

Before Santa Cruz County had the road southward to where it met Bear Creek Road built, anyone going that way used Mallot's Lane, a steep uncared-for track which the winter rains always washed into an almost impassable gully. At about halfway, it leveled off for a short distance. This was the sight of the Mallot home. They were a rollicking, rough-and-tumble sort of family. Because of disagreements with one man in the neighborhood who passed by frequently, the Mallot boys erected a tollgate. I doubt they found it profitable. There were stories of other young fellows, lifting the gate off its hinges and turning it on the padlock chain, or their father ordering that they open the gate and let Mr. So and So go through.

I only remember passing that way once and still have a sweet and pleasant memory of that occasion. While our parents were enjoying a friendly visit, two little Mallot girls came to our wagon and gave Lotte and me each a big slice of homemade bread generously spread with honey. It was hard to know on which side the honey had been spread; the whole slice was so saturated with sweetness—mmm, mmm, so so good. The little girls explained their brothers had found and robbed a bee tree that morning. One little girl ran away and soon came back with a wet towel for Mother to mop off the surplus honey. Stoltes were apparently in good standing for the boys went out, unlocked the gate, passed us through with friendly Irish grins and no charge.

BOX MILLS, VAN LONES, AND HOFFMANNS

Now forgotten are the box mills. As the orchards and vineyards came into bearing, there was a need for containers in which to ship the crops of table grapes, plums, pears, and apples to city markets: pears and apples in forty-pound boxes, grapes first in twenty-pound boxes, then in crates which held four-splint baskets which held five pounds each.

Two families on the Bear Creek Road operated both fruit orchards and box mills, just like lumber mills but everything on a smaller scale. A great deal of the material used was down timber left from lumbering operations. These containers were turned out by the thousands. For some years these mills were profitable. These families were the Van Lones and the Hoffmanns, both real pioneers.

Mr. William Van Lone came from Missouri by wagon train about 1850. He and Mrs. Van Lone, nee Romelia Allen, met and married in California, although Mrs. Van Lone too had come from the East by wagon train. They first settled in the valley on land later owned by the Cox family for whom Cox Avenue is named. The valley proved too flat, too hot, and too dry for them, so they moved to the hills in search of water and forests, finally staying put on the summit where I knew them, in the Brown School district on the Bear Creek Road in Santa Cruz County. Mr. Van Lone was a quiet, steady man, his wife a true frontierswoman, not an especially big person but being near her gave one a feeling of strength and security. She had the reputation of knowing what to do in time of trouble and doing it. In the event of illness, accident, or death, when often a doctor was not to be had, she was the first one to be sent for, and she never hesitated to lend aid. A week before her youngest son was born, a frightened young husband came in great haste, asking help for his wife. Mrs. Van Lone went on horseback in a howling storm for miles, over almost impassable trails to a cabin in the woods, where she helped the other woman's baby safely into the world.

In her everyday life, she always had something to share, a pat of butter, or a loaf of bread, something from her vegetable patch or flowers from her garden. From my earliest recollection, her hair was cut short just like the men in the family. This was very unusual at that time. She lived close to ninety years as did her husband. During the last years, she took into her home a brother and widowed brother-in-law, both eighty plus, because they needed someone to care for them. Although she suffered greatly from what she called her "rheumatiz," her one prayer was that she might live as long as her "boys" as she called these old men who needed her. Her prayer was granted.

There were six young Van Lones, five boys and one girl: Walter, Will, James, George, Lizzie, and Charlie. Lizzie married a neighbor's son, Henry Laddick. James died, still a schoolboy; George married and raised a family. Some of his children and grandchildren live near Campbell, but I have no touch with them. Charlie, with all plans for his wedding day made, still at work in the woods a day or two before the date set, was crushed by a falling tree and died.

Walter and Will I knew best. They lived at home, working there or in the lumber mills, also driving teams, hauling lumber or cordwood. Then Walter went away to the oil fields and followed that work until he came to Los Gatos after his retirement. Will always lived with his parents, taking an active part in community life. Serving as a clerk of the school board and deputy sheriff of Santa Cruz County, he was also fire warden, performing his many obligations faithfully and well. Like his mother, he always had time to help a neighbor. Physically, both Will and Walter were big men, six feet four inches, tall, broad-shouldered, and straight as ramrods with rather roughly hewn features. Stalwart is the best word to describe them. Before Will was forty, he was Old Bill to all who knew him, except his mother. To her, he was always Willie. When past fifty, gray headed and according to him, getting old, he married Martha Vernova, who taught Brown's School, was twenty odd years younger, and stood five feet tall. They lived happily until Will's death many years later.

The Hoffmann family I did not know so well. They too were pioneers, coming into the mountains in the early days, taking up land some miles beyond the line in Santa Cruz County and still in the Brown School district. The children attended school there, and their fruit was shipped from the Alma Express Office, as was everyone else's. There were four boys—John,

Louie, Ernie, and Hugh—and two older daughters I never knew as they succumbed to pneumonia early in life. The youngest daughter Irma and my sister Josephine were good friends.

When they moved to their home on Bear Creek Road, there was really no road, and Mrs. Hoffmann was too ill to ride a horse. So she made the journey from the valley on a sofa, lashed to saplings, which were in turn secured to a pair of steady pack horses. When I knew her she was a handsome, spry, and hardworking gray-haired lady. Mr. Hoffmann and his sons worked in the woods and also developed some fine orchards and vineyards on their home place. They also set up a good box mill to supply their own needs and those of anyone who came to buy. Their boxes like those from the Van Lone mill were well cut the right size and thickness and all the ends square. It was a pleasure to put them together. I nailed them by the hundreds and filled them, too.

Louie made a name for himself for being the best saw filer in the country. He worked in the big mills near Boulder Creek. Ernie, a six-foot-four young giant, was accepted as the best shake maker anywhere. He could spot a good shake tree with little effort. It had to be just so, straight of grain and free from knots. Working alone, he would fell the tree and cut and split the shakes in record time. Irma was a talented musician. Having no voice for singing, she whistled beautifully becoming almost a professional performer. She married a young man of like taste, a good amateur violinist. Unfortunately, lacking the urge to be gainfully employed, he caused the marriage to end in divorce. The three older boys, being rather turbulent individuals, also found themselves in and out of the divorce courts. No matter what happened, the parents went quietly along their appointed way, living long and respected lives.

Religion and Dancing

There were, of course, scattered through the community the usual assortment of religious beliefs. It was generally accepted that the people living in Lakeside were more inclined toward the Church than those at the top of the mountains. Even along the Summit there were those who believed in church on Sunday.

I remember one Sunday afternoon going to the Sharps where a number of neighbors were gathered to meet and hear Maude, their oldest daughter, tell of her work with the Salvation Army and join in her program. Dressed in her blue uniform and wearing her poke bonnet, Maude stood on a big rock of which there were many embedded in the yard; the guests found seats on other rocks or fruit boxes and listened to her. I suppose she told of her work in whatever city she was stationed and tried to coax her present audience into the fold. Everyone joined her in singing. I can only remember one song, "Pull for the Shore, Sailor, Pull for the Shore." Father must have heard it before and lent his good bass voice with a will. I believe Maude continued in this work for many years. I know the next sister Hattie, who had been blinded in one eye in childhood, also joined the army because over the years I occasionally came across her name in the newspaper, connected with reports of the work being done by the Salvationists. Her title I do not recall, but she held a position of higher rank. The third sister Mittie died in her teens. Wilbur was in business in San Jose for many years, but I did not know of it until one day, I saw his name listed in the funeral notices. Jamie and Barney I know nothing of. Winnie, the youngest girl, became a kindergarten teacher and many years later married a childhood schoolmate, George Thomson.

Now and then a minister from some Los Gatos church would come out to someone's home in Lakeside District or to the schoolhouse and conduct services. It must have been about 1890 that Rev. James Martin came to the Lakeside community. Mr. Martin, a Scotch Presbyterian minister, had for many years worked as a missionary in Jamaica. He was a quiet old man with white hair and whiskers. He was well liked and respected by all who came to know him. Mrs. Martin, I think, was a victim of arthritis and seldom left the house. My only recollection of her is seated in a rocking chair with a heavy shawl over her knees. There was a daughter Etta who played the piano beautifully, a son Tom, who lived at home. He was a carpenter, and James Martin Jr., who tried his hand at farming. They purchased land and built two homes, Mr. Martin and his family establishing themselves in an attractive cottage quite near the Howell Reservoir, a man-made lake built and owned by the San Jose Water Company. James, the son, with his wife and I think ten children, built his home in a newly planted prune orchard on the Gist Road. The Martins also brought with them a number of colored people who had been their servants in Jamaica. These people stayed a year or two; the men tried their luck at farming on a rental basis, but were evidently disappointed in the returns. I believe they later found work and established homes in San Jose.

Soon after they were settled in their own homes, Mr. Martin set out to build a church. It was generally known that he had received an inheritance of some hundreds from a relative in Scotland and intended to use this money for his church. Mr. Newell, who was an excellent carpenter and worked at that trade when not busy with his farming, and although not a churchgoer, said, "If Mr. Martin can give this money, which his family could use, for the good of the neighborhood, I guess I can spare the time to help him build his church." There were naturally other volunteer helpers, and a nice little church complete with bell tower was soon standing beside the road in a little corner of Baker's orchard. It served the needs of the community for many years.

My guess is that Father was the only one of Mr. Martin's new neighbors that had ever seen Jamaica or the Tropics. They would have long conversations expounding their opposite points of view on life in that part of the world. To tease the old gentleman, Father would contend that the water in Jamaica was unfit for human consumption unless purified with a good shot of rum. Mr. Martin in turn explained that rum was the invention and tool of the devil, spelling harm to anyone who touched it. Despite this difference of opinion, they were very good friends.

Along with the church, a Christian Endeavor Society was organized which met in different homes once a month in the evening. Everyone roundabout was welcome regardless of religious ties. Most often the meeting was at Raymond's since they had ample room. The refreshments of cake and sandwiches were brought by the families attending, coffee furnished by the host. There would be a very short business meeting opened and closed with prayer; the rest of the time passed visiting, with a little music and games. Kissing games were allowed, but dancing was taboo.

On the other side of the social picture was the group of young people, and some not so young, who liked to dance, perfectly willing to attend Christian Endeavor parties, even show up in church; but above all else, they loved to dance. To organize a dancing party was simple. All it needed was a floor and a bit of music. A new house finished to the point of having the floor laid, a room added to an old house, a barn or fruit house answered the purpose. There was always someone who played the violin, piano, or organ. I remember Bill and Walter Van Lone, Charlie Thomson and one of his uncles as playing violins; even Harry Winchell who lived near Central School, but he was called upon only as a last resort—it was too difficult to keep him sober enough to hold his fiddle, which someone described as a cigar box with strands of baling rope stretched across it. A harmonica and someone to play it were always welcome. The time and place of a dance were passed along verbally. It was amazing how far and fast the news traveled.

There is the story of a group of young people who had come ten miles or more on an unfamiliar road to attend this party. They finally reached a point where they could see the lights and hear the music far below them. The young driver, telling his passengers to hold their hats and sit tight, turned his horses off the road, heading straight for the lights, through the brush and over rocks, in the end arriving safely. I am sure it was the horses' good sense that took them there; the driver certainly hadn't used any. That party lasted until daylight, so they were able to see the road to go home.

If someone brought food to such a gathering, fine; if not, whatever was available in the host's pantry was consumed. There was always coffee, and sometimes wine or whiskey turned up. That was frowned on by the mothers. The waltz, schottische, and polka, interspersed with Virginia Reels and Lancers were the old-time favorites; later, the two-step became popular.

Wishing for a permanent place to hold dances, a number of young men canvassed the neighborhood for money to build a platform on an open flat beside the Thomson road, just a smooth floor with a bench all around and sort of a fence or bannister behind the bench to lean against. It was a lovely spot, redwoods all around, a chattering brook nearby, with a moon overhead; it was as romantic a setting as anyone could wish for. Sometimes in order to compensate a musician for his time and talent, a hat was passed among the dancers and everyone tossed in a coin. The resulting collection, large or small, was given to the musician.

I hadn't yet grown to the dancing age but remember going to a Lakeside school closing program there one evening, but we went home before the dancing began. Once there was a Magic Lantern Show by a traveling entertainer in the old schoolhouse at the junction of the Thomson and Black roads. School had never been kept there. The building had been brought from somewhere and put together again on that spot. Later Professor Rainey of San Jose lived there. Anyway, this night the room was crowded and dark, and these pictures appeared on a white place on the wall. It was the story of the Johnstown Flood (Johnstown is in Pennsylvania, and the flood occurred in 1889)—water everywhere, pouring over everything, people running around carrying things; a man on a horse galloping along at the edge of the water, houses floating in it, some with people on the roofs, some barns with small animals and chickens on them. After the lights were lit again, the man said there would be two contests with prizes to be decided by vote. The first one was to choose the prettiest girl present. Flora Thomson won that without any opposition. The second contest was to choose the homeliest man; that fell to Mr. Frank Baker, who wasn't homely at all.

CHRISTMAS AND THOMSONS

When I was a very little girl, Christmas meant a tree decorated with shiny ornaments, colored paper, baskets for candy and nuts, and lighted candles, real wax candles that burned and flickered beautifully, and when blown out had a fragrance all their own. There were gifts for everyone. Father played his accordion; we all sang "O, Tannenbaum," and Mother always made eggnog, flavored with vanilla for Lotte and me, with brandy and nutmeg for the grown-ups. Usually, one of the uncles was present.

One year we had an extra Christmas party at the Thomsons. They lived some miles away; the night was cold and frosty with great big silver stars shining in the sky. We were well-wrapped in blankets, enjoying every step of the way. When the horses shattered the ice on the puddles, we shrieked with delight. When we arrived at the house, it was overflowing with people. Soon everyone crowded around the Christmas tree, and there were whispers of Santa coming. Sure enough, he did. We heard him on the roof, everyone watched the fireplace, and suddenly he was in the room. I was never sure whether or not he had come down that chimney. Amazingly, he wore an overcoat and a fur cap exactly like my father's, but I knew it wasn't him for I was sitting on his knee at the time. Long after, I learned that Santa was my friend Lute Sabin, who passed out gifts and candy to all the children. Soon after Santa had said goodbye, Mother took me to the bedroom and laid me on a big white bed where a number of other little people were sleeping, and that's all I remember of my first Christmas Party away from home.

The Thomsons were a wonderful family, the father John a Scotch Canadian, the mother, daughter of a German couple named Jarrisch. There were seven pretty daughters and three good-looking sons: Flora, Jennie, Mary, Charles, George, Elsie, Nettie, Nell, Leland, and Agnes. The following bits of Thomson family lore were told me by the youngest son Leland, a delightful storyteller, and corroborated by his sister. I will try to retell them as accurately as I can.

Canada, I think Leland said Montreal, was the birthplace of four Thomson brothers, Tom, Charles, George, and John, commonly called "Jack." Tom the eldest was the first to come to California, into the Santa Cruz Mountains to work in the woods cutting redwood timber. I believe the first redwoods cut were made into bridge timbers and ties for the railroads then building toward the West. Next came lumber mills, of which there were quite a few always located where the redwoods were the biggest and best. There was a mill at Lexington owned by Henning, Chase Mill was somewhere in Lyndon Gulch, another somewhere near Patchen. As one mill cut off the available trees near its location, its owner moved to a new spot or went out of business. Then someone else would come along and put up a mill on the next ridge or stream, as water was important in this work; there was usually a stream nearby or water was brought from the distance in a V flume.

Just when Charles and George came, I am uncertain. I do know they lived in Lakeside for many years. Charles remained a bachelor. The thing that always fascinated me was that he wore gold loops in his ears like a gypsy. Late in life, George married a widow, Mrs. Cardew. The youngest John joined his brothers at about seventeen, coming by steamer to Aspinwall on the Atlantic coast of the Isthmus of Panama to the city of Panama on the Pacific coast. At the Atlantic side, according to Leland's story, the Steam Ship Company would rent the passengers a donkey for a dollar to carry them across the isthmus to Panama City. From there, they continued their journey up the coast on another steamer. The trouble with this donkey transportation was that the little beasts would go along nicely to a certain point, suddenly become unmanageable, buck their riders off, and run for home, leaving the travelers to go on as best they could. Other transportation was hard to find and expensive. John, being a canny Scot, saved his dollar and walked all the way. On joining his brothers in the Santa Cruz Mountains, he too worked in the woods.

After his marriage to Miss Jarrisch, whose parents farmed a place on the Skyline which they had purchased from someone named Henning (whether this Henning also owned this mill at Lexington, I don't know), he took his bride to Oregon where he intended to make his fortune raising wheat. Some years and five babies later, convinced wheat was not the moneymaker he had been led to believe and his wife anxious to return to her people, they came back to Lakeside and established a home, developing some fine orchards on a place at the end of what is now the Thomson Road. This was in the spring of 1881, so to me the Thomsons were always there.

There was also a brother-in-law of Tom in the group, another Canadian, Archie McIntyre. Archie worked in the woods during the summer, being skid boss at Chase's mill in Lyndon Gulch. In the winter, he lived and worked for an older man, Mr. Renowden, a farmer and close friend of John Thomson. His land also lay between the Black and Bear Creek roads across a canyon from the Thomson place with ingress from the Bear Creek.

ROADHOUSE KEEPERS

Along with the woodsmen, farmers, and others who now populated the surrounding hills and the valley, there were the roadhouse keepers. A roadhouse differed from a city saloon in that both man and beast could find food and shelter there.

When a place was run by a responsible person, it became a welcome addition to the neighborhood. Besides drink, usually beer served in glass mugs at $.05 or $.10 a serving, depending on the size of the mug. Hard liquor was also available. There was always a horse trough out front where horses and dogs could slack their thirst and humans too could fill jugs to carry with them or drink from the faucet or open spout. As in every human enterprise, there were also unscrupulous men among the roadhouse keepers. Such was the case at the Ten-mile House, ten miles from San Jose at the junction of San Jose-Los Gatos and Almaden roads. The worse the reputation of a place, the more no-account hangers-on were found there.

To return to Leland's story: since Mr. Renowden was a sober and industrious man, it was falsely rumored that he had large sums of money hidden on his farm. Majors who ran the Ten-mile House conceived the idea to rob Renowden and picked a pair of his cohorts, Jule and Showers, to do the job. These two made their way to the Renowden place; hidden in the woods nearby, they waited for night before approaching the house. Their plan was upset when they found the old man was not alone. Because of an injured eye, Archie had not gone to his job at the mill as they had been led to believe. So these two pretended to be lost and asked for food and directions to town.

Having been given food, they asked Mr. Renowden to come outside and show them the road, which he did. When they had him by himself, they threatened him with guns and demanded his money. Refusing to believe that there was no money, one of them shot Renowden but did not kill him.

McIntyre, realizing that something was wrong, started to go to his friend's assistance; one of the robbers saw his move, fired through the window, and killed him. Renowden tried to make his escape, but the robbers overpowered the wounded man; after brutally torturing him, they left him dead in the grass some distance from the house. Showers and Jule, panic-stricken by what they had done, rushed back to Majors and told him all about it. Knowing that the blame for the whole affair would fall on him, Majors made plans to hide the evidence. Giving the two men a bottle of whiskey and five dollars each, with orders to head for Mexico and make it fast, he drove to the Renowden place and set the house on fire, thinking it would look like an accident and not knowing there were two dead men, and one of those not in the house. Another thing he didn't know was that a Mexican who had appeared to be fast asleep in a corner of the barroom had, in fact, overheard the whole story and at daybreak had gone straight to Los Gatos and spread the news.

In the meantime, the first thing John Thomson saw that morning was the smoke rising from his friend's burning house. He went at once by way of a path through the intervening canyon to give help. He found the house a heap of ashes. A neighbor, Jack Lindsey, and another man were already there. The three men, finding Renowden's mutilated body, realized it was not an accident but a cold-blooded murder.

John returned home, at once hitched up a horse and was off to town to report the crime and alert the law. One of the first he met was the Mexican who told him all that he had overheard. He also met Majors who expressed great shock at the news and promptly became very busy organizing a posse to trace the murderers. The sheriff overtook the fugitives at Gilroy and also arrested Majors. Jule turned states evidence. After a court trial, he was sentenced to life imprisonment, the other two, to be hung. John Thomson was so incensed by the whole thing that he went to San Quentin to see the sentence carried out. Jule was killed in a prison brawl, stabbed with a file by another prisoner.

Over the years, the story of the Renowden murder would be retold; it was the worst piece of villainy ever committed in those hills. As time went by, tales of the place being haunted were heard, and youngsters dared each other to pass by the deserted yard at night.

As I said before, the Thomsons were always there, a good and dependable family.

LAKESIDE CLUB

A step in the way of civic and cultural advancement was the formation of Lakeside Club. I think its underlying motive was community improvement; an effort was made to bring in everyone, the churchgoers as well as the dancers, also the third group which belonged to neither of the other two. At this time, too, there had developed quite a home business, keeping summer boarders. People living in towns or cities would spend their vacations on a farm often spending the whole summer as paying guests, becoming part of the farm household at seven dollars a week for grown-ups and half that for children. Some families managed the equivalent of small hotels, taking care of anywhere from ten to fifty people. More than one mortgage was paid off by summer boarders.

Mr. Jeffs was president of the Lakeside Club. I never heard of anyone paying dues. The monthly meetings were held from house to house, with refreshments brought by the members. Every meeting, there was someone appointed to present an idea for community betterment. I remember a few: Mr. Hunter was for roadside beautification, and he defended his point of view by planting a cypress hedge on his property line along the county road. Mr. Beggs, some years earlier, as the family orchards came into bearing, had set up a cannery placing his youngest son Sam in charge with the intention of marketing all the fruit they produced that way. They soon learned to be a successful venture; it needed a much greater volume of fruit and other material than their farm could supply and a more available location than one on the side of a mountain, on a poor road, six miles from the nearest railroad. So they gave up the cannery and turned to summer boarders, with a big dining and general purpose room in the converted cannery, numerous small cottages nearby. They soon had a flourishing business. Sam drove a four-horse carryall to town every day to meet the eleven o'clock train. Anyway, when it was Mr. Begg's evening to talk to the club, he stressed cleanliness and explained there should never be traces of the breakfast eggs on the noontime dishes. In my little-girl mind, I thought to myself, well doesn't everybody know? Dishes have to be washed clean!

Mr. Chittenden was all for entertainment. These strangers in our homes should be kept happy. Mrs. Raymond felt one must be careful to have the right sort of people, which was what everyone wanted, only the right people were different by different people's standards. One family comfortably settled for the summer was politely told that dance music would not be tolerated on the household piano on Sunday, not even Strauss waltzes. As the guest's young son was a well-known and sought-after pianist, the whole family left next morning.

Of all the neighbors who engaged in the boarder business, the Raymond Resort was the best known and continued to be active longest. My great ambition at this time was to grow up and be a "summer boarder" preferably at Raymond's. Nothing to do but eat when the meals were ready and the rest of the time swing in a hammock and read books. The younger members of the club were to furnish programs for entertainment and report the happenings of the area.

I was one of those detailed to write and read a report on something of interest. So I wrote this rhyme about a young neighbor:

> A nice young gent
> A calling went
> On a night all dark and dreary.
> He sang and laughed
> Till he cracked his voice in half,
> And then to make it better,
> His hostess kind
> Some stuff did find,
> Which was called
> Molasses candy.
> A chunk he took,
> Which to his fingers stuck,
> And from chewing it,
> His jaws grew weary.
> Now this young gent
> Was not content
> With what he had devoured.
> The rest in his coattail he secured,
> And then prepared to leave.

But when he came to the garden gate
Where his restless steed for him did wait,
Everything was with raindrops hung.
Quickly he to his saddle sprung
And joyfully galloped away.
But when he came to his stable door,
All the joy was sadly o'er,
For John was fast to his saddle stuck.
Did ever a man have more bad luck?

Everyone clapped, but it's a question whether John was pleased.

The club continued for some years. The last meeting I recall was a picnic at the Withrow home. That day it was a stranger who talked to us, a Mr. Williams from Saratoga, an old friend of Mr. Jeffs. A retired minister, he urged us to appreciate and care for the bounteous gifts of beauty and plenty that God had lavished upon this part of the world. He was the man known as "Sunshine Williams" who was instrumental in starting the renowned Saratoga Blossom Festival.

A CAMPING TRIP

During the summer vacation of 1894, the Stolte family went on a camping trip. What prompted such an excursion, I have never understood, for any talk of a vacation or change of scene was always considered the height of foolishness by the head of the house. Anyway, whatever the reason, we went—with a tent, mattresses, blankets, cooking utensils, extra clothing and our family of five, all packed and tied on to a spring wagon drawn by two horses.

From home, we followed the old Summit Road to where the Saratoga Turnpike, now Big Basin Way, crossed the summit; from there down the San Lorenzo Road, which followed the canyon on the opposite side of the ridge from the present Big Basin Highway, fifteen miles to Boulder Creek, through beautiful country, huge redwood trees, ferns, everywhere azaleas in bloom along the banks of the San Lorenzo which we crossed again and again on long narrow plank bridges with no rails on the side; they swung and swayed with our comparatively light outfit. The horses didn't like them, nor did I. How the men with four or more horses and heavy loads of lumber dared to cross them, I can't imagine.

Upon reaching Boulder Creek, we spent some time at the Rambo home. Mr. Sam Rambo was County Supervisor at that time. Toward evening, we found a campsite beside the road which led to the Cowell big tree grove, not far from the river. There was a footbridge across the San Lorenzo at this point, but horse-drawn vehicles forded the stream. Lotte and I decided to wade across with the horses and look inside the gate. We made it across safely and peeked into the grounds but saw nothing different from the trees we had seen along the road to Boulder Creek that day. On our way back to camp, Lotte waded in first and had no trouble, but I must have gotten off the beaten track, and for a dreadful moment I thought I was going to float down the river. A few desperate steps took me into more shallow water, and I scrambled onto the dry roadway. A Negro couple had just come from the park. They were standing near the river drinking from a dipper of water to which they had added something poured from a brown bottle. I often wondered whether, had I been carried downstream, would that man have jumped in and fished me out?

The next day we went on to Santa Cruz and again made camp near the river, almost under a covered bridge. That evening we went to see the water carnival. A grandstand of wooden seats had been built on one side of the river and across from it a stage where I know now the dignitaries of the town and others responsible for the affair were gathered. The entertainment was a concert by what Father called a brass band, led by Philip Sousa, wonderful music, and a procession of floats, with pretty girls, flowers, and lights, really lovely. These floats really floated up and down the river all during the concert. The queen and her court of course were leading the line. I believe the queen was a member of a historical family, Anita Gonzales; I know she was dark and had beautiful dark hair. I clearly remember the Chinese float with its many lanterns and flowers, parasols, and girls in their silken costumes and the Chinese music which you could hear whenever the band was quiet. The grand finale was a display of fireworks that started with a loud bang, frightening Josie, so she hid her head on Mother's shoulder and couldn't be coaxed to look anymore. I watched the rockets climb upward and wondered why someone was shooting at the stars.

The next day we continued our trip along the old Soquel Road toward Watsonville and made camp that night by the roadside somewhere between Aptos and Freedom. We went to a farm home, a very nice one, not pretentious but tidy and painted, with every shrub and blade of grass, just so; and bought milk. Father said the people were Hollanders. The next day in Watsonville we arrived at Zmudowski's. We spent a happy day and night with them. No need to make camp that night; their home was spacious and well-equipped with big comfortable beds. Leaving Watsonville, we returned to Soquel taking the old San Jose Road toward home, camping one more night by the roadside. We reached home in midafternoon; I was delighted to be there and felt as though I had been away almost forever. I hurried about checking on the animals and chickens. Uncle Julius had looked after things during our absence, and everything was in fine shape.

Uncle Julius was an eccentric man, always doing things for the good of his health, like fruit for breakfast and the use of native herbs, about which he had studied a great deal. He was always trying to persuade Mother to try them. There was Yerba Santa for colds, either as a tea, which was black and almost impossible to swallow, or as syrup, well-loaded with honey. This a sore throat accepted gratefully. There was also horehound cooked to what might be called an essence and used in candy. That was good too. Mother had tried yerba buena for tea at mealtime, but Father would have none of it. Pine pitch, the sap of the Douglas fir, could sometimes be caught in a container of some sort as it dripped from a freshly cut tree. Golden colored and far stickier than honey, it had wonderful healing powers. Spread over an open cut or other wound, covered with a strip of clean old sheet for a bandage, it had both sanitary and antiseptic qualities nothing else could match. Father accepted the pine pitch and cough syrup, but Uncle's idiosyncrasies were scoffed at which led to arguments. Finally, Uncle built himself a house on some land he owned near Grizzly Rock, and, as the storybooks say, he never darkened the Stolte's door again.

MISS SCOTT TEACHES

The next school year, Miss Edna Scott of Santa Cruz became the teacher. Nickels were then living in a big house at the top of their place and asked to have her board there. There were now four Nickels children in school, Bell and Theodore, having reached school age while Miss Sobey had been presiding. I had reached the eighth grade, and Josie came in as a beginner. Miss Scott was young, a rather "prune and prisms" sort of a person, unfortunately not adapted to teaching young children, so the first and second graders had a bad time, especially my little sister, who was painfully shy. Because she was unkind to Josie, I never felt really at ease with her; although in the end she boarded at our house, and the two families became friends.

Her change of boarding place came about because of a very tragic happening. Before school one morning, Joe Mini rushed in saying, "Ada was awfully sick and said she was about to die." Sad to say, she told the truth; for some reason, known only to herself or perhaps for no reason at all, she had taken strychnine on her way to school. None of the emergency measures, which hastily called neighbors, tried were of any use. Her brother Will rode pell-mell for a doctor, but he came too late. Ada's death was a terrible shock to everyone. Miss Scott's mother insisted she move from a home where such a thing could happen, so she came to live with us. Mrs. Nickels was offended and hurt by the move, so she took the other three children away from Central and enrolled them at Lakeside. Poor woman, she was so distraught and confused by what had happened she had to strike at someone. As Ada's death seemed in some way connected with the school, the teacher and the school became her target.

Aside from Ada's death which was heartbreaking to her family, squabbles over personal notions and dislikes were not unusual in the public schools. Such foolish things as: So and So is making money off the district! He gets all the repair jobs. The fact that no one else was willing to do these odd jobs carried no weight. Or Mr. O always collects pay for the wood he hauls to the school. Or perhaps someone else felt slighted because "that teacher always appoints Nellie J. to be lunch monitor, and my Mary never gets a chance." It might be that the teacher went riding on Sunday with Mrs. Brown's son, leaving Mrs. Black's son twiddling his thumbs, and everybody knew the Blacks's horse and rig were far better looking than the Browns'. That teacher would have to go, or Mrs. Black was surely going to raise particulars! One fuss in a neighboring district went so far, a militant little woman nailed the schoolhouse door fast; her opponent hurried over and boosted teacher and children through the window so school could start on time, went home for tools, and pried the door open. The first party wrote the School Superintendent a thirty-two-page letter giving her point of view. Such goings-on could disrupt a whole district and often did. Many years later, the two families were still living on adjoining farms in reasonable harmony.

After Ada's death, school soon returned to its usual routine. The withdrawal of the Nickels children was felt on the attendance records, as the number of pupils had dwindled over the years. Sometimes families moved away, others allowed the youngsters to drop out of school to go to work, or just because it was too much bother to send them.

At home, everything was much the same except for something none of us was smart enough to see or understand—Mother's health was failing. She had always worked too hard, never complaining, always doing a little more, which added up to much more than any woman should have tried or been allowed to do. Part of her trouble was digestive. Dr. Knowles prescribed bismuth mixture before meals. I doubt whether it did any good.

This was the year that the school's liquor-loving neighbor staggered over to the path one morning, emptied the pail of water being carried up from the spring, and told the children in very positive language to keep the h—off his property. After that, each child carried a bottle of water to school, along with books and lunch. In June, Lotte graduated. The folks made quite a thing of it. Mother had made her a lovely white dress. The Blaich family was with us at the time, and Mrs. Blaich made an elaborate wreath of flowers for her. Fred, the oldest son, took part in the exercises. Aunt Emilia came from the city bringing her a gold ring set with a red stone, probably a garnet. After the program, everyone came to our house for a picnic which we had prepared. There were dozens of cream puffs. I am glad to remember that the shells came from a bakery in Los Gatos; we had only whipped the cream. All this wonderful excitement was promised to me—white dress, gold ring, everything—when and if I graduated the next June. Needless to say, it didn't materialize, although I did graduate.

The Scotts and Stoltes held to a friendship of sorts for a long time, and when in Santa Cruz, we always called on them. Mr. Scott, an old man, told fascinating tales of the early days—how he and his brother took up land in and gave their name to Scotts Valley. He said when they first rode into the valley, it was one beautiful expanse of wild oats, growing so lush they could take the oat heads from either side and tie them together over the saddle on the back of a standing horse. For a time, he was driver on a stage that ran between San Jose and Santa Cruz. There were then two roads from Los Gatos to Lexington; one about where Highway 17 is now a toll road, the other on the opposite side of the Canyon along the Jones Road, down through the Lyons's property across Los Gatos Creek and joining the main road just on the north side or end of a bridge over Lyndon Gulch. There were also two rival stage lines, one using the Toll Road, the other the Jones Road. When the drivers saw each other across the canyon, it was the signal for a race and a wild one at that, each man aiming to be first at the Lyndon Gulch Bridge, for the first man over had the lead into Santa Cruz, there being no other chance to pass. I always had a hunch that Joe Scott drove the Jones Road Stage; he sounded so jubilant when the story ended with that man leading.

MY LAST YEAR OF SCHOOL

When schooltime came around in September, Lotte went to San Francisco to live with Aunt Emilia and attend Cogswell College. I was now in the ninth grade with a new teacher, a Santa Cruz girl with a San Francisco Irish background, Bessie Gillen. She boarded that year at Withrows, to the great delight of their young son Washington; it gave a young man such standing in the community to escort the school ma'am about, at least Wash thought so. For the spring term to help bolster the attendance, Miss Gillen's young brother came to live at our house, attending school and working for his board. This was a good arrangement. Will was a nice lad of about fifteen. He cheerfully took over some of my outdoor duties, giving me more time to help Mother.

It was at this time that numbers of Japanese men came into the mountains, being employed mostly for woodcutting. They came in groups, as many as ten or fifteen, never less than four or five. One man who knew a little English would do the bargaining and boss the work. Father hired one such group to cut oak stovewood. They set up camp near the woods, ordered quantities of rice, onions, flour, and a little cured meat, and were in business. They did good work and gave good measure. There were numbers of other camps on adjoining ranches. At times they all got together and staged wrestling matches and other athletic contests which the natives like to watch.

Another pastime that seemed to please them greatly was catching squirrels. The pasture fields near our place were overrun with ground squirrels. These men having no guns would literally dig the little animals out of the ground with picks and shovels. When a squirrel was caught, there was a burst of shouting and jabbering as was never heard before or since. They left excavations in those fields deep enough to bury a horse in.

We children had a much simpler method to catch the squirrels. On the way to and from school, we would often see the young ones out away from their nests, throw our straw hats over them, and, at the risk of nipped fingers, reach under and get them. Before leaving the field, we let them go again, as they were not welcome in either place, at home, or at school. After a few seasons, the Japanese men left the woodcutting; many became fruit, vegetable, and flower growers in Santa Clara County. There was one I knew, Charlie Takamoto who stayed and took over the care of Mr. Pitman's farm.

One morning as I entered the schoolroom, Miss Gillen met me with the announcement that I was an honorary graduate. That meant I need not take the county examinations. My response was not a feeling of joy. My first thought was, "I can't go to school after this term."

Graduation Day I recited the poem, "Maude Miller," sang the appointed songs with my schoolmates, and received my diploma. A few neighbors had come as usual, so picnic lunches were shared, and the day was accounted for. Lotte had returned from her year at Cogswell and Rose Regan whose sister had been Miss Gillen's classmate at San Francisco State came to spend the summer, having been advised by her doctor that country air and rest would correct her run-down condition.

Country air was frequently prescribed by physicians of that day; sometimes a cure was effected but not always. The truth of the matter was, if the condition was not serious, fine; but if, as was often the case, the trouble was tuberculosis or consumption as the ailment was then known, fresh air and sunshine might prove a deterrent but seldom a cure. Patients were advised to sleep in the open, to live on fruit, to take plenty of exercise, and to consume great quantities of milk and cream. One unfortunate woman I met was on a raw egg diet, a dozen a day—Ugh! Strange to say, to have a member of a family ill with consumption was almost a disgrace, something not admitted, at best spoken of in whispers, and worst of all, very little done about it.

Rose was our first visitor suffering this way, but over the years there were other strangers all complaining of the same "run-down" condition who spent months with us. Why Josie and I escaped it, I don't know. There were certainly no special precautions taken to avoid contagion.

At Christmas that year, my gift was an Eastman Kodak which took 3 1/2″ x 3 1/2″ pictures. This became my most valued treasure. I still have nearly all the films and albums of prints taken with it. Ed Johns, a Los Gatos druggist, from whom the folks bought the Kodak, came to dinner one Sunday and spent the afternoon showing me the mysteries of picture-making. Having no dark room, we hung blankets over the windows. For a red light, we placed a candle in a five-pound starch box and covered the opening with orange colored paper. Then we snipped the film apart on the dotted line and put the pieces one at a time through the chemical bath. Wonder of wonders, they all came out. Then we stuck them on the windowpanes to dry. I learned to print them on Solio paper by following printed directions. I held the printing frame in the direct sunlight. Blueprints too were fun and easy to make. I have since owned a number of other cameras, in which I found great pleasure, but none gave me the feeling of pure joy and accomplishment as the little Kodak did.

As Lotte was home and of real help to Mother, I was always outdoors with Father working at whatever came next. I remember he had a lot of pine cordwood cut on the North Side, a steep and rocky hillside facing toward the valley. There had been a beautiful stand of Douglas fir there, but by then most of it had been cut. To get this wood to the county road where it could be loaded on wagons was quite a job; for this purpose we had a remarkable vehicle, a wheel-sled called a Go Devil. There was an axle with small sturdy wheels under the back. The front was built up on short runners making the bed almost level. It was a most unwieldy implement, but a team could haul a bigger load on a wheel sled than an ordinary flat sled, or as the Easterners called them, "stone boat." When the wood lay above the road, it wasn't too bad getting it down to where it could be loaded even if it took two or three throws to get it there. When it lay below the road and every stick had to be thrown uphill with all the strength you had, it wasn't much fun.

That was the summer also when Mother bought the organ; no one in the house could play, but we all intended to learn.

In October, Rose returned; Miss Gillen was living with us and teaching school, the Connolly girls, Mary and Ida, came because of Ida's need of country air. These girls were old friends and all of San Francisco Irish background. Despite illness which no one believed at all serious, they were a merry group. To everyone's delight, Ida could play that organ and sing, which she did by the hour, such songs as "I'll Take You Home Again, Kathleen," "Someday I'll Wander Back Again," "Come All Ye Faithful," which she sang in Latin, and many others. In the end, both Rose and Ida succumbed to TB.

The End Of Childhood

By November, Mother's condition had worsened so much that Dr. Knowles insisted she stay in bed and advised a visit to the Women's and Children's Hospital for observation and spoke of the possibility of the need for an operation. So she and Father went to San Francisco to see the hospital doctors. After a day or two, Father came home feeling assured that Mother would be given the needed care and everything would be all right. On my fifteenth birthday, I received a brave little note from her saying that was the day she would go to surgery, that she was not afraid, and her girls mustn't worry. We hadn't the faintest comprehension of the seriousness of her illness.

I at least believed that Mother would come back to us well and strong. Not so; Father went to San Francisco to bring her home, taking Josie with him. Lotte and I drove to Los Gatos Christmas Eve morning and met them. When Father lifted her from the train steps and I saw what a frail, white shadow of herself she was, I nearly died. That long cold ride home after hours by train must have been agony for her. We were all hopeful for her, but by spring, at least she knew that it was not to be. One day in April, I was sitting beside her couch on the vine-covered porch, when she asked me to promise to take care of Josie and my father, as Lotte would go to San Francisco to live with Mrs. Blaich. I was puzzled and asked what she meant. She explained that her time was fast running out and soon she would leave us. I promised, of course, although I could not grasp the idea that she must go. That promise held me for many years.

On Saturday, April 23 at midday, Mother slipped quietly away, and the bottom fell out of the world for me.

Her funeral was on Tuesday, April 26; Uncle Louie Dettmann and Mr. Blaich came from San Francisco to be with us, and many of our friends and neighbors were there. Mr. Martin spoke. I remember the sound of his voice, but not what he said except that he read the Twenty-third Psalm. A lady, Mrs. Elliot, sang "Nearer My God to Thee," and Mr. E. E. Place took care of other details. She lies buried in Los Gatos Cemetery, now Blossom Hill Memorial Park. Her fortieth birthday would have been on May 16 of that year, 1898.

We returned to an empty home that evening and took up the task of going on. Nothing mattered that summer; the work was done as it came before us, and the months passed. In August, Lotte went to San Francisco to become a member of the Blaich household. I think she was happy there. She was fond of them and they of her. I now had the job of doing for my family. I knew what had to be done about most things but had never baked a batch of bread, not from start to finish. So Lotte had me do the last baking before she left. It turned out fairly well; it was edible. She also insisted that I put my hair up. When a girl put her hair up, she was considered "grown up." It meant the end of childish things, the acceptance of responsibilities and no more nonsense.

LIFE GOES ON

When the press of the harvest came that fall, I slowly began to adjust to life as it was. I stopped saying to myself, "I'll ask Mama what to do" and accepted the fact that she was gone forever, that if my problems were to be solved, I would have to solve them myself. This made for self-reliance and resulted in some remarkable blunders.

Father too was coming out of the daze Mother's death had caused; without her gentle influence, he soon reverted to being Captain of his ship, a very stern and often unreasonable one.

I was acknowledged to be, and accepted as, keeper of the house, but somehow the housekeeping in his estimation was to be accomplished by some sort of hocus-pocus or magic; his one-girl crew would continue to take care of all the outdoor work he was accustomed to her doing. So he made an effort to organize the housework. One must remember he was not the man who lent a hand when things bogged down, but like many others, knew just how things should be done and never hesitated to tell you.

Because "scrubbing deck" was a daily chore on shipboard, he decreed that the dining room and kitchen floors should be mopped every morning. Mopping a floor in our house meant getting on your knees with a pail of soapy water and a mop rag, (a mop rag was usually part of a worn-out woolen garment), and going carefully over every inch of that floor.

Father had comfortably forgotten that on shipboard, a couple of able-bodied men would be assigned to this job, because the Captain was looking for something with which to keep them busy, and they accomplished the task with brooms or deck swabs and lots of water, any surplus of which drained away through the scuppers.

While here, he had one lone girl with a little sister to get off to school, with her hair combed and her lunch packed, first thing after breakfast, as well as many other things waiting to be taken care of, till the whole lot looked impossible. The floor mopping was soon changed to once a week and often longer.

To be sure, from five o'clock in the morning to nine at night is sixteen hours, and much can be accomplished in that time if one goes at it right.

Despite my ailing babyhood, once I recovered from that whooping cough, I was blessed with excellent health and really did not mind working.

Still harking back to his "cabin boy" days, Father thought a weekly schedule for meals would work, like bean soup on Monday, stew on Tuesday, ham and potatoes for Wednesday, and so on through the week; but to have this repeated week after week soon lost its charm for him as well as for everyone else.

The bread I baked improved, so did the meals I put together.

Before and after school and on weekends, Josie was my faithful little helper.

Washday rolled around once a week no matter what. This was no simple operation of tossing an armful of soiled nylons into an automatic washer and snapping a switch.

When breakfast was cooked and the stove top clear, the wash boiler was placed over a freshly replenished fire and filled with water carried from the kitchen sink in a big enamelware pan, and a cake of Queen Lily laundry soap shaved fine with a paring knife added. By the time breakfast was finished, this water was hot, so it was dipped from the boiler and carried to the tub on the back porch in the same enamelware pan, because the boiler was too heavy and too hot to handle; the boiler was refilled to heat again.

Everything to be washed had been gathered and sorted as to color and degree of dirtiness. The winter washing was by far the worst, especially the underwear which was either woolen or fleece lined cotton, ankle length and long sleeved.

Every piece was thoroughly soaped and rubbed clean on the washboard and often wrung very damp dry by hand; if a wringer was available, it was a great help.

A clothes wringer was a wooden frame equipped with two solid rubber rollers that could be adjusted tighter or looser by means of a set screw and were turned by hand with an attached handle. The wringer was fastened to the side of the tub by small clamps.

The washtubs, if wooden, were made of wooden staves held by hoops, about twelve inches deep. Some tubs were made in one piece of heavy galvanized metal.

As each tubful was finished, the wet things were carried back to the kitchen, put into the boiler with a portion of what I believe was the first soap powder made, "pearline," and boiled. After that, it went through two rinsing, the last water having been blued so white things would be whiter. None of this tattletale gray in our house.

This bluing material first came in balls like small marbles; a few of these balls were tied into a bit of cloth and swished about in the water till the desired shade of blueness was reached. If the swishing was overdone, all the white pieces come out very, very blue. Later bluing came in bottles, but one could use too much of that too.

A short piece of broom handle was used to lift the pieces out of the boiling water.

This process was continued till everything was finished and on the line. Colored things were not boiled.

Sometimes on cold winter days, washing would freeze and rattle like paper while being pinned on the line.

While the washing was being done, there was sure to be a pot of stew, white bean soup, or plain brown beans simmering on the back of the stove or a batch of bread on the corner table ready to be made into loaves.

Baking a batch of bread was quite a job; every step had to be attended to at the proper time or the finished product was nothing to be proud of.

The day before baking day, the water in which the noontime potatoes were cooked was set aside. That evening it was heated to lukewarm, while a cake of Magic Yeast, a commercial product of flour, cornmeal, and the element which caused fermentation derived from hops.

These little cakes, about one and a half inches square by about three-eighths of an inch thick, came five in a package and cost, I think, a nickel a piece.

As I already have said, one cake of Magic Yeast was crumbled and left to dissolve in a glass of warm water; this was added to the potato water along with a little sugar and enough flour to make a rather thin batter. This batter was set in a warm place near the stove and left to develop until morning.

Then the proper amount of flour, about six quarts, and a handful of salt were sifted into a big bowl, most of the now bubbling yeast added, also some warm milk in which a chunk of butter had been melted. This mass was thoroughly mixed with a wooden spoon, covered with a white cloth and a small quilt, kept just for that, and set on a table behind the stove away from drafts.

By ten o'clock, the covering would be puffed up into a rounded mound, and it was time to work the dough into loaves. While this was being done, flour was added till the dough no longer stuck to one's fingers and the loaves could be shaped properly. As a rule, there were six loaves, three to a pan. Usually we made one loaf of rye bread flavored with caraway seeds and sometimes a shallow pan of coffee cake topped with sugar, cinnamon, and bits of butter.

These loaves were again set to rise to the right size, an hour or longer. When ready to bake, the fire was adjusted and the heat of the oven tested by holding your hand inside. It took an hour to bake the six loaves, another hour for the rye bread and coffee cake. Sometimes the oven was too hot, and heavy brown paper placed over the loaves saved them; sometimes there was a nice crust of charcoal over at least part of the loaves.

Mostly it was good, better in memory than any loaf now available in any supermarket.

Washday was of course followed by ironing, lots of it. Everything from handkerchiefs to linen tablecloths, Turkish towels, and everyone's underwear was ironed with old-fashioned solid iron, "sad irons" heated on the kitchen stove.

Women in those days, at least for dress-up occasions, wore long skirts which cleared the floor by an inch. It was every young girl's hope that her next dress would be made longer.

These skirts were often three yards or more around, trimmed with ruffles and supported by equally voluminous petticoats which were also adorned with dust ruffles and over-ruffles of embroidery.

All cotton apparel was starched on washday. Corn starch was used for this; it came in small lumps, sold in five-pound lots in nice wooden boxes. The desired quantity was dissolved in cold water in a large bowl and then cooked by adding boiling water while stirring briskly till it became clear and reached the desired consistency. The wet garments were dipped in this, rung by hand, and hung on the line to dry.

To iron a set of starched clothing took both time and patience.

KIND NEIGHBORS

While Mother was so ill, the neighbor ladies had been very kind and thoughtful, coming often to see her and being as helpful as possible, especially Mrs. Pelton and Mrs. Hunter; but by the end of summer, things had changed for both.

Mrs. Pelton's husband died very suddenly, and she and her little boy went away, to her parents I think.

The Hunter family had come from the Midwest some years before: father, mother, and six boys, Harry, Fred, Roy, Walter, Vern, and Clarence, three blonds and three redheads.

Trouble developed between the parents, and they parted. Mrs. Hunter soon moved to Los Gatos with the younger boys, so I seldom saw her. The older boys found work and took care of themselves. Mr. Hunter stayed in the community and later married again, a widow, Mrs. Flockhart, who had three teenage children, Mary and two boys.

Anyway, these ladies had their own problems and no time to worry over the Stolte girls.

Mrs. Newell, who had been very ill at the time of Mother's death, found time to look in on us now and then. Her kindly words of counsel helped a great deal.

As the road to town led by their door, I always brought their mail from the post office when I went to deliver the eggs and butter and do the needed shopping. This gave me frequent opportunities to visit in her kitchen, which helped too.

That winter Mr. Newell died. The oldest son James, who was then living in Weaverville, came with his wife, Fanny, and baby son, Oscar, to take charge of the farm and care for his mother. Young Mrs. Newell and I soon built a lasting friendship.

Josie had of course been attending school all this time. During the spring term, a young Los Gatos girl, Ida Sund, had been the teacher. She made her home with the Ben Cushings.

The teacher who came in July was Miss Bess Bailey, daughter of a Santa Cruz jeweler. She too stayed at the Cushings'. Having made plans to go home one weekend, which turned out to be cold and wet, somehow Mrs. Cushing failed to meet her with the horse and cart, so Miss Bailey set out to walk the six miles to the railroad station at Alma.

After braving the storm for several miles, completely soaked and shivering with cold, she met Jack Petty, the father of three of her students. He turned his team about and took her to her destination. The result of this experience was a severe case of double pneumonia for Miss Bailey. So Emma Martin came to finish the term.

In the spring, Beatrice Boston of Santa Cruz took the school. Upon the insistence of Mr. Bixby, a one-time druggist in Los Gatos and an acquaintance of Father's, we agreed to have Miss Boston live at our house. Mr. Bixby did not know that we had lost Mother.

Having Miss Boston with us was wonderful. She was sensible and cheerful, a good teacher and to my great joy a musician, having studied both piano and voice. So she looked upon the organ which had stood closed and silent since Mother's death, as a useful part of the furnishings of the house. When not otherwise busy, she would sing and play tirelessly to everyone's delight. It may have been practice to her, but to me it was pure joy.

I still have an old blue songbook titled "Gems of English Song" which she gave me at the end of her stay with us. It was old and falling apart then and more dilapidated now, but still one of my cherished possessions.

Her father had owned one of the first tanneries in Santa Cruz, and the family had lived in an adobe house with walls three feet thick which had been built by Indians from the Santa Cruz Mission. When I knew them, they were living in a two-story frame house on Mission Hill not far from the spot where the adobe house had been.

Although Miss Boston's stay at Central was a short one, our friendship lasted through the years. We came to know her mother and sisters too.

A Tricky Soldier

Matilda Prusch, from Evergreen, near San Jose, followed Miss Boston and lived at Cushings; being busy at home, I did not know her very well.

She was a tall, blue-eyed blonde. Josie went to school every day; she and the other pupils seemed happy.

One fine day a soldier, Harry Goldsworthy, in his spic-and-span blue uniform and shiny brass buttons stopped at the school and explained that a company of United States soldiers from San Francisco's Presidio were making a march to Santa Cruz, that they were coming along this very road, that he was the advance guard, and it was his duty to see that the road was clear for them.

He thought that surely the teacher and the children would want to be out to see them marching by. Marching soldiers! Hurrah! What could be better? Matilda gathered her little flock and started up the road to meet them.

My sister, always ready to share any pleasure with me, hurried ahead of the rest, accompanied by her best friend Belle to tell me all about it. The two excited, breathless little girls coaxed me to come as far as the Black Road with them, for the soldiers were surely coming.

Something warned me the whole thing was a hoax, so I persuaded them to return to school, which they did, arriving there a few minutes after the rest had resumed work and were marked tardy; this they never forgave.

Harry Goldsworthy stayed in the hills for some time, working wherever he found employment.

Whether he was an honorably discharged soldier or had merely taken French leave, we never knew. He certainly thought himself "pretty smart" for having fooled that school teacher.

Some years later, Miss Prusch, now Mrs. Hart, and her husband, a victim of TB, returned to the mountains where she taught at Brown's School.

Mr. Hart made a fair recovery and for a time was in business in Los Gatos, but Matilda succumbed to the dread disease shortly after returning to her valley home.

FATHER'S ACTIVITIES

All during these years, Father served as clerk of the School Board of Trustees; because he wrote a legible hand, he was also always appointed clerk of the election board, whenever a county, state, or national election came up.

These elections were always held in Brown's School. The precinct was made up of the entire Brown's and Central School districts. It seems to me the polls were open from sunup to sundown. When the ballots were counted and tabulated, one of the younger men, often Harry Cushing, because he lived nearby, was dispatched with the sealed records for the county courthouse at Santa Cruz.

This was a three-hour drive, even if driving a good horse hitched to a light rig.

Father also took part in other affairs concerning the neighbors. One I recall was a lively boundary argument between a couple of families on the Bear Creek Road. Finally, someone suggested that they ask that Dutchman over in the other school district to come and settle the matter. Amazingly, they both agreed to the suggestion and abided by his decision, thereby ending the fuss.

Another time Mike Weaver, who in the early days of our life on the ranch had been a woodchopper nearby, and once in great indignation had come storming into the yard and told Mother that "Be-gorra and Be-jabbers ect and so on"—he was going to shoot that old brown cow and "may the devil fly away with the beast." He finally calmed down a bit and explained that Stolte's cow had come to his cabin, pulled his best red woolen undershirt off the line, and eaten it.

Of course, Mother Boss hadn't really swallowed that undershirt, just chewed on it to get the sweaty salt it was loaded with, and no doubt ruined it for further wear. Mike didn't shoot the cow.

Anyway, Mike now had found himself a wife and acquired some land way down in a canyon off the Bear Creek Road. He wanted to become a citizen of the United States of America, for this he needed a witness to testify to his good character and the fact that he had lived in this country the required length of time.

Father was of course pleased and willing to do this for him; on the appointed day they appeared before a judge in Santa Cruz. Everything went along smoothly; Mike answered all the questions correctly in the broadest of Irish brogues, causing quite a bit of amusement in the courtroom. When the judge asked the question about the place of his birth, Mike replied, "Sure, and I was born in a fine city in Germany."

The judge was astonished, and Father tried to argue the point, but Mike calmly produced papers from his pocket which showed that he spoke the truth, and so another native of Germany became a citizen of the United States of America.

Strangers In The House

As I look back over these pages, I find much space devoted to the school and the teachers. This is because these women stayed longer in our lives than anyone else not related to us. They brought us in touch in varying degrees with a part of the world beyond the walls of our own home.

Other strangers often came to us, such as the School Superintendent, Mr. Linscott, Sam Rambo, the County Supervisor from Boulder Creek, the County Assessor and the man who delivered the election supplies. City drummers and commission men all found it convenient to reach the Stoltes at nightfall, knowing there would be stalls and feed for their horses as well as a bed and food for themselves.

After supper, they would sit with Father and talk, but we girls were supposed to go about our household duties, not sit idly listening to what didn't concern us.

Sometimes the strangers in the house were men or women, acquaintances of acquaintances, who came as paying guests for a week or two, interested in their own problems, health, business, family troubles, or just a desire to get away from where they were. To most of them, Jo and I were just there to look after their needs, serve their meals, and keep their rooms in order, if the days were cold, keep the fires burning, or warm days, tell them where shady walks and resting places could be found.

But the teachers of necessity settled deeper into the family life and turned to us for company, which was fine, for we needed them as much as they us.

Social Activities

About now the storms of the past winters had changed the course of the gentle stream that flowed beside the dance platform on the Thomson place, into a raging torrent, carrying away the road and heaping boulders all about. Therefore, the young men of the community again canvassed the neighborhood for money to carry out more pretentious plans; this time they wanted to build a hall, so dances could be given during the winter as well as summer.

Mr. Thomson was willing to give a bit of land near Lakeside School for a building site. By using the money collected, what lumber they could salvage from the platform and all volunteer labor, they soon had a hall; quite a large building, unfinished inside with permanent benches on each side, a stage at the west end with curtained dressing rooms on either side, and an old square piano in place for the musicians, at the other end near the front door, a counter for serving refreshments and a stove on which to cook coffee and to furnish warmth on winter nights. This place was known as Lakeside Hall and for years was the scene of many a happy party.

Sometimes a group of young people would get real fancy, hire professional musicians, issue formal invitations, charge admission, and use printed programs. Most often these musicians were Miss Tillie Brohaska and her brother, she playing the piano and her brother, a violin.

At other times when the music was furnished by local volunteers, their compensation was whatever was collected by passing a hat among the men, or if the attendance was light, they played for free.

Refreshments and coffee were always donated by the local mothers and daughters.

The music was supposed to start at eight or eight thirty and continue till about two a.m.

It was sometime before I attended any of these affairs, although asked to do so. Father would not go, declaring he had no interest in such frivolous nonsense, as for going just to take his daughters, that was ridiculous.

Finally, he agreed that I might take the horse and buggy, my sister and the teacher if she cared to go, if we felt it was so important. The possibility of being escorted to the dance by some young man was definitely out.

I think Harriet Bailey was with us when I first ventured down to Lakeside Hall without any knowledge of dance steps or etiquette. Fortunately there were always a few kindly souls present willing to lead beginners through the changes of the lancers; I especially remember the good-natured help of Mr. Thomson in that.

Bill Van Lone was another who, for all his size, was light on his feet and enjoyed dancing and would patiently count 1, 2, 3, 1, 2, 3, till you got some idea of what you were trying to do.

The waltz and the two-step were easy, and I enjoyed them very much, but I never did learn to do the schottische.

I must admit, I was never the Belle of the Ball; no one who took life as seriously as I did could hope to be. There were always other girls present, better dancers, prettier, and far better versed in small talk and the simple art of being sweet and helpless. This I accepted as being as it should be. I was too well drilled in doing for others to know how to let others do for me; nevertheless, I had a fine time.

So about once a month, when the moon was full so as to give light along the road, if the weather was favorable, a horse in the barn, and it hadn't worked too hard that day and if my own work was pretty well in order, and the request caught him in the right mood, Father would agree that we might go, but seldom without a lecture on the folly of our ways.

If the musicians were local like Charlie Thomson or Bill Van Lone, there was no set time for the music to stop; of course no one dreamed of going home till the musicians said "no more." So then, if you didn't get home till daylight, the thing to do was to change to working clothes and take up the duties of the day and hope to go to bed with the chickens at dark.

Although Father would attend no gathering where dancing was the order of the evening, it was not because of any inherent or religious reason, by his own telling, he had cut quite a figure on the dance floor in his younger days.

He paid his dues promptly in the Los Gatos Lodge of Odd Fellows and never attended meetings. With another fraternal organization, "Der Deutsher Krieger Verien" it was different, seldom missing a meeting, for which he went all the way to San Jose.

Their yearly picnic was a must. Jo and I were not enthusiastic about these affairs, but we went. The best description of these picnics is a German Beer Bust. Good music, much singing, plenty beer.

I remember one at the Forest House now under Lexington Lake, one at Sunset Park at Wrights, now Water Company property and others at Schutzen Park on the Monterey Road, also lost to progress.

BILLY MCGEE

One summer we became acquainted with Father Townley, a San Francisco priest, summering in a cottage on the Gist Road. It had long been a common occurrence to have groups of students from the Jesuit Novitiate at Los Gatos, when out on their walking trips, stop at the house for drinks of water, perhaps to ask where the road led, often just to fill their pockets with pears or apples and rest awhile.

Father Townley was older, quite settled in his cottage and usually had a younger priest as a companion. These men found it a pleasant walk as far as our house, and frequently spent the afternoon on our vine-covered porch with Father, settling the problems of the universe over a plate of bread and cheese and a jug of wine.

Father Townley was in some way connected with the Father Crowley Home for Boys in San Francisco, so they worked out a plan, unbeknown to Jo or I, to the effect that upon his return to San Francisco, Father Townley would arrange with the Boy's Home to send one of their older boys to the ranch, to be taught farming, become a member of the household, and in general, be a great help and companion to the head of this women-dominated family.

The day of the boy's arrival, Father went to meet the train and that evening brought home Billy McGee.

Poor Billy, about seventeen years of age, certainly one of San Francisco's most neglected orphans, stunted in stature and, as another Irishman remarked, perhaps unkindly but nonetheless truthfully, "If ever a human being looked like the missing link, it was Billy McGee."

His unfortunate appearance was of course no fault of his nor was the fact that he was also mentally retarded. The whole situation was impossible; he could not comprehend the simplest explanations, the country's space and stillness frightened him, and the gentle old cows looked like raging wild beasts to him.

The simple rule of yours and mine meant nothing to him, so all sorts of things found their way into strange hiding places. Most of the back rows of preserves and jellies on the cellar shelves vanished, and the empty containers turned up in the horses' mangers or the hens' nests.

Billy being as he was and Father not noted for patience or understanding, this became a very unhappy state of affairs.

Billy finally left us for a neighbor's, where he said they wanted him. I doubted the truth of his statement, but Miller's was a household where a young man, married to the eldest of a family of eight, cheerfully made a home for his seven orphaned in-laws. I suppose they figured one more wouldn't make much difference. After a few weeks at Millers, he drifted back to San Francisco; we heard nothing more of him nor of Father Townley.

Mountain Schools

Alma Osterhaus was the next one to take the school; her home was in Santa Cruz, Central her first school, and she boarded with us.

Alma was well liked by the children, as she asked very little of them. She loved parties and picnics and was popular with the other young people, a pleasant person to have in the house.

With the passing of time, children growing beyond school age and families moving away, sometimes the daily school attendance dwindled almost to the vanishing point. According to the state school laws, when the average daily attendance over a given time dropped below five and one half, the school would lapse. This meant that for a period of years—I think five—the district had no teacher and no money, but if in the meantime enough children came into the district to make the desired attendance possible, the school could resume without further to do.

This had happened to Castle Rock School, as it was never reopened at the end of the given time that district was divided between Central and Fairview.

Fairview was a school located at the junction of Summit Road, now Skyline Boulevard and the Saratoga Turnpike, now Big Basin Way. It was always known as a joint district as its attendance was drawn from three counties: Santa Cruz, Santa Clara, and San Mateo.

Fairview came into existence to take care of the children of the families connected with the Hubbard and Carmichael lumber mill. For most of the years it existed, the teacher was an older lady from Boulder Creek, Miss Sterling. When the mill closed, the school too was discontinued.

The name Fairview brings to my mind the story of a surveying party, told to me by a Mr. Butler who at one time worked at the mill and knew the surveyors.

It seems these men were camped near the school site; their purpose among other things was to locate the corner where the three counties met, as stated on a map made by the surveyors who had done the original work many years before.

The weather was miserable; every day a cold wet fog hung low to the ground making it impossible to see from one point to the next.

They were a disgruntled lot, all but one young fellow who insisted on prowling about with his gun in search of game.

One evening he remarked very casually, "There must be someone buried on yonder hill—I found sort of a tombstone today." Sure enough he had come across a sort of a monument, with the letters SC and a date on two sides. He had found the object of their search without the use of transit or chain.

The division of Castle Rock School District put the Moodys, Scotts, Smeads, and Herrings in Central. Only the Moody boys, Earl and Wallace, came to school. There were no schoolchildren in the other families at that time.

Lotte's Summer Home

One summer the Blaich family made a visit to Germany, and Lotte came home to be with us during their absence.

She had made several quick visits of a day or two, during the past year and a half, but this time she would be home for several months. So in older-sister fashion, she decided we needed reorganizing; there seemed to be endless things we had been doing wrong.

Poor Sis, she had adopted city ways at an alarming rate, and now found much she just couldn't understand.

The first time she took over the, to me, pleasant duty of delivering the butter and eggs and attending to the weekly shopping, she arrived home a very indignant young lady.

Every teamster on the road, men she had never seen before, had greeted her with great familiarity, and the storekeepers and clerks were just as bad. Naturally this was all my fault; I should develop more dignity and self-respect and not let it happen in the future.

The truth of the matter was, these men, young or old, recognized the horses from a distance, and not until they had given voice to their usual friendly and often jovial greeting did they realize that it was a different girl driving.

These men were all good friends of mine. A woman alone on the road would sometimes find herself in need of help. Harnesses could break or horses get into difficulties or a poorly tied load could shift and need adjusting. No matter what the trouble, any one of these men would cheerfully climb down from his high perch and put things right.

Anyway, what was wrong with resting your horses while you exchanged a quick rundown on community gossip with some driver going in the opposite direction? It was amazing what a variety of information one could gather in a short space of time.

The next thing I knew, Mrs. Pearson, one of my butter customers, knew a lady in great need of help, someone to look after her home and care for her frail little mother while she went to her daily work of school teaching.

Mrs. Pearson thought this would be just the place for Lotte. Not so; Lotte and Father decided it was just the place for me. They felt I needed to learn how other and better housekeepers managed.

So I found myself in a strange home with people I had never before seen and believe it or not, never in my life had I spent a night away from home without a sister with me. I was about as homesick as anyone could be. Nevertheless, I managed, aside from being considered extravagant with butter and eggs, my cooking pleased them.

Although I had been told there would be no washing to do, that little old lady found a surprising number of things to be hand washed because the laundry might ruin them.

At the end of the second week, Lotte stopped by to tell them I was needed at home. I stayed till they found someone to take my place.

I was paid for the time I spent there, but I was so happy to be going home, I wouldn't have noticed if they hadn't.

By late summer, Blaichs came home, Lotte went back to San Francisco, and Josie and I reverted to doing things the wrong way.

GROWING UP

With the passing of time, my sister and I, of course, drew nearer to adulthood. No matter what, Father could not keep us children, although we continued to accept his word as final.

We nevertheless, as all young people do, developed opinions and plans of our own. These did not always meet with his approval.

Don't think for a moment that we were unhappy, far from it. There were endless pleasant things to fill our leisure time when we happened to have any. Every day brought something to be enjoyed. It might be a glorious sunset over Grizzly Rock that gave us a half hour of joy and peace, or we could sit for a while on the road bank and listen to the wind in the great fir trees; this was quite as delightful as some organ recitals I have heard in later years.

To spend some time on a rainy day over on the "North Side," to listen to the drip, drip, of the rain on the deep carpet of fallen leaves and twigs, to smell the indescribable perfume that rose all about, sheltered from the storm but hearing it roar and thunder some hundreds of feet above us, was well worth the discomfort of the storm going and coming as well as the scolding awaiting our return.

Trees and flowers had always been of great interest to us, the trees we knew as permanent parts of the landscape always there in the same place year after year. The flowers were different. Our interest in them was not scientific, so many petals, sepals, and anthers, but just lovely friends that would be waiting for us at given spots at certain times, fresh and beautiful and surprising.

Many flowers had names never found in botany books. Wild iris were flag lilies, mariposa lilies, honeycups, cyclamen, roosters, fritillaria, dogheads, Johnny Jump-ups, pansies or Stiefmutterkin, the rare lady slippers were Chinese Shoes.

The birds too, we knew. The blue jay and his top knotted cousin, the Stellar Jay, the Baltimore Oriole and various hawks were counted as enemies as they destroyed fruit and fowls, so we shot them at every opportunity.

In this program of extermination, single-shot .22 rifles were the standard weapon, but one day when a particularly obnoxious hawk had been after my chickens, I took the twelve-gauge shotgun and some shells and followed Mr. Hawk across the orchard and onto an uncultivated hillside. Taking aim, I tried to follow his flight as he turned slowly in the air above me; finally I had him right in line. What I forgot was, as I turned, I had placed myself facing uphill. So when I pressed that trigger, bang! I found myself some distance from where I had been standing with a very sore shoulder and numerous scratches and bruises, to say nothing of hurt pride. The hawk? Oh, he flew away.

The house wrens, black-headed chickadees, woodpeckers, flickers, quail, doves, and wild pigeons did little damage and were nice to have around.

Not to be forgotten were the owls, especially the big gray horned owl. At dusk or on moonlit nights, they could be heard carrying on long conversations from one ridge to another, their mournful whoo-o-oos echoing up and down the canyons. To hear Mr. Owl calling to his lady love on a quiet summer evening is the most lonesome sound I know of.

Moving about the woods, intent on their own affairs and seldom seen, were foxes, coons, chipmunks, and tree squirrels, sometimes a deer or coyote, and not so shy and to whom everyone willingly gave the right of way, the big black polecat or skunk with the two white stripes along his back.

There were also numbers of lizards and some snakes, the grass and ribbon snakes usually near water, the harmless gopher and not so harmless rattler, turned up in all sorts of unexpected places.

You can see there was always something to keep us interested and alert.

The way sounds carried in the clear mountain air was quite surprising. There was a busy agricultural enterprise near Saratoga, the Hume Ranch, known as the biggest prune-growing operation in the world. They had a whistle that blew morning, noon, and night, one long hoarse blast of sound, which could be plainly heard on the mountaintop. No matter where our team was working when that whistle blew at noon, they stopped stock-still and waited to be unhitched and taken to the barn for dinner.

Another sound that carried up from the valley was the marching beat of the drums as the Native Sons of the Golden West of Los Gatos practiced on Main Street on Saturday evening.

From the other direction, after a heavy storm when the wind was still blowing from the west, we could hear the steady glumph, glumph of the buoy off Light House Point near Pescadero.

Strangers who came to the house, especially women, would look about and ask questions. How near were our neighbors? How often did we get to town? In short, why didn't we curl up and die of loneliness?

These were questions beyond my comprehension. Loneliness had no place in my scheme of living.

Woodwardia and finger ferns in Sheer Creek

My Neighbors
To The North

My early-day schoolmates, like myself, were now grown, some with families of their own.

It was always pleasant to spend a Sunday afternoon or an evening, just visiting.

One of the families I knew best was the Herrings. These people were true pioneers, having come into the mountains in 1878, six years before the Stoltes, in search of better health for Mr. Herring. He, a Union Veteran and a native of Maine, had come to California as a very young man and had engaged in various types of work until his enlistment. After the war, he took up newspaper work and became owner and publisher of *The California Agriculturist*. When failing health forced him to give up this enterprise, he sold to the Pacific Rural Press which is now known as the *California Farmer*.

Mr. Herring and his six-year-old son, Fred, came to the ranch to prepare a home for the coming of his wife and second son, three-year-old Joseph.

Mrs. Herring had medical training and did a great deal in helping her neighbors in time of need.

As the two boys grew up, there was no one better versed in field lore than they. Both became excellent taxidermists.

Joe left home at an early age, but Fred stayed on through the years. He married Miss Luella Case of Santa Cruz who had come into the community as teacher of Castle Rock School.

Fred and Luella had a family of five, three boys and two girls: Georgia, Norman, Ralph, Freda, and Joseph. Despite a number of tragic happenings among their children, they remained a quiet steady couple accepting life's vicissitudes as something to be faced with courage and faith. Theirs was a friendly, cheerful home to visit. I spent many happy hours there.

The Scott family moved to the place just beyond Herrings. This was a lively group of six girls—Lula, Linnie, Hattie, Florence, Ada, Georgia—and their parents. I did not learn to know them well. There was nothing to hold them on that small farm, so they went away one after the other while still in their teens.

On the farm next to the Scotts lived the Smeads, a pioneer family, the father having taken his land from the government during the 1870s.

There were five Smead boys, Amos, Charley, Albert, Harold, Percy, better known as "Pat" and Almon. They had always attended school at Castle Rock, so I did not know them as children. As men, they followed various lines of work: farming, teaming, and operating lumber and box mills.

Not long after coming to the mountains, their father was attached by a jersey bull which he owned and was attempting to bring into the stable. After Mr. Smead's death, the older boys took on the responsibility of caring for their mother and younger brothers.

The last family I knew to the north of us was that of Charles Moody. I think Mrs. Moody, a very small, black-eyed woman, represented authority in that household. It was generally understood that her six-foot husband and two big boys, Earle and Wallace, moved when their mother said to. There were tales told of the many capers cut by the two boys when they should have been working. I have no firsthand knowledge of them. There was a third son, Frank, who grew up as the foster son of a family in Oregon or Washington. He returned to his mother when a grown man.

Besides the usual early day activities in the woods and mills, they planted and developed a Bartlett pear orchard, still flourishing on the Skyline.

I knew Mrs. Moody's mother too. One day while in search of our horses, I came upon a wagon stopped in the roadway. It was loaded with what looked like household or more likely camping equipment and many sacks filled with moss. Next I noticed a man high up in a big oak tree busy pulling off the short brown moss which grew on the bark, paying no attention to the long gray festoons of moss near at hand. When I asked what he meant to do with such quantities of the stuff, I learned he was gathering it for the florist trade.

At that time, florists used this type of moss to bind to wire shapes to be used as foundations for floral arrangements. When thoroughly wetted then allowed to drip awhile, it would still hold enough moisture to keep flowers fresh for some time.

What he realized per sack, I have no idea. It had cost him nothing to rise, only his own time to harvest it. I also learned that his name was Louie Ziek, he lived over the hill from the Carmichaels, that he was an old sailor, and that he had heard of another old sailor living near here and was going to visit him.

As I moved on past the wagon, I smelled tobacco smoke and heard a voice say "Where do you live, dearie?" I turned and looked. There in one corner of the load in a small rocking chair sat a tiny, withered old woman smoking a pipe. She told me she was Mrs. Ziek and mother of Mrs. Moody, she always traveled with her present husband, and that he was on his way to visit a friend, and I should come to see her sometime.

I went on my way, found the horses, and took them home; when supper was about ready, my new acquaintances arrived and were invited to join us, which they did and stayed for a week.

During this time, Mr. Ziek was outdoors with Father, lending a hand at whatever was being done or passing the time exchanging stories of their seafaring days. The little old lady sat in the corner of the living room sofa, smoking her pipe, which she said was the only good thing she had ever learned from her son, and playing solitaire, only moving when asked to come to meals.

She was just as Scotch as Scotch could be. I liked to hear her talk. When they left, she exacted a promise from me—that I would come to her house and let her make me "a dish of tea." Having an errand in their neighborhood some months later, I did just that.

Mrs. Ruggles was a newer neighbor who came summers to live in a small built overbarn on Ed Richardson's land quite near us. She came because of a frail little son, Howard, who certainly needed the freedom and sunshine of country life. Because she felt the country was a lifesaver for Howard, she suffered with unfailing patience the misery of poison oak infection. She was never without a chunk of yellow laundry soap in her purse or pocket. Soap applied to the infected spots was all that ever gave her any relief.

The remedies for this trouble are endless, both home cures and those prescribed by doctors. Unfortunately, what gives relief to one has no value for another.

Mrs. Ruggles was one of the people I enjoyed very much, but when she no longer came to spend the summers, we lost touch with each other.

AUNT LIZZY

Our troublesome school neighbor, Harry Winchell, having enjoyed one spree too many, was carried away to a pauper's grave by the coroner. His land reverted to the county and later purchased by a maiden lady, Miss Lizzy Donnelly.

It was not unusual for a widow to take up the task of making a home and living for herself on a farm; after her husband's death, if there were children to help her, they made things easier, for country children learned to take on responsibility at a surprisingly early age. But Miss Donnelly was all alone and no longer young, at least nearing fifty, so her coming drew forth both attention and criticism.

I'm sure her whole life's savings went into this ten-acre hillside with its few prune trees and nondescript house. She came with her worldly possessions in a light spring wagon, drawn by an elderly horse of which she was afraid. Besides the horse, which passed out of the picture the first winter, she had a few Plymouth rock chickens, which sad to say, soon were stolen by night prowlers, foxes, coons, etc.

For some years, she went away for the winter months to work for a family near Los Gatos as cook and housemaid. As years went by, she gave this up, staying on her farm the year round, finding what employment she could among the neighbors.

It soon became evident that she was another for whom the tensions of life had been too much, and now her mind was filled with vagaries, but she was neat and tidy about her little house and person, always friendly and anxious to be of help.

She was very fond of children, so her nearness to the school presented no problems. Everyone knew her as Aunt Lizzy. At last becoming ill and unable to earn enough for her simple needs, it was arranged that she go to the Santa Cruz County Hospital where she lived out her last years working in the children's wards. The little patients accepted her as one of their own, no more child minded than anyone else.

WHEN HARRIET CAME

Mrs. Graves came to teach Central after Alma Osterhaus. She was only with us two weeks; her heart really wasn't in the job. For one thing, she was engaged to marry a Los Gatos man who wasn't enthusiastic about her being way off in the hills. Second, she was frantically trying to finish a novel she was writing, *Kenelem's Desire*. I have a copy of it, but it is not one of the old books I like to reread. Her third reason was a spell of the hottest weather imaginable; she resigned her position and returned to Los Gatos.

Her going turned out for the best all round, for it brought us Harriet Bailey to take her place. Harriet was a sister of the former teacher, Miss Bess Bailey. In her, Jo and I found a truly kindred spirit.

She brought so much that was good into our lives. She liked the school and the people she met, enjoyed the same things we did; in short, she fitted perfectly.

We soon developed a Sunday afternoon routine of hurrying through the dinner dishes and going for a walk. This meant exploring some canyon or mountain, on a schedule of going away for two hours and returning in equal time.

Harriet liked to shoot a gun but never killed anything. Therefore, she always carried a light single-shot 22, just in case we came upon some vicious wild animal or a rattlesnake. We never did.

Jo always prepared a light snack of sandwiches or crackers which she carried and we were happy to consume before starting home. I took my precious Kodak and still have albums of faded prints made from those films.

We explored Sheer Creek and Deer Creek, Chilcote and Lyndon Gulches, and every other watercourse we could reach, as well as Grizzly, Castle, Summit, and White Rocks. We'd get home in time to do the chores and get supper, tired, dirty, and happy.

Of special interest in our explorations was the fern and flower growth along the shady canyons where the redwoods grew. There we found many specimens not known in the drier, more open country on the summit. The finger ferns and woodwardias often eight feet tall, were a never-ending delight; this is where the lovely azaleas and dainty wake robins grew as well as occasional clusters of the amazing tiger lily. Here the gray waterousel lived, flitting from boulder to boulder, never seeming to get wet.

I knew one man who lived in Deer Creek Canyon—Chris Muller, a German. He took up this land in the early days when men first came into the hills. He lived in a tiny split lumber cabin and made a living splitting and selling shakes. He always kept two or three donkeys to carry the finished shakes up the long zigzag trail to the wagon road. When I was a very little girl, I remember him stopping at our house, visiting awhile with my parents, and usually staying for dinner.

As far as I know, he had no relatives, at least not in America. He lived in his little house all alone for many years. In the end, he suffered a stroke and fell beside the trail. Some young men out hunting found him and carried him up to the road, and from there he was taken to a hospital. He did not recover.

The rocks I mentioned are great masses of sandstone on the summits of the ridges. Of the four, Castle Rock is the best known and most easily reached. The property surrounding the others has passed into new ownership. Now with fences and Keep Out signs, they are seldom visited.

Castle Rock is the biggest and most picturesque with caves of various shapes and sizes. The biggest cave is on the western side. A young lady, Miss Jones—a teacher at Castle Rock School which stood nearby—and her mother lived in this cave one school term. Many picnics have been held at its base and under the oaks surrounding it. A minister from Los Gatos, Mr. Wintler, conducted church services at its base one summer.

I'm not sure about the height, would guess seventy-five or a hundred feet at its lowest elevation. I have visited it many times. It stays always the same, always people have climbed to the top for the view and clambered around the base to marvel at the distance and still do.

I went to the top only once and persuaded Harriet to come along. Jo, who was always afraid of high places, stayed on the ground and worried about us. Looking back now on some of our excursions, I wonder why we didn't come to grief. There have been times when accidents did happen.

Some distance down the ridge west of Castle Rock perhaps a mile, where a water run is reached, there is a drop of forty or fifty feet known as the falls. Here one spring day, two children—ten or twelve years old, cousins, and grandchildren of the Fred Herrings—came to picnic. The details will never be known as they were by themselves, but that evening, after a long and anxious search, their grandfather found them at the bottom of the falls, clasped in each other's arms, both dead.

There were smaller, looser outcroppings of this sandstone in many places. Much of it was broken up and used to build foundations and retaining walls by the property owners.

There was a time when it was quarried commercially. This was when a group of Los Gatos men—Dr. F. W. Knowels and Ed Yocco are the only names I recall—decided to develop a tract of land in Union District for burial purposes, to be known as Los Gatos Cemetery, the old cemetery at the corner of Santa Cruz Avenue and Saratoga Road having reached full capacity.

Quantities of this stone were taken from the Herring property and also from that of Ed Cushing on the Bear Creek Road near Brown's School. After being cut into shape, some was used for curbing along the various avenues in the old part of the renamed Los Gatos Memorial Park. The Stolte plot is faced by such a curb. More of this stone was used in building the original chapel at Stanford University, and also to build the San Jose Post Office, now a library at Market and San Fernando in San Jose, California.

Through the generosity of Mr. and Mrs. Varian of Varian Enterprises, Castle Rock is now the property of the Sierra Club and may someday become part of a state park.

Besides enjoying the great outdoors which we were able to introduce her to, Harriet would cheerfully lend a hand about the house. Her help often meant getting a job done instead of having to face it again tomorrow.

Though not a trained musician, she could play accompaniments on the organ. Having a pleasant singing voice, she could lead us, and Father, never able to resist music, would join in with his good rolling bass.

An evening would pass oh so quickly. The standard college songs, very popular at that time and old favorites like "Then You'll Remember Me," "The Last Rose of Summer," "The Rose of Killarney," to mention just a few; we knew them all and sang them over and over.

Harriet also did beautiful needlework. I of course tried my hand at that, but found I did better working with gingham or darning cotton. It was because of her that I read many of the books of that time; novels it is true, but good books nevertheless.

Yes, Harriet did much for me. Through the years we corresponded but seldom met as she had married and lived near Fresno. Her friendship was very dear to me and lasted till her death at the age of eighty-three.

ROCKS—

Castle

Summit

Grizzly

CANNED MUSIC

It was while Harriet Bailey was with us that the Edison phonograph, with its cylindrical records and morning glory type horn, became available and very popular.

Herrings bought the first one; somehow Fred Herring had a way of being first in the community where mechanical innovations were concerned: the first motor-driven car, the first phonograph, the first gasoline engine to pump the water up to the house and not so mechanical, the first bathroom. Dick Zimmerman, who now lived on Tip Top, the old Sabin home, soon bought the second one.

Both were generous about carrying their phonographs to whatever place the next dance was to be. If Fred couldn't go, Dick would. Dick would even lend his to anyone he considered responsible; this took the music even farther afield.

Parties now being free of having to take up a collection to defray expenses were held in someone's home or farm utility building or a schoolhouse. Lakeside Hall fell into disuse and finally Mr. Thomson, on whose land it stood, dismantled it and rebuilt it as a fruit storage building where he now lived near Skyline Boulevard.

So the gatherings moved around the neighborhood, perhaps in Mrs. Herring's living room or in a funny old building on Tip Top known as the Cliff House because of its precarious position on the mountainside.

Sometimes, a phonograph was carried all the way to Fairview School which was really beyond the ordinary line of travel. Wherever the music went, the young people followed.

Cushing's fruit house on the Bear Creek Road was another favorite spot because of the popular young members of that household.

There one evening when the youngest son, meaning to do an extra good cleanup job, had given the floor a thorough soaking with the garden hose, the guests soon found it was impossible to waltz on a wet, unpainted lumber floor. However, the evening was not a total failure; it was spent pleasantly enough listening to records, singing, talking, and consuming the refreshments.

Chris Muller's split lumber house on Deer Creek

At the little settlement of Patchin on the road to Soquel, there was a fine big hall; I believe it was given to the community by the Averell family. This hall was generally known as the Patchin Opera House, but the builders having dancing in mind, had placed heavy wagon overload springs under the floor joists so that the whole floor responded to the rhythm of the dancers. This was considered very, very special.

I very seldom attended dances at Patchin, but this one time Georgia Beatty and I were invited to a masquerade there. This promised to be an exceptionally enjoyable affair, so off we went, wonderfully bedecked as colored ladies in costumes made from blue and white window curtains. Upon arrival, we learned the committee had changed plans and decided on just a dance. We felt somewhat embarrassed, but having gone all those miles to attend, it would have been foolish not to stay and enjoy the evening, so we did.

At Patchin they always had "live music," usually The O'Fallons—Irma Hoffman and her husband.

MAIL ROUTE

Early in the 1900s, a Mr. Edward Berwick, an Englishman living at Pacific Grove, had done much good work toward getting the government to establish Parcel Post in California.

Later Miss Marion Rouse, a longtime resident of Lakeside District and at one time a teacher there, became Mrs. Berwick.

When it became known that this postal service would be available upon presentation to the Post Office Department of properly signed petitions, Mr. Leudemann of Lyndon Gulch secured the necessary papers but found getting the signatures would be more of a job than he had figured on, so he gave the papers to Father.

Our neighbor, Mrs. Ruggles, too, was interested in getting this service. Mrs. Ruggles and I spent some very interesting days driving about the neighborhood, up and down all the little side roads, meeting people we didn't know existed, and finding others we hadn't seen for years.

Most people were willing and pleased to sign; a few thought we were off on a wild goose chase but signed anyway, and several others signed with reluctance because they didn't want anyone handling their mail. They preferred getting it once a week direct from the Post Office instead of having it delivered every day to a box on the county road near their homes. On being assured that they would not be compelled to put up boxes and take the service, they agreed to sign. Finally, we got everyone.

As we pictured the route, it would start at the Los Gatos Post Office, then located on West Main Street at the eastern corner of Lundy Lane a short block from the bridge, go up to Santa Cruz Avenue then the Old Toll Road to the Black Road near Lexington, up the Black Road to the Summit Road, now Skyline Boulevard, from there southward to Brown's School on the Bear Creek Road, down Bear Creek Road to the Toll Road and back to Los Gatos and the post office. This distance was estimated as twenty miles.

With everyone's name down, the petition was sent on its way. Before long, a letter came stating a Postal Inspector would visit Los Gatos shortly and report on the feasibility of our request.

The inspector, Mr. de la Montanya, arrived the first week of September. Father took him over the proposed route. He agreed the service was certainly needed but questioned the distance; besides, the Postal Department considered twenty-five miles minimum.

Country roads were sometimes measured by tying a marker on one spoke of a wheel then counting the turns as the vehicle moved along. By knowing the circumference of the wheel, simple arithmetic gave one the answer.

This time I offered to walk the distance wearing a pedometer such as used by the Boy Scouts of today. Mine had been a special premium for renewing the subscription to *The Youth's Companion*. The inspector promised to accept the result as I found it and said he would do his best to see the route established. I made the walk. The answer was nineteen and three-fourths miles.

When the final report came, the route had been extended north, past the Stolte place as far as the Lint ranch now Sunnyvale City Park and beyond Brown's School west to the Casella home, thus making the distance something over twenty-five miles.

That November, in 1904, Orson Rouse, the first mail carrier, with a pair of horses and spring wagon, delivered mail along Rural Free Delivery Route 2 out of Los Gatos, California.

Another carrier was Arthur Foster from the Bear Creek Road. He, finding the trip very hard on his horses even though he used two, which he drove alternate days, became interested in motor-driven conveyances. He answered an ad from a Middle Western city praising a horseless carriage, built like a wagon even to the high wooden wheels, with some sort of a motor and rods and gears to turn the wheels. This vehicle may have answered on the level plains of the Dakotas; it was hopeless on the mountain roads of California. So Mr. Foster returned to his buggy and his horses, always regretting his useless purchase. As he put it, "That thing had cost him quite a considerable."

For sixty years, storm or sunshine, good roads or bad, by horse-drawn rigs or autos of various names and makes, driven by many different carriers, someone has safely delivered the mail every day on RFD #2 out of Los Gatos, California. As the demand for service increased because of the greater number of people moving into the country, the route has been extended.

I inquired of Mr. Briggs, Postmaster at Los Gatos, as to what roads Route 2 now covers. This is what I learned: from the Post Office, which is now a bigger and better building on Santa Cruz Avenue near Royce, the carrier proceeds through town to Highway 17, thence to Black Road to Thomson Road, up Thomson Road some distance and returns to Black Road, continues to Gist Road after delivery on Gist Road, again returns to Black Road and proceeds to Skyline Boulevard, turns north, goes to Saratoga Gap, also known as Carmichael's or Big Basin crossing, about nine miles, backtracks to Black Road, follows Skyline south to Bear Creek Road, turns right and travels west to the Helwig place, returns to point of entry and proceeds down Bear Creek Road to Highway 17, then south to Idlewild Road, on Idlewild Road to Old Santa Cruz Road and on down to Alma Bridge Road and Aldercroft. In Aldercroft, he makes house-to-house deliveries up one road and down the other till he returns to Alma Bridge Road, from there going north to the Beatty and Feehan properties, returns along Alma Bridge Road to Soda Water Road, up that two miles, and back again to Alma Bridge, on that to the Old Santa Cruz Road, down that to Oakmont and more house-to-house calls, back to the Old Santa Cruz Road to Idlewild Road, returns to Highway 17, on 17 back to Los Gatos and the Post Office, having covered 61.35 miles of mountain roads.

When the route was established, Mr. Campbell was Postmaster of Los Gatos.

An Unexpected Change

All this brings me to the summer of 1904. I now found myself scolded more and more often for what was really no fault of mine.

Indoors or out, anything that went wrong was automatically due to my neglect, carelessness, or indifference. It seemed impossible for Father to admit he was in error, so I, always there, became his Whipping Girl. I can understand now that he was lonely, at odds with himself and the world in general, gaining little companionship from his daughters, and certainly taking no counsel from them nor anyone else. Here we were very much at outs with each other; he probably as unable to make the effort to talk things over with me as it was impossible for me to reach him.

One unlucky day, being, as I thought, unjustly scolded for something, whatever it was, I no longer remember, but in that unguarded moment I told him I didn't like housework, had never liked it and never expected to. Just for the record, I still don't like housework. Well, that settled the "cat hop"; shortly afterward he told me, since I was so dissatisfied and unappreciative of all he had done for me, I could jolly well go find something I liked better, as he had written Lotte to come home and take charge, and that she would arrive at the end of that week.

To say that his ultimatum was a jolt puts it mildly. My greatest concern was leaving my sister Jo, but with the other sister home, I figured things would not be too hard for her.

Whether by his own decision or Lotte's intervention, I'm not sure; anyway, someone decided I was to stay till the New Year, by then the grapes and apples would all be taken care of and Lotte established in her new regime. This delay gave me the opportunity to help establish the Rural Mail Route I have already told about. It also gave me time to think about what I would do when I left.

Jo graduated from Central that November, and it was that autumn that Ed Richardson sold his four hundred acres to the Reverend George W.

Beatty, a former Los Gatos Methodist minister. The place was to become the home of his younger brother William and family.

The William Beatty family was then living in Pennsylvania somewhere near the Ohio River. The father had been a school teacher until ill health compelled him to seek less confining work. This he found in the oil fields of that region. They arrived in October, father, mother, and eight children from seventeen down to eighteen months of age: Nellie, Billy, Jennie, Georgia, John, Josie, Pauline, and Reed.

In time, their presence was to be felt in the community; at this point they were just eight lively youngsters, somewhat surprised by the vastness of the mountains and overcome by the freedom they had suddenly acquired.

As for my plans, I was sure of one thing. I wanted more schooling, something which would perhaps take me into the business world; for this, business college seemed to be the answer.

I found tuition for a bookkeeping course at Healds Business College in San Francisco was, if my memory is correct, seventy-five dollars for the first six months. After that, there was a monthly charge. One could stay on indefinitely.

Through correspondence with my friend Mrs. Charles Lymbery, a one-time *Examiner* reporter and sister of Beatrice Boston, a former teacher at Central, I learned that her neighbor, Mrs. John Wetmore, whom I knew, she and her children Peter and Ruth had spent some time at the ranch with us while recovering from whooping cough, offered me room and board, plus one dollar and fifty cents a week in exchange for washing dishes and doing what housework there was time for mornings and evenings and Saturdays. With this and two hundred and eighty-four dollars in the German Savings Bank, I felt everything was taken care of.

That savings account had been a slow-growing accomplishment. Father had once agreed that money I received from any paying guests was to be half mine to spend as I thought best for clothing and personal needs for Josie and myself. Any leftover I could bank if I liked. The leftover never amounted to much. Added to this, if he felt the last year had been a profitable one, as a Christmas gift, there would be a check under the tree for me.

The first time it was fifty dollars, causing some neighbors who were our guests that evening to be certain sure that Mr. Stolte was a rich spendthrift. Those Christmas checks never reached fifty again and sometimes weren't there at all.

That was understandable, for after a farmer had cared for an orchard or vineyard all year and at harvest time purchased the proper containers and prepared the fruit for shipment to the city markets, found, after express and commission were deducted, that he had received less than the cost of the containers for some of the finest fruit ever grown. It was enough to make anyone discouraged and short tempered.

There was one season when our neighbor, John Cassella, through some buyer's urging, had sent a big shipment of grapes to New York and in return had only a freight bill for his trouble.

One year I went to the Jesuit Novitiate at Los Gatos to offer the cellar master the opportunity to buy the wine grapes. After some thought, he decided to take them at twelve dollars a ton.

Father was pleased to get that much, but he had to haul them all the way down one mountain and up the other to deliver them then reverse the procedure to come home with the empty boxes. A long day's work to deliver three tons of grapes, which was the quantity the hired man, Josie, and I could have ready to load and all the horses could haul.

We were fortunate in never having had to struggle against a mortgage. Aside from the main fruit crop, there were other things from which some cash was derived, eggs, butter, a dressed veal, a few gallons of wine, a cord or two of wood, a cow, all helped. As Father expressed it, "With hard work and frugal living, we managed." In fact, we managed very well.

On the whole, he did the best he could; had he been just a little more considerate of others, things would have been better for everyone.

The good ship Albert tied to an open wharf

TO SAN FRANCISCO

On January 8, 1905, with my clothing packed in a wicker telescope bag, my sisters escorted me to the train at Los Gatos, on my way to new experiences; to the last Father and Lotte were sure, going to school at my age was a mistake, I'd do better to find a place as household help.

At that time, the train from Los Gatos went to Oakland, and one crossed the bay to San Francisco by ferryboat; on the ferry that afternoon, I met Mr. Isiah Hartman, brother of our Santa Cruz County Supervisor who kindly carried my bag into the Ferry Building; there Agnes Boston, Mrs. Lymbery's sister and a student at the University of California, met me and took me to Bess's house for dinner.

Later that evening, Bess and I went by way of a stile over her backyard fence to the Wetmores. They both lived on Washington Street just below Jones, overlooking the bay.

The Wetmores were good and friendly people. I had no trouble adjusting to life with them.

I found Healds not at all like any school I had ever heard of or imagined, but soon learned the routine and began getting acquainted with other students, nearly all were younger than I, just out of other schools, while I had been away from school and studies for nine years.

Healds Business College was located at 24 Post Street, just off Market. A two-story building painted a weather-beaten gray, the classrooms too were pretty dingy, the stairways and floors worn from the scuffling of many careless feet. The desks and chairs were also worn and battered; by present-day standards, the whole place needed renovating badly; that generation of young people seemed unaware of this need.

The beginning classes were conducted on the first floor; the more advanced were promoted to the upper floor.

In the beginners' division, there were rows of tables; these had a slightly raised division lengthwise and a student seated on either side. The first two rows were reserved for girls, the other rows—I think there were four—were occupied by boys.

There was a teacher stationed at either end of the room. Mr. R. L. Rudy, first in command and Mr. Stearns, an elderly man, second.

In the upstairs department, the arrangement was about the same as to number of desks or tables; only these were higher with a rack in the middle where books could be placed. The student could either stand to do his work or use a high stool to sit on.

Many business offices were furnished with this type of desk at that time.

In this department, the students carried out all sorts of business transactions with each other, dealing in merchandise printed on cards.

Around three sides of the room were various offices, a bank, railroad station, wholesale houses, and all sorts of businesses which conducted business among themselves and with the students on the floor. When students were promoted to the offices, everyone knew graduation was just ahead for them.

Each student moved along at his own pace. There were no classes in the bookkeeping courses.

In this department, Mr. J. M. Davis was the head and J. P. Kiel second. Later, T. N. Titterington came to take the place of Mr. Davis. It was not a good change.

There were two other teachers, who both taught classes in arithmetic, grammar, and penmanship: one, a gentle older man, Mr. Stauffer, was an excellent teacher but lacking the ability to keep order, so J. P. Kiel would come in and patrol the aisles for him. These silly young men old enough to know better thought it was smart to play cards or shake dice during class just to aggravate the teacher; the girls with the same notions would just sit and giggle.

The other teacher was James Flannigan, as Irish as his name, quite equal to keeping any number of young smarties in line.

The shorthand and typing department was conducted by Miss Elizabeth Day. I tried her classes for a short time; I found I was making no progress at all, so I gave up.

A happy thing happened to me while at the Wetmores. A little package came to me by parcel post; in it was a pretty tooled leather purse, containing a collection of silver coins and several dollar bills and a list of names which told me that Mrs. John Thomson had contacted the neighbors for a show of appreciation for the work I had done toward getting the mail route.

A million dollars could not have pleased me more; I floated on clouds for days and still have that little purse tucked away somewhere.

During my stay with the Wetmores, I spent most of Sundays and sometimes part of Saturday afternoons walking. Thus I learned the streets from Polk to the Bay and south as far as Market.

Sometimes I made my way over Russian and Telegraph Hills and on down to the waterfront, the tumble-down shacks and goats on Telegraph Hill, and the open wharves with their ships and cargoes made fine subjects for my Kodak. Chinatown and North Beach with their strange shops and people were most fascinating.

Aunt Emilia still lived on Dolores Street in the Mission District; sometimes I spent Sunday afternoons there. It was a long ride on the street cars, and as riding on the cars always gave me motion sickness, I avoided them as much as possible.

At that time, carfare was five cents. If one knew just when and for which direction to take a transfer, a person could ride for hours and see most of San Francisco for one nickel.

Evenings I would often go by way of the stile to the Lymberys and visit with Bess and her sisters; sometimes Beatrice would be there as she was still studying music and often had singing engagements to fill.

Bess was the first woman I knew who smoked cigarettes, which she rolled herself with the standard brown paper and Bull Durham tobacco. Her husband smoked some fancy brand from a white and gold package. I often wonder what the people who criticized Bess so sharply would say now when the majority of women all smoke.

Upon being promoted to the upper division, I found students were expected to attend Saturday mornings, so I left Mrs. Wetmore and rented a room at 822 Leavenworth Street with housekeeping privileges for twelve dollars a month.

My landlady was Mrs. West; besides renting rooms, she told fortunes, either by cards or the lines of the hands. People came to consult her on all manner of subjects, from where they should invest their money to who they should marry.

She flatly refused to read my fortune by any method, saying it would be useless; I wouldn't believe her, but shortly after I moved there, she made prints of my hands, on paper smoked all black and sooty over a lamp chimney, to display in the front window. Because as she said, I had such excellent lines in my hands.

R. L. Rudy, a young man exceedingly proud of his fine physique, organized a physical culture class which met one evening a week, in a hall on Divisadero Street. About twenty attended.

A Telegraph Hill goat resting

It was fun, with someone to beat time on a piano, we would line up, and following Mr. Rudy's lead the lesson would begin with hands on the hips, thumbs forward, head erect, and shoulders back. With everyone in position, we went through the motions of exercising all the muscles of our bodies, no doubt good for us.

I had always enjoyed poetry often amusing myself doing parodies on the much better work of others. While among the beginners at Healds, I put together one I titled "The Psalm of Bookkeeping" which fell into the hands of Mr. Stearns who in turn had it printed in the school paper, it went like this:

> Tell me not in mournful numbers
> Bookkeeping is an idle dream
> That the student's wrong who grumbles
> And balance sheets as easy as they seem
> on and on through the nine verses.

In the upper division, I did another on the well-known "Excelsior." This did not reach the paper, which was just as well. It rambled along in this fashion:

> The ways of school are strange alas,
> And oft as down the aisles you pass
> You'll hear some youth say cheerily
> To another working drearily,
>   Stuff it.

> The other never stops to think
> But dips his pen into the ink
> And soon his voice, like the one before
> Sings this refrain forevermore.
>   Stuff it.

This continued through the entire poem; the young people in the department enjoyed it. By using the tune "Upidee, Upidae" it became the school song for a time. And the teachers became more careful than ever in checking to make sure none of the ledger columns showed evidence of having been stuffed.

New Friends

By the time I went to live on Leavenworth Street, I had become fairly well acquainted with the people at Healds and had at least a "Good Morning" and "Good Night" acquaintanceship with most.

My favorite among them was a brown-eyed little girl from Nevada City, Alyce Fenton, our friendship has held through the years; in fact, out of the many I met while in San Francisco, she is the only one I keep in touch with; all the rest are just shadows in my memory.

The Fentons lived on Larkin near Jackson. Mrs. Fenton was a widow with seven grown children, if I should call Alyce the youngest grown-up at not quite sixteen.

Mrs. Fenton was one of the finest women it has been my good fortune to know. She was the daughter of a French family; her father was a storekeeper in French Corral, Nevada County, at the time of the Gold Rush.

She told me how in the evening when her father closed the store, he would call her, then about four years old, from her play, pour the day's gold take into her apron and tell her to run along and take it to her mother.

I spent many pleasant evenings with them after Alyce and I had finished our homework. "Mom," as everyone called her, would have a pitcher of milk, gingerbread, and sometimes rhubarb sauce for us, a most delicious snack.

There were four girls: Maggie, married, mother of two daughters, living I think on Howard Street; Mame, a cateress in Nevada City; Desiree or Dee at home and planning soon to be married; and Alyce, the youngest member of the family.

The three sons were Will, who worked in the mines of Nevada County; Frank, the middle son was the mainstay of the family, a dependable young man with a quiet sense of humor and at times a surprising streak of mischief. His brothers and sisters called him "Judge" and usually abided by his decisions. Frank spent his winters in San Francisco; in summer, he managed a mine somewhere in British Columbia, near the town of Bullion.

The last son was Ben, older than Alyce, taking his time about growing up. He finally made it, working on cement construction projects for many years.

Another member of the Fenton household was "Bud" Wyllie, Dee's fiancé, a young man also from Nevada City of Welsh ancestry, a nice guy and a good friend.

There were three other girls whose homes and families I learned to know. Bess Wilbert, whose people were from New England. Mr. Wilbert owned a machine shop at Seventeenth and Mission; her brothers worked in the shop, and later Bess took charge of the office.

Sometimes on Sunday, Bess and I would meet at the entrance to Golden Gate Park at the end of Geary Street. From there, it was a pleasant walk through the park to the beach; after an hour or two on the sand, we would walk back the way we had come.

Once we took the ferry to Sausalito, then the train to Mill Valley, from there a footpath to the top of Mt. Tamalpais. This was something of a mistake for Bess; it was not only unused to this kind of an excursion, but somewhat overweight too.

Before we reached the top, I found myself carrying her coat, her hat, and her lunch as well as tugging her step by step up the last part of the trail. Fortunately, there was a railroad to the mountaintop, and we returned to Mill Valley by that.

I made the climb again with Alyce and Dorothy Money, a country girl from Napa. This was a carefree jaunt all the way up and down.

Fanny McConalogue, a pretty Irish girl, lived on a little street off Castro in the Twin Peaks district. Her father and brother Billy were marine engineers, away at sea much of the time. Her three sisters—Rose, Dolly, and Madeline—and their mother I learned to know very well.

One evening when I had stayed later than I should, after walking to the Castro Street corner, I found the last car had already gone by; rather than go back to the house and ask to stay the night, I walked, all the way down Market to Leavenworth about twenty blocks then up Leavenworth to Bush another eight.

The only people about at that hour were policemen walking their beats; several spoke to me to ask where I thought I was going. When I explained, each one told me that was no time of night for a woman to be walking about the streets alone. I agreed with them and walked on.

Then there was Eda Bauer, only daughter of a German couple, living in Oakland. Alyce and I would visit there, going by way of the Key Route ferry and train. Her people were as old country in their mode of living as anyone could be.

Mr. Bauer had a garden where he grew the most luscious loganberries I ever tasted.

Myra Hallet, I liked very much, but like me, her home was elsewhere. After she married our teacher, Mr. Flannigan, our paths no longer crossed.

Among the boys, there were a number that I learned to know rather well. Boys on the whole are easier to get acquainted with than girls, now as well as then.

Walter Bassett, a tall, good-looking, redhead was Bess Wilbert's devoted cavalier. Dick Shute, a good-natured self-styled comedian was a cousin of George Green, our Los Gatos druggist. The Farley brothers, Ernest and Clifford, were nephews of Mr. Eben Farley of the Los Gatos Bank.

Harry Wood, a restless youngster who had lost a leg while trying to jump on or off a fast-moving train, and could now travel faster and farther on crutches than any of his friends with two good legs.

A couple of seventeen-year-olds from Nevada were a lonely pair. I sort of adopted and occasionally cooked a meal for them. Elmer Wedertz was a sheepman's son from Wellington, and Oliver J. Trevillian was the son of a Cornish miner from Virginia City.

And not to be forgotten, Montgomery Thomas Scott, commonly called "Empty" from Pinole, determined to be my friend Alyce's steady and always among those present at Fentons.

I learned to like the city and enjoyed it, but for me, there will never be a lonelier place than a crowded city street.

I Go To Work

By October, I realized that my finances were dwindling so fast I could not continue to pay living expenses and tuition much longer. The problem was what to do next. I felt I had gotten all I was likely to from the bookkeeping course, and staying on to qualify for a diploma seemed useless.

My first move was to write home, explaining to Father that I had finished what I had set out to do, learned to keep books, and was ready to come home if I could be useful there.

The answer I received said that since I had fooled away the best part of a year learning something of no use to a farmer, I'd better find employment where I was, and a little financial help for himself would not come amiss. Now I had to do something else and do it right away.

The school office had a job-finding department; through that I was sent to Varney and Green, a billboard and general advertising agency. At Varney and Green, somewhere in the neighborhood of Valencia Street, I found myself in a place not unlike the schoolrooms at Healds.

Long counterlike desks with people busy addressing envelopes, I was assigned space at a counter, furnished pen, ink, and a great lot of envelopes along with several file boxes of addresses, house by house along the city streets. The one requirement for the job was the ability to write a legible hand. The pay was seventy-five cents a thousand.

The next step was folding advertising leaflets. The ones I worked on extolled the wonders of gelatin for desserts and salads. These leaflets of which there were two different ones were then put into the addressed envelopes, these in turn were given to men who carried loads of them in shoulder bags, to leave them one by one at the proper address. What we were paid for folding and filling, I've forgotten. I know it wasn't much.

A Mr. Simmonds and his sister were in charge of this activity. They were both nice and pleasant to work under. As I saw no prospect of advancing to Miss Simmond's job, I decided to try for something else.

With Mrs. West's friendly urging, I applied for work at Nathan Dohrmann's. Here I went to work as posting clerk on the hotel ledger at the munificent wage of ten cents an hour, ninety cents for a nine-hour day.

That Nathan Dohrmann store was a fairyland to me; it was located just below Kearney with the front door on Sutter and the back door on Bush, the sales rooms extending across the whole block.

In the retail division, they dealt in china, glass, art goods, lamps, clocks, and kitchenware; as the name implies, this department catered to homeowners, and the customers were mostly women.

The hotel department supplied hotels, saloons, and any public or semipublic institution that used their line of merchandise.

The wholesale part of the company did all the buying both foreign and domestic.

The Nathan part of the firm's name was just that, a name, Mr. Nathan having departed from this life long ago.

The Dohrmann name was well-represented by four men of a younger generation. At the head of wholesale was Bernard, known among his associates as alphabetical Dohrmann; his initials were ABCD.

Fred, younger brother to Bernard, a charming and capable man, was head of retail.

Julius, cousin to the other two, was responsible for the hotel section of the firm, and his brother Clarence was usually around, a part-time salesman.

THE ACCOUNTING OFFICE

The accounting office where I was assigned a desk was a busy friendly place. Mr. Allen Wagener was office manager, with Miss Appleton his assistant; the others in the office were Miss Alice Johansen and Jessie Pearson who segregated and recapitulated all retail sales slips.

May Kenard and Evelyn Sheldon operated Fisher billing machines, Lotte Killgore had the retail ledger from A to L and Effie Roseberry took it from M to Z. Alice Anderson had the wholesale ledger and I the one for hotel sales. These ledgers were not heavy unwieldy books but boxes of loose leaf cards.

For about a month, a Mr. Brunswick took the hotel ledger and Margret McDonald and I undertook the task of transferring all over two-year-old sales slips to new folders, as well as properly filing all the daily retail slips.

When Alyce Fenton completed her course at Healds, she came into the office to become the third billing machine operator.

I soon found I could work two and sometimes three evenings a week at overtime pay of twelve cents an hour. This helped a little money-wise as well as being pleasanter to spend the time in the office where others were also at work than alone in my room.

There was a lunchroom in the building equipped with tables and chairs, where the women who brought lunches from home would gather.

After Alyce came into the office and having the same lunch period, we would go to a restaurant on Kearney where they served an exceptionally good soup and a basket of nice crisp buns for fifteen cents, an ample lunch and much better than cold sandwiches. On the way back to work, we took turns in buying and sharing a nickel's worth of wrapped chews from Maskey's, the Haas Candy Store was on the same block, we considered it too ritzy for our money.

In February 1906, Lotte came to stay with me. Apparently one year on the ranch was all she could take; she felt Josie was now quite equal to managing the household, and she intended to live her own life from here on.

For some reason, she took exception to Mrs. West and her rooming house, whether it was the fortune-telling signs in the window or the geographic location I never learned. I had never found anything wrong with either one, but she wanted to move so we did to a basement room at Fenton's, which suited me fine; by this time, the Fenton family had become my own by mutual adoption.

After a few weeks, Lotte went to San Mateo to take over the management of the John's household.

THE EARTHQUAKE

I stayed on at the Fentons till April 18, the day of the historic earthquake and fire, when everyone in San Francisco moved.

The quake shook me half-awake but being something of a sleepyhead, I settled more comfortably under my covers and went on sleeping. I was soon wakened again by a voice just outside my window. Alyce was crying and pleading with Bud, her brother-in-law, to go in the house and see if I had been killed; this really wakened me, so I dressed and went out on the street to see what all the commotion was about.

The Fenton family and other people from both sides of the street were gathered in groups, many in their nightclothes, excited and frightened.

There was little visible damage; a few chimneys had tumbled down; that was all I saw.

We stood around and talked for some time; neither Bud nor I could coax the rest into the house, so I left them to walk up the hill to the Lymberys intending to go on to work from there.

At Bess's, everything seemed quite normal, a few dishes broken, nothing serious. She was alone, her husband due home from a business trip the next day.

We went downstairs to her kitchen, turned on the gas, prepared and ate a good breakfast, giving no thought to the possibility of broken gas or water lines. From the upper floor of the house, great clouds of smoke could already be seen, rolling up from different sections of the city below us. I left Bess, still intending to go to work; in Chinatown and along Kearney, people were gathered in excited groups, many already carrying loads of personal belongings, bent on reaching safer locations. Every now and then, the earth underfoot seemed to shiver and the surrounding buildings would creak and groan.

At the office, a number of people had gathered like myself expecting to go to work; we found that the door to the cement vault, where the ledgers and current papers were stored each night, had shifted, and no one could get it open. Mr. Fred Dohrman asked us to come to the art department and gather up as much of the unbroken stock as we could. We hadn't made much progress, when there was another heavy shock.

No bull in any China shop could have caused the havoc in hours that the next few moments accomplished. Stacks of dinnerware, hundreds of beautiful glasses, everything that hadn't come off the shelves during the first shock at six fifteen that morning came crashing and banging to the floor, the most terrifying noise imaginable. Mr. Fred came, calling to everyone to get out and go home, as he was afraid someone would be hurt, and that would be more than he could stand.

Leaving the store, I walked out Kearney Street to Market, a fire was burning furiously near the Call Building, people were coming from the south of Market District with whatever they could carry or move otherwise, in toy wagons, baby buggies, in chests of drawers or piled on tables and sewing machines, depending on the insecure casters to move them along.

I heard one young fellow, staggering under a load of household goods, say to another, "The cop told us to go to Golden Gate Park. I never heard of the place, have you?"

On O'Farrell Street, some men were trying to hitch a restless horse to a delivery wagon. It was easy to see they didn't know much about what they were attempting to do. I felt it wasn't my place to pass out unasked for advice, so I moved on.

Upon reaching home, I found that with the help of a fellow worker, who owned a horse and wagon, Bud had been able to bring his sister-in-law, Maggie, Mrs. Fenton's oldest daughter and her little girl, Eileen, from their flat somewhere beyond Market to her mother.

They were still sure that the house was about to collapse and refused to think of spending the night there, so we spent the afternoon moving food and bedding to Lafayette Square, a small park at Octavia and Clay about six blocks west.

Maggie had been ill a long time, far too weak to walk that distance, so Alyce and I, forming a chair with our crossed hands, carried her. A very lopsided chair it must have been, as Alyce stood a possible five foot two inches to my five foot almost nine inches. It is surprising what one can do in time of need.

Many others had the same idea as we. There were hundreds in that little park that night, few slept, everyone moving about, watching the fire, looking for others who might have made their way to this refuge.

I had seen forest fires, bad ones. I doubt if there was ever another fire like this one. At two o'clock that morning, I snapped some pictures with a Brownie camera, which were as clear as though taken in daylight.

Everyone talked to everyone else, telling of things that had happened to them and of others they had heard about, like the story of the Cliff House being shaken from its foundation and drifting to the Seal Rocks, it wasn't; it stood there on the edge of the cliff till it was destroyed by fire some years later.

Everyone seemed to have firsthand knowledge of the many people who lost their lives that morning, numbers running from hundreds into thousands. I saw no victims, but it is a fact that there were many casualties.

One story had it that the reason the city water system was completely disrupted and useless was because the Spring Valley Water Company dam back of San Mateo had broken, not only leaving San Francisco without water but had carried away most of San Mateo on its way to the bay. This too was a figment of someone's imagination; that dam stands today just as it stood before the quake.

In the morning, some of us returned to the house for a few personal belongings and "Gram's" canary.

Bud knew the Rushton family who lived way out in the sand dunes on Clement Street. He decided to walk there and learn if we could all come there to stay till the next move could be decided. They were willing to have us, so with the help of their horse and wagon, Bud moved his wife who was pregnant, Mrs. Fenton, Maggie, the little girl Eileen, and our possessions. Alyce and I walked.

We were to live in the Rushton yard in a tent and cook over an open fire; everyone else was doing that too. The word had gone out; no one was to make fires or lights indoors because of the danger of broken gas lines.

While Bud went for the horse and wagon, I returned to the Lymberys to see how Bess was faring. I found her sister Agnes and two of her newspaper acquaintances with her. The newsmen knew of a launch whose owner would take them across the bay to Oakland. Bess was anxious to reach Oakland as her husband was due to arrive there that evening.

Agnes had walked and hitched rides from San Mateo that morning, so I was assured that San Mateo and the surrounding country, though badly shaken and suffering its share of damage, on the whole was in fairly good shape. She also knew that Lotte and the Johns's household were all safe, which was a great comfort.

I stood on the front steps and watched them make their way toward the waterfront, with Sandy and Nora, a pair of Airedale terriers on leashes.

As she left, Bess asked me to lock the front door. I went into the living room, sorry because all her beautiful furnishings would no doubt be destroyed and wishing I could do something about them.

I noticed that Agnes had left her handbag; as it was too late to try to overtake them, I decided to carry it with me. Then I noticed a little silver vase which I knew Bess valued highly. I had seen it first in the Boston home at Santa Cruz and later in a place of honor here in the Washington Street house. So I took it from its place on a little wall bracket and tucked it into Agnes's handbag and left the house, locking the front door as I had been asked to do and returned to Lafayette Square. That little vase, about nine inches tall, has a story of its own which I think is worth telling.

It is made of silver taken from the Washoe mine in Nevada by Mr. Bull, grandfather of the Boston sisters. This silver was fashioned into a pair of slender bud vases by a New York silversmith, to be given as a wedding present to a favorite young sister-in-law by Mr. Bull. At the time of her death, this vase came to Mr. Bull's daughter, Mrs. Boston; from her it went to Bess, who treasured it over the years. What became of the second vase, no one knows.

Some weeks after the earthquake when I was able to go to Los Gatos and home, I mailed the handbag and the vase to the Boston address in Santa Cruz, thereby returning it to its owner.

Forty years later, when Bess had become a frail little old lady with a heart ailment, one day when I had gone to see her—which I did as often as I could—she gave me the silver vase to give to my daughter Louise who has it now and who will, no doubt, pass it on to her daughter, Barbara, some day.

We got ourselves settled at the Rushtons that afternoon; everywhere, people were moving toward the public parks, each one trying to save something they valued. One old Chinese man I remember was carrying a big wicker wash basket half-full of irons, a hundred pounds or more, he no doubt intended to set up a laundry at the first opportunity.

Another man was hurrying along with a huge parrot cage unaware of the fact that the bottom had fallen out and his parrot no longer there.

The streets were being patrolled by men in uniform, some from the Presidio, some National Guards, and I believe some were Marines. I didn't know which were which; they certainly did their best to keep law and order and to help the bewildered people.

At the fire lines, men were working desperately to stop the fires which were moving on block after block; without water, the men were almost helpless. Dynamite was being used to clear a space ahead of the flames in an effort to halt the conflagration, but it was not until whole blocks were flattened along the east side of Van Ness Avenue and Valencia Street that they finally succeeded.

While the struggle to stop the fire was going on, efforts were being made to care for the displaced people everywhere in the unburned part of the city.

Transportation was rapidly being reestablished; this was before the time of automobiles, what few there were, were novelties, motor trucks unheard of. Street cars even in the outlying districts were still out of commission so supplies had to be moved with horses.

Food, including carloads of hard-boiled eggs, was sent in from many sources and supply stations set up, food lines soon formed, as no one could have carried much food had they had it on hand.

Everyone cooked over open fires, where the houses could be lived in; people were not permitted to light fires indoors because of the danger of gas pockets exploding. Kitchens were built on the sidewalks often using telephone poles for anchorage and were quite snug and secure. Others were just little campfire affairs with the pots balanced on bricks, if the wind came up suddenly the lids at least, sometimes the whole meal would go rolling down the street.

When the fire was finally under control except for flare-ups in the burned-over districts, where the big warehouses had been the ruins smoldered for weeks, especially some coffee mills and their storage places near the bay. The smell of that burning coffee seemed to be everywhere.

The tremendous task of cleaning up was already begun, groups of men at work clearing the debris from the streets even though the bricks they handled were still hot.

Day after day, Bud and I walked through the ruins for no special reason, just moving. There were many little signs, just scraps of paper tucked under a brick or chunk of mortar telling where the people who had lived there could be found.

A man walking alone about the streets often found himself commandeered by the soldiers and put to work for an hour or more on the cleanup job. If accompanied by a woman, he wouldn't be bothered; perhaps I did Bud a good turn by tagging along.

Restaurants began to spring up in all sorts of locations, one I remember in a big tent down where the business district had been, flaunted a sign "The Fly Trap"; it was literally that, the whole city swarmed with the nasty things.

I believe that same restaurant continued in business, under that name, but in very fine and sanitary surroundings in downtown San Francisco for the next fifty years.

As it was becoming possible to move in and out of the city in an almost normal way, we pooled our resources and arranged for Bud to take Maggie and Eileen to her sister Mame, who had a home in Nevada City. Poor Maggie was growing worse steadily and passed away shortly after reaching Nevada City.

One day I walked to the Mission District to visit my relatives, the Spiering family on Dolores Street, which had fortunately escaped the fire.

I found them in an uproar; my cousin Henry, their oldest son, was just leaving the house with a bundle on his shoulder. He gave me a curt greeting and muttered, "I'm leaving." His mother in tears told me Henry was married that morning and according to her to the wrong girl.

The young sinner had, for some time, devoted himself to two loves, both named Anna. One, the daughter of German friends, about eighteen, she met with his parents' complete approval, the other a widow with a sixteen-year-old daughter. As Henry was just twenty-one, I can see why his mother objected to the marriage.

He had made a practice of telling his parents, "I am taking Anna" wherever he happened to be going, because they wanted it that way. They thought he was referring to the younger Anna, so when he announced his marriage to the other Anna, there was one grand row.

After he left home that morning, I seldom saw him. They had one child, a boy they named James, whose whereabouts are unknown to me. Henry died during the 1918 flu epidemic a few days after being drafted for World War I.

As soon as transportation out of the City had been reestablished, I had of course written home, telling the folks of my safety and whereabouts.

During all this time of disruption and excitement, it had never crossed my mind that the quake could have reached into the mountains near home.

The San Francisco daily papers were being printed in Oakland and sold on the streets by newsboys. They contained many personal ads, families searching for each other, and business houses trying to contact their employees. Through this, I found the Nathan Dohrmann people were asked to report to 1090 Page Street. This address was familiar to me, it being the home of old-time friends of my parents, the Fritz Plagemanns.

The store had been one of the last blocks in that neighborhood to burn, and with the delivery teams and drivers who came to help, most of the records had been saved and were now housed in the Fred Dohrmann home. Mrs. Fred was the former Millie Plagemann with whom I had played as a child when my parents made their yearly visits to San Francisco.

I found the hotel ledgers ensconced on the stationary tubs in the basement laundry. My first task was sending statements to out-of-town customers in the hope of gathering in some ready cash.

We all left Rushtons, the others going north to Nevada City. I rented a room on Lyon Street which was quite near my work.

CALLED HOME

Then one day I got a most distraught letter from my father telling me of all the damage done by the quake, especially on the ranch and demanding I come home at once and help my own people instead of enjoying myself among strangers, inconsistent as could be—my father.

I talked to Mr. Fred about leaving; he suggested I go home and see for myself how badly I was needed. If after a week or two I wanted to come back, they would be glad to have me do so.

The mountains in general looked safe and secure. The house had suffered little harm; one section of the front retaining wall had crumbled. Josie and Harriet Bailey, who was again teaching Central, gave me the details of the morning of the quake.

How the furniture danced all about and the organ and the Morris chair both low heavy pieces were upset, and dishes, jars of canned fruit, pans of milk and cream all shaken from shelves and cupboards. The biggest loss was the fruit house, as the cellar walls gave way, the whole building had slowly leaned toward the west and collapsed like a house of cards.

The water system was disrupted, the underground pipes pulled apart, leaving spaces of several feet between the broken ends. The whole line had to be replaced. Springs where water had always flowed freely vanished, never to flow again even in the wettest winters. By great good luck, the one from which the water supply for the ranch had always been pumped was not disturbed.

There were all manner of reports of cracks opening in the earth from a few inches to many feet in width and depth, in which animals were lost. I did not see them.

I did see what came to be known as "the big slide" on the Beatty place, somewhat west of Grizzly Rock, a section of landscape, estimated as forty acres, broke from its place on the mountainside and rumbled off down the canyon toward Deer Creek, carrying everything before it for several miles, except for destroying the forest and leaving a great gash in the mountainside with a sheer precipice about a hundred feet high at its beginning; it did less harm than one would think.

The worst damage was to a shingle mill on the bank of a small stream which emptied into Deer Creek from the east; this mill, owned and operated by the Hoffman Brothers, stood directly in the path of this great mass of moving earth and trees. I understand it was completely buried. As far as I know, it has never been unearthed. There was one fatality there that morning. A man hurrying toward the cook shack to warn others of the coming danger was struck by a falling tree and killed.

Farther down the creek was another mill bigger than the first one, engaged in cutting lumber. This mill and its service buildings had been built off to one side on higher ground and thereby escaped destruction.

At Lake Ranch, a Water Company reservoir near the Bernard home, Emile Bernard told me the water splashed back and forth in an east-west motion till it was carried across the road and up into the vineyard on the east side.

My stay at home was short; there seemed no great need for my being there. Josie was doing fine as housekeeper; Harriet being there was good too. Father's brother had returned to make his home on the ranch for an undetermined time and now did much of the work and chores that had always fallen to me.

Father, since the first shock had worn off, was busy, with the help of Uncle Bill, salvaging what could be reused of the lumber in the fruit house and preparing to build a similar building before the next fruit season. This they did with the help of a carpenter and stone mason.

A good enough building, it filled the harvest and storage needs for a long time but lacked the nice finish of Fritz Wherner's expert hands. Fritz had built the first one but not the cellar walls under it. It was not his fault that the first one fell down.

I returned to San Francisco and my job with Nathan Dohrmann Company.

SAN FRANCISCO RECOVERS

The accounting office continued to operate from Page Street until Nathan Dohrmann and many other retail houses erected great barnlike structures in a burned-over part of the City, which is somewhere between the Potrero and Army Street and the streets are all named for the states. The street cars were running to this new development. It seemed a long trip from where I was living.

Some of the men found time to dig in the store's ruins and came to the office with various souvenirs which they generously passed out to the office people. I still have a number, a tiny pitcher from a doll's tea set, a Tom and Jerry mug, a bread and butter plate, and a statue of a lady which has been broken twice since by other quakes and glued together again. All discolored and rough from the heat of the fire and the blowing sand.

Salesmen from the eastern manufacturers began to appear with their trunks and suitcases of samples. The Homer Laughlin man was the first to come.

Our next move was to a better building also built of lumber, with all the requirements of a retail store, which Dohrmanns had built on Van Ness near California. Van Ness Avenue had become the retail shopping district; the White House, O'Connors, the City of Paris, and all the rest were there.

I rented a room for twelve dollars a month at 1745 Bush Street with cooking privileges. This meant there was a wooden box about 2 1/2 feet long, 18 inches deep, and 18 inches wide nailed to the windowsill. This was equipped with a two-burner gas plate, the gas supplied by a hose from the overhead light fixture in the center of the ceiling. When the window shade was down, the kitchen was invisible. It answered the purpose; I was not an enthusiastic cook.

The office was on the mezzanine and my desk under an unshaded skylight, which brought on eyestrain. An optometrist advised glasses; with variations in shape and strength, I have worn glasses ever since and have now progressed to trifocals.

Alyce and her family had returned from Nevada City and located in Oakland where Alyce found employment with the Sunset Grocery.

I now had the choice of two pleasant things to do on Sunday. I could ride or walk to the ferry building at the foot of Market Street and take the Key Route ferry and train to Fentons on Aileen Street in Oakland and spend a happy day there. The trip across the bay plus the train ride cost a dime. If I stayed the night as I often did, I would go directly to work from there.

The other possibility was to go to San Mateo to spend the day with my sister Lotte; from Fifth and Market, the Interurban Electric Line made hourly trips out Mission Street, through Colma, past the cemeteries on to the downtown section of San Mateo. From there I walked to the Johns's home on Crystal Springs Road. On this car line, there was the regular five-cent fare to the county line then the conductor collected twenty cents more for the rest of the way.

I had my first automobile ride that summer. Autos had become more common; sometimes there were several to be seen at the same time. This was quite an event. There was a company picnic being given at Larkspur, a summer place across the bay. Two other girls and I were waiting on a corner of Van Ness for a down car when Mr. Fred came along in a shiny red auto and offered us a ride. We were delighted of course, but going down that hill to the bay I had some very doubtful moments about the advisability of using this type of transportation.

The picnic was a great success, but I was glad to go home from the waterfront to Gough Street on a Sutter Street cable car.

There was an endless amount of building going on everywhere, all lumber structures. Any man who could swing a hammer or use a saw was sure of a job.

Parks, such as Jefferson Square, which covered four big blocks from Eddy to Golden Gate one way and from Gough to Laguna the other, were given over to rows and rows of little houses painted green, to take care of the refugees; the same type of buildings were put up by the hundreds at Daly City and Colma, I think by private land owners as rental units.

There was much said and written about what was to be done. The Mayor, the Supervisors, and men of financial importance, according to the rumors, were bringing trained advisors in the business of building cities from the East.

These advisors were to formulate a complete plan for a perfect city. No more queer triangular lots where streets met, no more blind alleys, everything smooth and perfect. The catch to this dream was the property owners didn't propose to give up any ground, what they owned they intended to use no matter what shape the corner lots turned out to be.

So San Francisco was rebuilt on the same old lines. I'm sure most of the people wanted it that way. A pretty fine and much loved city it still is.

There was a freely quoted poem written to the rhythm of "The Road to Mandalay" by Lawrence W. Harris which seemed to express the spirit of the average San Franciscan better than other printed opinions.

The Damndest Finest Ruins

Put me somewhere west of East Street where there's
    nothing left but dust,
Where the lads are all a-hustling and where
    everything's gone bust,
Where the buildin's that are standin' sort of
    blink and blindly stare
At the damndest finest ruins ever gazed on anywhere.

Bully ruins—bricks and wall—through the night
    I've heard you call
Sort of sorry for each other cause you had to
    burn and fall.
From the Ferries to Van Ness you're a godforsaken mess
But the damndest finest ruins—nothing more
    or nothing less.

The strangers who come rubberin' and a-huntin'
    souvenirs.
The fools they try to tell us it will take a
    million years
Before we can get started, so why don't we come
    to live
And build our homes and factories upon land
    they've got to give.

"Got to give!" Why, on my soul, I would rather
bore a hole
And live right in the ashes than even move to
Oakland's mole,
If they'd all give me my pick of their building's
proud and slick
In the damndest finest ruins still I'd rather
be a brick!

Lawrence W. Harris

There were those who thought the "Quake and Fire" were sent to
punish the City for its wickedness.
Thereupon Charles K. Field asked this question:

If, as some say, God spanked the town
For being overfrisky;
Why did he burn the churches down
And save Hotalings Whisky?

This question is still unanswered.
I too tried my hand at putting the story of the earthquake and fire into
verse; after lying hidden all these years in an old notebook, here it is:

How It Happened, April 18 to 21, 1906

I was sleeping so soundly one morning
In sweet dreams my tho'ts were wrapped
The day was just a dawning
The first sunbeam at my window tapped.

I tho't sweet music was beating
In dear old Golden Gate Hall
It seemed the night was fleeting
At a good old College Ball.

When O! What a start awoke me
What a bang and crack and roar
The plaster seemed to choke me
My bed danced about on the floor.

From the street I heard voices calling
Come out, oh do come out quick
The house is surely falling
And you will be hit by a brick.

On the street live ghosts were walking
At least each one looked like a ghost
And each to his neighbor was talking
Telling which one had lost the most.

Bricks over the street were scattered
The houses seemed creaking with pain
Both windows and nerves were shattered
Pray God—it never happens again.

But low the trouble was only begun
Great smoke clouds appeared in the east
Like a blazing red ruby arose the sun
The fire of our city was making a feast.

It burned; how it burned, no pencil can tell
From the fire's wild advance all were flying
In hopeless despair, knowing too well
Beyond human aid the city was dying.

Three days and three nights the big fire lasted
And all in its path was swept to the ground
Many a life and bright hope was blasted
And fortunes lie buried in that ashy mound.

From parks and hilltops we watched the burning
From block to block the wild flames leap
From the awesome sight our eyes ne'er turning
Too exhausted to move, too excited to sleep.

'Tis over at last the city lies gasping
Struggling bravely to regain its breath
It may be hurt, but the hurt is not lasting
It has gained new life in its fight with death.

And better and fairer than ever before
Old Frisco will rise from the ashes
We will have a new city as gay as before
E'er the next quarter century over us passes.

Emma Stolte

My young friends from Nevada, Wedertz, and Trevillian found me again some weeks after the quake by inquiring at Dohrmann's. They had been employed as timekeepers on a steam shovel, part of a construction project, building a railroad along the coast from San Francisco toward Santa Cruz.

These steam shovels were huge pieces of equipment propelled by old-fashioned steam engines which were fueled with wood or coal, and for which track had to be laid foot by foot as they chewed their way along.

By the middle of April, the work had progressed as far south as Pedro Point, due west of Colma.

The way the boys told it: the morning of the quake, the finished roadbed, quantities of smaller equipment and the steam shovel, all slid into the ocean, gone beyond recovery.

The loss was so serious to the men financing the enterprise, the work stopped right there, and the vision of a Coast Line Railroad, forgotten.

HELENE'S EXPERIENCE

This is a story of the time of the 1906 quake which I heard a short time ago, told by a dignified, gray-haired lady who moves about with a cane, while a group of us senior citizens were passing a pleasant evening relating tales of the "I remember" variety.

As a young woman in her early twenties, Helene lived with her mother in San Jose at the time of the earthquake.

Word came through from Salinas that the quake had taken the life of her aunt, wife of her mother's brother. Circumstances were such that her mother could not go to Salinas herself, so she sent Helene in her place to give what help she could to the bereaved household.

After a short stay, she was returning home by railroad train; when they reached Gilroy, she learned to her dismay that that train was going no farther. While casting about in her mind for a solution to her problem as to how she was to get to San Jose, a relief train en route from Los Angeles to San Francisco with food and clothing for the destitute stopped for water at the nearby tank. Helene quickly decided that she would manage some way to get aboard that train and home.

Making her way quickly past the many people gathered at the depot, she hurried along the edge of the track beside the train. One person in the crowd attracted her attention, a man with an awkward parcel in his arms who seemed to keep pace with her saying over and over, "I must get to San Jose and preach my sermon."

As she hurried along, the ladderlike handholds on the box cars came to her notice and she thought to herself, "I can climb to the top of the car that way and ride to San Jose." Suiting action to the thought, she proceeded to climb up. Just as she reached the top, there came a brakeman shouting, "Lady, lady, come down from there. You can't ride on the car roof." "Oh yes!" said she. "I'll hold on tight. I must get to San Jose." The brakeman won the argument by promising to take her to the conductor to tell her story.

The conductor listened to her story for a moment then said, "Your uncle is an old friend of mine. There is room for you in the caboose." He asked if anyone was with her. As she looked up, there stood the man with the parcel and the sermon he was determined to preach in San Jose. She pointed to him saying, "Yes, that man." They were both given seats, and the train started on its way.

Next she learned the train would not stop in San Jose. It was scheduled straight through to San Francisco. What to do? Here was another problem which the conductor solved by asking if she could jump off while the train was moving. Helene was sure she could. When the train neared Second Street, the conductor gave the slow signal, jumped off first, and gave her what support he could by taking her hand as she left the train. She landed safely on her feet and made her way home without further adventure.

The man with the parcel and the sermon following her example also left the train safely and went on his way without a backward glance or thank you.

AFTER THE QUAKE

The year 1906 ended, and 1907 moved along. I was now being paid fifteen cents an hour, which with three evenings overtime, gave me about $37.50 every four weeks.

I tried sharing my room as an economy measure. My first partner was Margaret McGillicuddy. She stayed two weeks, leaving to marry a man from Bakersfield.

Then there was Carrie Lockie, dark, quick, and fun to be with; we were together quite a while. It was her seagoing sweetheart, insisting on marriage and a home of their own, that took her away.

Carrie had a childhood friend, John Malone, a Petty Officer on the naval training ship at Yerba Buena Island. Occasionally, he would send her invitations to ball games or other daytime affairs always on Sunday. We could invite groups of girls, the more the merrier, meet the official launch at the wharf, and be transported to the island for a wonderful day of being waited on by squads of young men in uniform. One special evening Carrie and I attended a dance there, in a beautifully decorated hall, music by the Marine Band and bounteous refreshments. A truly gala evening.

After Carrie became Mrs. Charlie Norton, I had Beatrice Tenny to share room and expenses for a time. She was a little widow with some strange principles. Lotte definitely disapproved of her, though I objected to some of her ideas of right and wrong, like matching one of her young admirers a copper penny against a twenty-dollar gold piece, and keeping the twenty; there was much about her that I enjoyed. Financially, I was the loser. When she left having lost her job. I found she had established credit in my name at the corner grocery and I had the bill to pay.

So when one of the Nathan Dohrmann bill collectors told me of a job at Kelly's Stables that paid $75 a month, which could be mine if I liked, as their bookkeeper was leaving, I made the change. The amount $75 looked like the mint to me.

There had been two girls in that office, the one that stayed was Constance McAullif, a very nice person to work with a gray-haired, twenty-three-year-old Irish, Colleen.

Kelly's was a boarding stable for businessmen's horses and hack service. Hacks or cabs were two-or four-seated enclosed vehicles, the forerunners of taxis. The driver's seat was high up in front, separate from the passengers. Kelly's drivers wore long double-breasted coats and stovepipe hats.

The men working here with a few exceptions were an entirely different type from those I had known at Dohrmanns, or anywhere else for that matter.

Monday was payday. Had they been paid on Saturday, as most working people were, there would have been a great shortage of drivers on Monday.

There were four Kelly brothers, the oldest Ed, a man about fifty, called "Bullets" by the men, took little interest in the days' activities, spending most of the time asleep in an armchair in the entryway. The second brother was Frank who carried most of the responsibility and worried about everything. The next was "Dud," short for Dudley, busy and cheerful and never seemed bothered. A fourth brother supposedly managing a stable in San Rafael, I never saw.

They were the most talented liars I ever met. It was always "my brother" who had given an order, made a promise, or owed a bill.

I think I had been there three months when California suffered a depression, a bad one. Some business houses paid their obligations in script. Real money was not available. Kelly's solved their problems by letting help go, so I found myself out of a job. Kelly's survived and remained in business for a long time. I believe there is still a business called Kelly's on that corner of Pine and Franklin. It now reads Kelly's Garage.

It was useless to look for office work just then, so I took housework with Mrs. T. deWolf at 1929 Broadway at $35 a month. This was not what I wanted but, the deWolfs were nice people and the work easy, so I stayed through the winter and into the spring.

Mrs. deWolf was sister-in-law to Miss Elsie deWolf, at that time the foremost lady interior decorator in the United States. Mrs. deWolf had a little daughter, Winifred Shaunessy, who was often left in my care. I grew very fond of her; even then she was always dancing about the apartment to phonograph records.

As she grew up, she studied interpretive dancing and made her way to Hollywood where she met and married the renowned matinee idol,

Rudolph Valentino. After a short and stormy marriage, they were divorced. She never married again but later changed her name to that of a Russian dancer, Natasha Rambova, whom she had known and admired.

This much I had known about my little friend for a long time. Now in 1966, I find an article in a San Jose paper telling of her death at the age of sixty-nine, after a busy life having been premiere danseuse with the Kosloff Imperial Russian Ballet, as well as master of many languages and translator and editor of the materials of ancient Egyptological studies. It was good to know her life had been so worthwhile and satisfactory.

While I was with the deWolfs, Lotte met the young man who was to become my brother-in-law, Henry Frahm.

Henry's people were German. He and I think one brother was born in Hanover. There was a sister, Kate, and a younger brother, Charlie, born in America. The parents and Charlie were at that time living near Colma where Charlie was a well-known hog raiser. Kate became Mrs. Coleman and the other brother, Alfred, was away working somewhere in the California oil fields.

Henry lived and was employed in San Mateo. His work was connected with the Jenning's Livery Stables. Sometimes he drove a carryall stage over the mountains to Half Moon Bay where some real estate men were developing a subdivision right on the beach sand.

One Sunday, Lotte and I went along for the ride. A beautiful ride all the way, especially to me, as I had had no opportunity to get into the country all winter. The salesmen tried to interest us in buying lots, but we resisted their blandishments.

It was cold coming home, so Henry gallantly tucked a horse blanket around us. I knew about the fleas in San Francisco, having known them in the various rooming houses where I had lived, but the ones in that blanket were more numerous and hungrier than any I had ever met with. Such is the power of true love. My bemused sister never knew that fleas were fellow passengers on that trip.

As spring advanced, I became more and more anxious to get away from the city, so I answered an ad offering pleasant employment in the Yosemite Valley for the summer, put out by Camp Curry. I soon received word that Mrs. Curry would be in San Francisco shortly and would then look me up, which she did. It was agreed that she would let me know when the camp would open. This seemed to depend somewhat on the weather and the road conditions. When ready, she would furnish me transportation, and the job would be there for me.

In the meantime, Lotte and Henry had settled on May 6 for their wedding. They were to live in a house Henry owned which he had had repainted and generally refurbished. It was located at 314 The Crescent, San Mateo. At the end of April, I bade the deWolfs goodbye and spent the first days of May washing windows and helping to put the finishing touches on the new home.

Their wedding day fell on Sunday. Josie was maid of honor and Charlie his brother's best man. A Lutheran minister officiated; the guests were all members of the Frahm and Stolte families. Mrs. Frahm Sr. and Alfred Frahm were unable to attend.

That evening Father, Josie, and I went to San Francisco to visit the Spierings and also to see the Pacific Fleet which was coming into the bay next day. We made a tour of the bay to get a closer view of the big ships and stayed to see the sailors march up Market Street, a beautiful parade with many bands and flags and thousands of marching men.

After all this excitement, we went home, where I intended to stay till time to go to Camp Curry. Father surprised me by asking that I change my plans and stay home permanently, using the old plea, "I am growing old and need younger shoulders to lean on." I was pleased to be reinstated in his good opinion and more than happy to be home. I wrote Mrs. Curry that circumstances had changed for me, and I would not be able to take the job she had offered.

HOME AGAIN

The spring following my return to the hills was most delightful, having missed the preceding four or at best seen, smelled, and heard mere shadows of the coming to life of the growing things which are so close to one in the country; I reveled in every phase of it.

Armloads of hothouse roses in a floral shop window can never compare with one pink duchess rose peeping from under a blanket of late snow on a bush in the backyard.

If there is anything more lovely than a cherry tree in snow-white bloom, it is some gnarled old apple tree covered with myriads of tiny pink and white corsages each with its own cluster of green leaves, so honey sweet all the bees go mad over them. Rows of prune and pear trees too stand in breathtaking beauty.

A vineyard in the spring, though not as spectacular as an orchard, has a beauty all its own, so clean and green. When the tiny grape buds burst and shed their faint perfume, the result is like nothing else in this world.

The baby chicks, calves, pigs, and kittens hidden away in nooks and corners where they had no business being, all demanding care and responding so beautifully when it was given, filled each waking hour to overflowing. No city can offer anything to match spring in the country.

I fitted into the old order of life as though I had never been away; with this difference, Josie now took charge of the kitchen. It was mighty nice to come in at mealtime to well-cooked food all prepared without any effort on my part.

There were of course changes in the neighborhood. The Zimmermans on Tip Top Ranch had a new baby as did the Stewarts. There had been some deaths; a few had moved away to be replaced by strangers.

Some of the young people had married and set up new homes, among them the two older Beatty girls. Nellie was now Mrs. Walter V. Newell, and Jennie had chosen Isadore Miller. Their brother Billy had gone off to the goldfields of the Nevada and California deserts. I soon learned that my little sister watched the daily mail for letters from that direction.

During my absence, several of the Central's teachers had made their homes at our house. Miss Florence Cunningham of Saratoga divided her stay between the Stoltes and Posts. Then Harriet Bailey came back and was there at the time of the earthquake.

As sometimes happens, the center of population in the district had shifted to the northern end of the district; the parents of these children felt it was too far for them to walk to the schoolhouse on the Mini place, so temporary quarters were set up in a small service building on the Gamble property then owned by Fred Herring. After a term, another change was made; the trustees moved a cabin which had housed the Stolte's woodchoppers for some years from its location on the far end of the ranch to a spot beside the county road at the edge of the vineyard and a short distance from the house. School continued here for several terms. Agnes Thomson, John Beatty, and Emma Moniere graduated there.

Two teachers presided in this building; Dr. Alice M. Parker, an older woman, difficult to do for, dissatisfied no matter what. I don't know what the Dr. stood for; I doubt that it meant medicine. She was a firm believer in home remedies. For a cold, she would shut herself in her room with a dish of burning sulfur; when the fumes became so heavy that she was all but suffocated, she would rush outdoors gasping for breath, leaving her dish of sulfur for Jo to take care of. Luckily, the room never caught fire. She soon took herself back to Elks Grove, for which the household was thankful.

Dr. Parker was followed by a little Italian girl from Los Gatos, Martha Vernova. She stayed several terms and was there when I came home, a pleasant friendly person and a capable teacher; from Central she went to Browns School. She taught there till she resigned to become Mrs. Will Van Lone.

The little building by the side of the road had never been considered adequate. The trustees now decided to acquire a better site, dismantle the building at Mini's, and rebuild it in the northern end of the district.

The main requirement for locating a public school was that the land on which it stood must border on a county road. To accomplish this, Father gave the use of a piece of land on the northwest line of the ranch, not an ideal location being below the road on a rather steep hillside, but it answered the purpose.

The procedure was for the landowner to give the use of the chosen plot free. If at any time the school was discontinued, the land and building reverted to the owner.

A road was built to the chosen spot and the building site leveled. A young carpenter, Bert Moore, engaged to dismantle the old building and build the new one.

When the lumber was hauled from the old to the new site, the men piled it all near what looked to them like a heap of dead ashes. Next morning, the carpenter found nothing but a bigger heap of ashes. This of course made new problems as finances had to be found to buy new lumber, doors, windows, everything needed to put together a building. However, their efforts were successful, and a new schoolhouse stood ready in time for the beginning of the next school year.

There being no water on that little piece of shale and chaparral hillside, the children carried a daily supply from our house.

Miss Isabel Martin had the honor of opening the new building. She was not a stranger, having lived in Lakeside district since early childhood. She knew the country, the people, and their ways. We enjoyed her stay in our home. As a teacher, she was conscientious and patient; the children did well and liked her.

After Miss Martin left, I think to take a school in Willow Glen, Ida Kruft came from San Francisco and taught for a year. She was very much a city girl; country life just wasn't what she wanted.

The next year, Ethel Case from Los Gatos took over and managed nicely. She too lived at the Stoltes. At the end of her year, with children growing up or moving away, the attendance stood at zero and Central went on the county records as lapsed, automatically granted five years to reestablish itself if enough children came into the district at any point during the five years to justify such a move.

The children came, and the school resumed.

People

New people were coming into the mountains all the time. Dr. Hector of Berkeley purchased the original Herring place. They had three small children, a daughter Louise and two boys, John and Fred, all suffering from whooping cough. Dr. Hector continued his practice in Berkeley, spending weekends and holidays with his family. A baby girl, Roberta, joined the family soon after they came to the mountains. The Hector family was a worthwhile and delightful addition to the community.

The Ellisons of Campbell bought the Lint property, and George Lint moved to Twin Lakes near Santa Cruz. In turn, the Duncan McPhersons of Santa Cruz took over the N. W. Scott place as a summer home and later lived there permanently. Joe Favre of Boulder Creek brought his young wife and two little boys, Henry and Louie and established a home on the ridge beyond Grizzly Rock.

The same sort of changes were taking place in Lakeside District, with the difference that many of the original holdings were broken up into smaller parcels, going to people of strictly urban backgrounds and ideas. Invariably the first sign of new ownership was evidenced by an array of No Trespassing, No Hunting, and Keep Out posters which were very disturbing to the old-timers.

One young man, who had grown up in the neighborhood always at liberty to come and go as he pleased, just as all others were accustomed to doing, only Johan had been somewhat deaf all his life and sometimes misunderstood when spoken to by strangers.

One evening walking quietly along a familiar path after a long day of hard work, he was hailed by the new owner and told in no doubtful terms that he was trespassing on private property and to get to H-back to where he had just come from. Johan listened to all the man had to say, then replied, "I'm not trespassing, I'm just going home," and home he went. In time, the new man learned better manners.

Now and then there were misunderstandings between the old-time settlers too; who certainly knew better, for example, there was young Ernie, six foot four, son of pioneer parents, and the owner of a yearling steer, inclined to wander from his pasture and invade the neighbor's orchards; and there was William, an elderly and crotchety Englishman who lived nearby and didn't propose to put up with any nonsense.

After several sharp warnings to the young owner, he sent the final message, "Take your animal off my premises or I will call the sheriff." When Ernie went to comply with the demand, he found his steer very, very dead, it having been shot some unknown time before and now presented a most unpleasant disposal job. Ordinarily, the outcome would have been a knockdown and drag out fistfight to settle the matter once and for all. But no self-respecting husky twenty-five-year-old would lower himself to the point of striking a wizened sixty-year-old man half his size.

Things simmered all summer, till one day meeting at the local shipping point, each with a load of fruit for the San Francisco market, with other men near to give him a feeling of safety as well as courage, William had no better sense than to twit Ernie about his steer and how he had gotten the best of him. When the young man reached the limit of his patience, which didn't take long, he picked William up by the back of his collar and the seat of his pants, carried him squalling and protesting to a nearby horse trough and gave him a thorough ducking.

They never became pals, but William learned not to plague Ernie anymore. They lived on adjoining farms for years under an uneasy truce.

MISHAPS, ETC.

These had been the years of automobile development and encroachment, all very much resented by the farmers, especially those living in the hills; the motor-driven vehicles were given all manner of uncomplimentary names, like "stink bugs" and "skunk wagons" according to the team driver's disposition and imagination.

Almost all horses at that time were really afraid of the noisy things and would rear and fuss and often take their drivers and wagons off the road into all kinds of difficulties.

Efforts were made to have laws passed to keep motor-driven vehicles off all mountain roads, such laws were of course never passed. Now if one meets a horse-drawn rig on any road, it is as much of a surprise as the automobile used to be.

The first auto I remember passing our house on the county road was a big touring car of some kind, going along at a great rate of speed, probably doing as much as twenty miles an hour, which was considered tops at that time.

The people were apparently having a fine time as we could hear them singing. Jo and I watched them disappear southward. Later we heard they missed a turn of the road before reaching Browns School, one woman dead and a young girl badly hurt.

When neighbors who heard the crash reached the spot to give what aid they could, they found the head of the party who turned out to be an Oakland newspaperman, stumbling about taking pictures of the wreck, paying no attention to the dead and injured who happened to be his wife and daughter.

Mrs. Van Lone took the injured girl into her home and cared for her till she could be taken to her home in Oakland. For her trouble and kindness, Mrs. Van Lone received not so much as a simple word of thanks, a very black mark against all city automobile people.

Of course the horse and wagon days had not been free of accidents, some tragic, others just inconvenient or funny. There were men who lost their lives on poor roads, where neither horse nor wagons were equal to what was expected of them, Joe Olave and Charlie Anderson to name two.

The first mile of road from the Bernards's yard toward Saratoga was very steep and very narrow. It was necessary when leaving the place to close the yard gate to keep the barnyard animals from straying away. If there was no one else to do this, the driver had to climb down from the wagon, after passing through, walk back and close the gate.

Emile Bernard had a way of wrapping the reins around the brake lever when leaving his seat; upon returning to his perch, the signal for the horses to move out was the sound of the brake lever striking the ratchet guard when it was released by the driver.

This morning with a full load of cordwood and six horses strung out in front, he was the one to walk back and close the gate. Before he could return to the driver's seat, one of the horses bobbed his head too hard, pulling the brake lever free of its ratchet with the usual sharp snap. At this signal, those six horses promptly leaned into their collars and walked down the road. It was impossible for Emile to get past the wagon and gain control of the reins and stop them. It was an amazing feat, but those horses took themselves and the loaded wagon safely down that mile of narrow road coming to a stop at the bottom, where they were overtaken by a badly shaken but thankful young man. Some months later, two of these horses pulling a spring wagon up that same road one dark night went too near the outer edge and plunged to their deaths; luckily, their driver was able to jump to safety.

Sometimes young people at a dance or party found, when ready to go home, that their horse or horses had untied themselves, sometimes making their way home, sometimes having taken a wrong turn of the road, were found next morning patiently waiting by a neighbor's barn door. At times it was unfair to blame the horses, for as it was often irately expressed, "Some—smart-aleck tied that horse loose."

A young lady from the Bear Creek Road always drove a fat and gentle roan horse, hitched to a rig known as a phaeton. Four-wheeled vehicles had the back axle and wheels fastened securely to the body, but the front axle, wheels, and shafts or pole were on a pivot centered by a bolt called the kingpin so as to make it possible to turn right or left. One day, the kingpin in Tessie's phaeton broke; the horse trotted calmly along the way to town with the front wheels, leaving a much embarrassed young lady helpless in the middle of the road.

Another girl driving a horse hitched to a very light spring wagon and accompanied by a young city friend was trotting comfortably toward town on the Gist Road which is a series of hairpin turns, when rounding one of the shortest turns, perhaps a little too quickly, suddenly found themselves tipped out into the road. The horse, being a sensible creature, stopped upon hearing a decisive "Whoa."

The young people picked themselves up unhurt but dusty; the young man's first concern was to whip off his fine white Panama hat to make sure the cigars he carried there were undamaged.

There were two young men, very good friends, Jack and Johnny, both accustomed to working with horses and not above playing jokes on each other. Jack was driving team for Tip Top Rancho; this day on his way to town with a four-horse team and a load of fruit, well down the Gist Road at the most difficult reverse, he locked one front wheel under the wagon bed. Seeing no safe way to free it, he left everything right there and walked to the nearest house for help. Soon along came Johnny who was perhaps a little more experienced and certainly more inclined to take a chance.

After looking the situation over, he unhitched the leaders and used them to pull the wheel out of its locked position, put the leaders back in place, tied his saddle horse behind the wagon, and took the load down the road to a safe stopping place, tied the team to a tree, and went on his way. Imagine Jack's consternation upon arriving with tools and help to find that horses and wagon had vanished.

Another happening that called forth much glee in the community concerned a young newly married couple living on the Skyline, both accustomed to country living, but neither of farming background. One day returning from a shopping trip to Los Gatos, upon reaching Lexington at the corner where Black Road began its climb to the summit and also the location of Monte Shepard's Saloon, an accepted stopping place for most men before starting into the hills, they stopped as a matter of course. The young man liked a glass of beer as well as the next one; his wife, not caring for this type of refreshment, was however willing to wait in the wagon while her husband fed the horses a ration of grain and refreshed himself at the bar.

The young man made two mistakes; he failed to tie the team to a hitching post, and he removed the bits from their mouths before putting on the nose bags. Time passed, the grain was all eaten; and the horses, becoming restless, started for home. The young lady in the wagon was of course unable to stop them. She might have quickly jumped from the wagon, gotten in front of the slow-moving horses, and stopped them; she just wasn't that much of a country girl.

Soon her husband came from the bar, realizing what had happened, rushed off in great haste to overtake them, but no matter how he hurried, the team steadily gained distance. Meanwhile ahead on the road, another man was traveling toward home.

Charlie drove a heavy slow-moving pair of bays, hitched to a wagon on which he had that morning taken a load of lumber to town; he used only the running gear of his wagon and rode on the load for a seat. This day he had a loose lumber floor on the running gear and was taking back a load of hay. Not wanting to sit up high on the bales where overhanging tree branches would catch him, he had left a ledge at the front of the load to sit on using the hay for a backrest.

The faster-walking, uncontrolled team came up so close to the slower rig that the tip of their wagon tongue thrust itself into the baled hay, and their momentum was enough to push the whole load so far forward that Charlie was shoved from his narrow seat onto the wagon tongue and double trees close to his horses' heels. In his fall, somehow or other, a chain with a hook on the end fastened itself into a loop made to adjust the belt line of blue denim jeans at that time. This loop was at the center of the back, so there hung Charlie unable to manage his team nor free himself. Finally, someone coming down the road stopped the horses, rescued the poor man, and sent the young people safely on their way.

THE FARMERS UNION

Early in 1909, Mr. and Mrs. Ede, from somewhere in the Middle West, rented the J. B. Stewart home, the Stewart family having moved to Lexington because of Mrs. Stewart's health.

Mr. Ede's purpose in coming to California was to organize the farmers of California under the leadership of the Farmers Educational and Cooperative Union of America. The effects of the 1907-08 depression were still being felt, and at the same time labor unions were making steady headway.

The idea of a Farmers Union was welcomed with great enthusiasm, and Locals, as the local groups were called, were established in many of the Santa Clara County school districts. The nearest were Union, Evergreen, Saratoga, and Lakeside. Lakeside was the local that Father and I joined.

The setup was the head of a family or a single man over twenty-one paid dues of three dollars a year, women and children were free, everyone could attend the meetings, only adults could vote, if there were refreshments, the women furnished and served them. Just what they thought such a union would gain for them, I am not sure, some sort of Utopia I guess.

Beyond the Locals there were county, state, and national units. In some states, commercial enterprises for buying and selling were set up and at times were quite successful.

The Santa Clara County Locals developed a cooperative dried prune marketing business which operated for a few years, when it was taken over by the then newly organized Prune and Apricot Growers Association, now the well-known Sunsweet.

At the beginning, Lakeside Local had forty members with Mr. William O. Post as president and Orson Rouse, secretary-treasurer. There were also a warden and a doorkeeper, their names I have forgotten.

Despite the first enthusiasm, attendance soon dwindled, the few faithful ones met from house to house, then the president and secretary agreed to disagree; Mr. Secretary didn't propose to have any old man tell him how to keep his records or write his letters. To keep peace and save the Local from breaking up completely, someone suggested that Miss Stolte be made secretary. I held that doubtful position until Lakeside Local's membership reached the vanishing point.

At one meeting at Mr. Post's home, I was handed a legal-looking document full of whereas's and therefore's to be read to the assembled members. It was a proposed contract to be used by farmers in dealing with dried fruit packers. It probably had good points, but Mr. Post explained it was being proposed by a young fellow from the Saratoga Local whom he had seen and heard at the county meetings, as he always had much to say. But Mr. Post wasn't at all sure the young man had what it took to carry out his proposals, so he advised the document be returned to its sender with the information that Lakeside Local could see no value in it.

Upon Mr. Post's urging, I began to attend the county meetings, which were held in the San Jose Chamber of Commerce Hall at Santa Clara and Market Street upstairs over Springs Clothing Store.

Attending these meetings was quite an excursion. It meant driving to Los Gatos where I would leave my horse in Gertridge's Livery Stable and take the Interurban electric car to San Jose; in the afternoon, I would reverse the procedure and reach home about dark.

There was always a fair attendance at these quarterly meetings, perhaps fifty delegates from all parts of the county. The young man from Saratoga usually was among those present. One meeting he was exerting all his persuasive powers trying to have the county Local print its own newspaper, with a Mr. Clump as editor-manager. The members voted it down.

As I left the hall, I told him I was sorry he had lost the argument. Not that I cared whether or not there was a paper; the poor guy had tried so hard I thought he deserved to win. He seemed pleased to learn that I had taken that much interest.

At one state meeting while acting as doorkeeper, he met my father; while checking his credentials, the young man remarked that the Lakeside secretary was present, to which he got the answer, "Yes, that's my girl," which led him to think, "Huh! Here's another old fogy who thinks all unattached females fall for him."

One member from Campbell kindly advised me not to pay attention to anything that fellow from Saratoga said as he was just a cheap tinhorn politician. A serious-minded, kindly man from Evergreen remarked he just couldn't understand that fellow from Saratoga, as he seemed sensible enough but was always coming out for the wrong side.

Despite these adverse opinions, when I received a note one day saying he would like to call on a certain Sunday after church, I was pleased to reply that I would be happy to see him. This was September 14, 1914.

In the meantime, the seasons rolled on and changes took place. Billy Beatty came home from his wanderings over the deserts of California and Nevada, a handsome, self-assured young man with many entertaining stories to tell of his adventures. Josie was overjoyed by his safe return, and everyone accepted him at his own appraisal.

They were married in their own home on the Bishop place near Alma, on December 18, 1910. Josie asked me to be her bridesmaid, and Isidore Miller stood as best man. Billy's uncle, Rev. George Beatty, read the marriage lines. In time they became parents of three sons, William Ferdinand, George William, and Joseph Jay.

Unfortunately, Billy had not and never did overcome the wanderlust; always seeing greener fields across the fence, sure of millions to be made elsewhere but failing to see the surer though smaller opportunities close by. It also developed that he had a most explosive temper and would give way to unjustified fits of jealousy all of which caused my sister much distress and unhappiness. Due to their mother's care and good sense, the three boys grew up to be honest and capable men.

After a stay at an oil pumping plant in the San Joaquin Valley and a business venture running a "jitney" bus service between San Jose and Morgan Hill, as well as a garage in San Jose, these both proving unprofitable; he volunteered for World War I. He just couldn't resist the appeal of the army posters nor the beat of the recruitment drums.

For some queer reason of his own, he enlisted as a single man, leaving his wife and three babies in a difficult spot, which took a long time and much correspondence with Washington to straighten out.

He came home from the service, without seeing action, an invalid because of pneumonia. After several years of patient care and nursing by his wife, he drifted off again in search of gold in the Sierras and at the age of sixty-five died of a heart attack.

Fanny McC.

Fanny McConologue one of my business college friends came to spend her summers at the ranch, as others had done before her, in an effort to overcome what was known as a run-down condition due to winter colds.

She was a happy, cheerful little person; we enjoyed each other very much. She would follow me about from place to place when my chores kept me near the house, claiming it was fun to watch me work. She always enjoyed being along when I went to town or to a neighbor's with a horse and buggy.

Not up to much physical exertion, she would take short walks by herself, accompanied by the two collies, Pick and Nip. One day when quite near the school, the dogs discovered a snake, a big rattler, and promptly gave battle. Hearing the commotion, Norman Herring came from the classroom and disposed of the snake, but not before it had struck Nip on his mouth. Fanny hurried the dogs home to me, but there was nothing I could do, and to take Nip to San Jose to a veterinary was out of the question.

Nip was a very sick dog for some weeks, helpless because of the terrible swelling of his head and forequarters. He was unable to move or eat; after several days, he began to lap a little milk or water. In the end, he made a good recovery and was again ready to meet any challenge that came his way. Mr. Thomson told me he had known other animals, both dogs and horses which had been struck by rattlesnakes, that they had been very sick but none had died from the poison.

About September, Fanny would return to her home in San Francisco, upon her return the next year, one could see the gain of the summer before and more had been lost during the winter.

Her mother and sisters made short visits to the ranch to be with her, and her brother when his ship was in port, would spend weeks with us, in sailor fashion declaring that when he retired from the sea he was certainly going to be a farmer way off somewhere in the wilderness. I never heard of him doing so.

I feel sure neither Fanny nor any of her family suspected that she was suffering from that dread disease consumption.

Life for me at this time was rolling along very nicely.

1913

After Josephine's marriage when Father became convinced that his new son-in-law was not to be persuaded to take the responsibility of the ranch off his shoulders, he cast about in his mind for another solution to his problem. He was determined to get away from the daily demands of farming.

So he turned again to his eldest daughter for help. As he saw it, her husband had many qualifications to fit him for the job: (1) his family background was German; (2) he was young; (3) he was not afraid of work; and (4) he was not in business for himself, so stood to gain by making such a change.

With some correspondence and several conferences, the deal was made. We three young people, Henry, Lotte, and I would rent the ranch for four hundred dollars per year and between us do the work and divide any profits. Father would of course continue to live with us. The Frahms moved in on March 13, 1913, Lotte, Henry, and their pretty little four-year-old daughter, Anna.

This change was a mistake. I think we all tried, but nothing worked out as we hoped. Henry naturally was given the responsibility of being head of the enterprise. He was a good and capable man, but somehow could not adjust to the give-and-take of our household and community. A day's work to him was a day's work at some appointed task with no breaking away to tend to something else that was suddenly more urgent, either at home or some neighbor's need.

Other things also interfered; Fanny McConologue had returned for the summer as a paying guest. In a losing battle to regain her health, she, as I have told of others, had fallen victim to tuberculosis and each summer when she came back to us, it was evident that she was slowly losing ground and one bright Sunday morning of this troubled year she passed quietly away.

Though he did not say so, I think Henry had a great fear of this disease, so her presence had always disturbed him. On the other hand, I could not say to my little friend, "Go away, we are afraid of you."

Father, in trying to start the gas engine which pumped the water, somehow hit himself on his shin bone with the handle as it slipped off the flywheel, after limping about for several days a quick turn as he was walking caused the bone to break all the way, and he was confined to his bed or chair the rest of that summer. Lotte and I were able to care for him, but having him helpless certainly complicated matters. He made a good recovery, not even a limp.

The Frahm Family—1913

Picnic near Castle Rock

One thing after another came up to upset routine. That was the year our brother-in-law, Bill, decided to try his luck in the oil fields at Taft. It wasn't feasible for his wife and small son to accompany him, so they came to stay with us. Happy as I was to have her, her presence did not ease the situation, too many people, too many mouths to feed, too much general upset. Josie's second son was born January 17, 1914, and named George William.

There was nothing for it, but to put an end to our agreement. One year to the day from their coming, the Frahms moved away again. I had kept a record of the year's income and expenses. The final figures gave us a credit balance of nine hundred dollars—six hundred to Frahms, three hundred to me. I thought it a very good showing for the year's work.

Henry Brown

Father and I picked up where we had left off the year before, depending on whatever help was available, either local or transient.

During the harvest season, a young Russian, who said his name was Henry Brown, came from the employment agency in San Jose. He fitted in nicely and stayed till the work was done.

As we wished to spend a day in San Jose and knowing that meant a late return, Father asked Henry to stay another day to look after things and feed the animals before dark. When we returned at about ten o'clock that night, we found the animals all waiting for attention and Henry Brown nowhere about.

We soon found he had made a thorough job of ransacking the house, making off with some antique guns, a German saber which once belonged to my Uncle Louis, a few pieces of jewelry of no great value, about five dollars in cash belonging to the Farmers Union I was secretary of, and a suitcase to carry his plunder in.

The wages he had not collected amounted to far more than he could possibly get for the stolen articles. I reported the matter to the County Sheriff but got no results.

By now the biweekly visits from the young man from Saratoga had become a well-established routine. On the alternate Sundays, he took his mother to church.

This was the year Mrs. Philbrook of Santa Cruz spent some time with me. Although contemplating divorce at the time, she was a great advocate of marriage. She was also an accomplished artist and did the small unframed landscape in oil for me.

THE PANAMA PACIFIC FAIR

After the unpleasant experience with Henry Brown, different plans were made for the next year. John Beatty with his wife, the former Agnes Thomson, and his sister Georgia whose husband was Steve McLoughlin—a bright and industrious redhead who had come into the neighborhood with the Hectors—took over the orchards on a share basis, the details I have forgotten.

I continued to take care of the cows and chickens. I had developed quite a little business selling butter to private customers; as most of them lived in Los Gatos, I made two trips every week. This with the feeding and milking, caring for the cream and butter as well as the usual housework and occasional guests—some paying, some just friends—I was kept busy.

This was the year of the Panama Pacific Exposition in San Francisco, located near the bay on what is now known as the Marina. Being my first introduction to fairs, it seemed a virtual fairyland, with its lights, colors, statues, and fountains, its domed buildings surrounded by lawns and gardens. Everything combined in a beautiful whole centered by the Tower of Jewels which sparkled and glittered in the sunshine by day as well as at night when the electric lights were lit, because of the thousands of colored glass medallions with which it was hung from its base to the very top.

I remember the Hawaiian Building where fresh pineapple was a specialty, and the Guatemalan Pavilion where coffee was served in very small cups without cream or sugar, the blackest black coffee ever brewed.

The Canadian Building was most fascinating. Among its exhibits was a colony of beavers busy as could be cutting trees and building dams.

The lumber interest had a fine structure devoted mostly to hospitality and known as the Hoo-Hoo House. After the fair closed, this building was dismantled and rebuilt as an amusement enterprise—dance hall, restaurant, and bar in Monte Vista near Cupertino.

In the floral culture division, my friend, Mrs. Bess Lymbery, won most of the prizes for dahlias, which she was then growing in a nursery in San

Mateo, in partnership with Sam Shuda, her one-time Japanese houseboy. Their place was known as The Bess Boston Dahlia Gardens.

The Palace of Fine Arts was a place of unbelievable beauty; although now fallen into woeful disrepair, efforts are still being made to have it restored to its original splendor.

The motif of the fair being the completion of the Panama Canal. Naturally one of the special attractions was a panorama of the Canal. Here you were seated on bleacherlike seats on the edge of a simulated canal while a photographic view of the landscape slowly passed before you, giving the impression that the landscape stood still and the audience moved as though passing that way by boat.

I was able to make two visits of several days each to the fair, once with Father at the time of a German conclave in San Francisco, and again with my Saratoga friend who found it convenient to make a business trip to the city the week I had arranged to spend with the Spierings at their home on Dolores.

Summer

Winter

Fog in the valley

Someday We Will _ _

Before Christmas, we reached the decision that someday we would marry, just when or what would be done about our respective families were questions neither of us had the answer for.

I had only Father to be concerned about; there was no question but that he depended on me for the daily comforts of living; on the other hand, he was in good health, and common sense told me he could adjust to change as well as anyone else.

Way down deep, I knew I would be the one to do the most adjusting. Father knew it too, having always been a staunch advocate of the theory, "The man knows best"; despite this, he still hoped that something would cause his prospective son-in-law to offer to establish his new home on the Stolte place.

However Vince had greater family responsibilities than I. As far as I know, he spent no time nor thought on completely disrupting his life by moving to the mountains.

The Garrod family lived on a foothill farm five miles out of Saratoga, some years before Father and I, returning from a visit to some friends in the valley, took the Pierce Road as a shortcut to the Big Basin Road. As we passed along, we looked into the hills off to the west where we could see orchard plantings on what seemed to be very steep hillsides and commented on the strange and out-of-the-way corners of the world people chose to live in.

Now I was seriously considering leaving my beloved mountains to share the ups and downs of life with the man who lived in the farthest corner of this strange and out-of-the-way bit of the country.

Vince had come from England with his family, father, mother, sister Mary and brother Harold, in 1892 at the age of twelve. After two years of change and uncertainty in the matter of financial partnership with a relative, they had in 1894 gained title and moved to this sixty-five-acre farm in the foothills near Saratoga.

The place was partially planted to prunes, apples, Moorpark apricots, a few pears and peaches, a little hay land and the rest still covered with chaparral.

His parents had had no farming experience, at least not of the California variety. Mr. Garrod's failing health had been the reason for the change from English school teaching to California agriculture.

Vince, the eldest son, soon found himself at least partly responsible for the welfare of the farm and the family. This responsibility he had cheerfully carried on through the years up to the time of our marriage and for many years thereafter.

Now here I was, thirty odd years old with a goodly number of years of housekeeping, farmwork, and whatnot to my credit, no different than any innocent sixteen-year-old preparing to embark on the matrimonial sea.

I had long been accustomed to having some wag introduce me as "the best preserved antique on the mountain" or to being told, "You've been on the shelf so long, you are dusty." Nor had I reached the mature age of thirty plus in a single state, without having had opportunities to change into double harness.

Somehow widowers with grown families never appealed to me, and the single men who had looked my way, bless their dear hearts, wanted to take me to some far-off place like Alaska, Canada, the Islands, most any place away, and I wasn't about to go. Guess I didn't want one of them forever and ever under any circumstances.

This time it was different, knowing better all the while, I forgot that promises—like pie—are made to be broken. If this man had offered to reach up and pluck the stars from the sky for me, I would no doubt have believed that he could do so.

Broken promises or not, I was not like the girl in the story who walked down the lane and through the woods searching for a good straight stick to lean on, when she reached the end of the woods she seized the very last stick within reach and found it crooked and of little use.

Not so with me, the last stick that came to my hand was straight and dependable.

The spring of 1916 was devoted to adjusting the affairs of myself and Father to a complete change. Father decided to put the ranch up for sale, this he had often threatened to do; this time he really meant it.

All but one cow was sold; several yearlings which were mine, my saddle pony, a little blue roan, Fanny, from the Nevada deserts and a flock of chickens plus a brown collie, Pollo, I planned to bring with me.

We settled on Sunday, April 30, 1916; at 2:00 p.m. as the all-important day and time.

Now we had three different points of view: I said," Let us be married by a Justice of the Peace, as I have neither hard and fast religious convictions nor any church affiliations."

Vince said "We will be married by an Episcopal minister. That has always been my faith; I wouldn't feel right about being married any other way."

Father said, "Now see here, my girl, both your sisters had their weddings away from home, the way they wanted. I'm not letting you get away with anything like that, whether you choose a Justice of the Peace or an Episcopal minister is your affair, settle it between you. You will be married here at home, invite relatives, friends, and neighbors and have a real jollification." Now guess who won. So we went through the whole routine.

As we now knew the wedding was to be at home in Santa Cruz County, it was necessary to get our marriage license in the same county. So we traveled to Santa Cruz by autobus from Los Gatos over the new Santa Cruz highway, now the Old Santa Cruz Road, by way of Glenwood. This road had just been completed and was not yet black-topped. It was a very dusty trip.

We went to Los Gatos one evening to see Mr. Bray, the Episcopal minister at St. Lukes. Mr. Bray was a frail little man who looked as though his greatest need was for someone to say, "Rest a bit while I untangle some of life's problems for you and ease the load generally." However, he talked to us at some length as to the seriousness of the step we were taking and promised to come at the appointed hour to conduct the service, which he did.

I sent invitations written by myself—Mr. F. Stolte, requests the honor—etc., etc., to the prescribed relatives, friends, and neighbors with the exception of one neighbor of whom I was really fond. I had told her some weeks earlier what my plan was. To my surprise, she exclaimed, "Good Lord, I'd rather go to your funeral than your wedding. Marriage is a delusion anyway you look at it." So I didn't invite her, and she was deeply offended. She will never attend my funeral as her own took place many years ago.

We expected a hundred guests, and they were all there. The house being too small for so many, we tidied up the yard and the fruit house and made tables and seats of trays and boxes.

Father had decided on cold roast pork and potato salad with the usual assortment of extras with wine and coffee to drink. Vince arranged for two young men from a little coffee shop in Saratoga to help serve. I can't remember how the salad was produced. I do remember very clearly who helped dress that nice fat young pig, and roasted the resulting pork. It was good, too.

The Wedding Party

Elsa Klutz, an elderly neighbor's young wife, came Friday and Saturday to help with the last hundred and one things to be done.

The weather that day was perfect; the cherry trees under which we gathered for the ceremony were green and lovely. My bridesmaid was a little Italian girl, Vera Panighetti, and Vince's Uncle Ralph Creffield stood as his best man. After the ceremony, everyone adjourned to the fruit house for refreshment, good wishes, toasts, and merriment.

Vince's father and young cousin came; his mother stayed home for this strange reason: "her mother had not attended her children's weddings, so neither would she."

Lotte, who now lived at Evergreen, was also absent; she was momentarily expecting a baby and therefore better off at home. Her son Walter was born the following week.

Josie came from Morgan Hill with her three small boys and stayed on for about a week. As her husband was to return to San Jose that evening, we went with him to take the eight o'clock train for San Francisco. Thereby reversing the usual procedure, we saw all our guests off before leaving ourselves.

Understanding Father

As I think back over what I have written in my effort to give an honest picture of my youth, now so long gone, I find that I have painted Father in rather dubious colors, which is wrong; he wasn't a tyrant, because he really didn't mean to be; he felt he had a job to do, namely two motherless daughters to guide along the path of life, and was doing the best he knew how.

Jo and I loved him dearly, felt he was always right, and accepted his decisions as law, whether we liked them or not.

He held the respect, if not the love, of other men, but our own generation, like ourselves was all just a little afraid of him. As his sister used to say, "When Ferdinand starts with Himmel Donner Wetter. It's time to get out of the way."

In a manner of speaking, he was a handicapped man, born the eldest of five brothers and one sister twelve years younger than himself. He left home at the age of fourteen for a life among men at sea.

I have no recollection of him ever speaking of a woman living on board any of the ships he sailed on. I believe a woman on shipboard was considered an omen of bad luck by the crew.

For seventeen years, this was his life and when on shore leave in foreign ports, I suppose he was no different than any other sailor. At the age of thirty-one, he met and married Mother, left the sea, and bought an interest in that saloon at Fourth and Townsend.

A saloon was strictly men's business; some had a side or family entrance through which a man could escort a lady, presumably his wife, and be served at a table; no self-respecting woman would enter by the swinging doors, walk up to the bar, and order a drink.

There were no stools at the bar, just a polished brass rail a few inches above the floor where the customer could rest one foot while he consumed his mug of beer and the free lunch that was always there for him. The floor was often strewn with clean, white sand in flower patterns and nice polished brass cuspidors set about at convenient intervals. How do I know all this? My bartender uncle told me.

When we moved to the ranch, we girls were mother's responsibility and minded Father when spoken to; his life away from the house was still pretty much in a man's world.

At the time of Mother's death, he was fifty years of age, and as he often told us, growing old and in need of help to carry the load that was too heavy for him alone. To make this burden worse, here he was left with three daughters, seventeen, fifteen, and nine.

There had been two stillborn sons which he could not forget. Nor did he ever realize that if Mother had not tried so hard to carry so much of that heavy load he liked to talk about, he just might have had his sons and his wife as well.

When you think about it, it was impossible for him to understand and sympathize with the desires, dreams, and notions of a couple of growing girls.

Lotte, as you know, went away the first summer to make her home with Blaichs in San Francisco, as Mother had wished. To him, Josie and I were still children; in fact he never entirely accepted the fact that we were adults, although he was still with us when we were both gray-headed.

In my late teens, his sharp "sie ruhig" ("be quiet") was most disconcerting, enough to silence a much more self-assured person than I ever dreamed of being.

However, I grew up and reached a point of self-determination where his continual nagging (not a pleasant word, but there is no other that expresses the habit into which he had fallen), poured over me like the water off the duck.

I had made a promise to my mother and went stolidly about the task of caring for the physical well-being of my father and sister, but lacking gumption enough to bring about better rapport.

He often quoted old proverbs when he thought the time was appropriate, some from his seafaring days, some from his German childhood, for instance:

Let's have more work and less talk on this job, or work while you're living, you'll be a long time dead.

From here to there is the same distance as from there to here. Handy when you wanted to visit someone who hadn't come to visit you.

When you want to go dancing, your feet don't hurt. Easy to see where that applied.

One German proverb I liked and to a degree endeavored to keep in my life, "Halte maas in allem dingen" ("Keep measure in all things"); in short, "be moderate."

With the years came better understanding. A time or two when he thought I was somewhere else, I could not avoid overhearing conversations in which he extolled the virtues and abilities of his daughters far beyond their just deserts. I finally concluded that my father did an awful lot of bluffing.

I have used the name Father all through these pages, but it was not the name that came easiest to our lips. While Mother lived, he was always Papa; later as most families do, we varied it with Pa, Pop, Daddy, or Dad and at the last, Gramp.

Because of his seagoing background and the stories of that part of his life he loved to tell; many people called him Captain.

It is said that men and good wine mellow with age. This was certainly true of F. Stolte; with his daughters all married and other men's responsibilities, the ranch sold and that mythical heavy burden off his shoulders, he became a good-natured, genial, well-loved old gentleman, retaining good health and mentality to the venerable age of ninety-five.

MR. AND MRS.

As Mr. and Mrs. Garrod, we found ourselves in San Francisco late that Sunday. The name of the hotel escapes me. It was somewhere way downtown.

We spent the week enjoying the city and also made an overnight trip to Napa to visit old-time friends and neighbors of Vince's, the Don McNairs. Another day we visited the Ed Brown's at Fruitvale where Mr. Brown owned a grocery store, which Vince had supplied with dried fruit for many years.

Mrs. Brown's maiden name was Marcum. I was surprised to learn that her people had owned a farm on the Black Road in the early days and had sold to the Rouse's at about the time that my father bought the property on the Skyline.

While at Fruitvale that day, I had a few minutes with my cousin Henry Spiering, now a pharmacist manager of a drugstore there. This was the last time I saw him; he was drafted for World War I and died in the flu epidemic of 1918.

The following Sunday we returned to Saratoga and the Garrod ranch on Mt. Eden Road where we were to make our home with the Senior Garrods until a house then being built would be ready for occupancy, at which time Mr. and Mrs. Garrod Sr. would move to the new house and we would take over the old one until the following year when we would build a new house for ourselves.

Promises, promises; little did I dream that it would be thirty-two-long years before that new house became an accomplished fact.

The old house deserves a chapter all to itself which I will leave till later.

As one left the back door a pathway led to the right, this took one down a rather steep bank through a wooded gully very pretty with second growth oaks and laurel; at the bottom a short bridge crossed the streambed where water flowed only during the winter rains. It was a very nice bridge with a church-pew type of seat on one side at the halfway point. This was a fine place to sit and relax on a hot summer afternoon, if one ever found any time to relax in.

After following the path up the other side of the gully one came upon a pleasant open yard, a place for storage and repair of farm implements and equipment, and much of the harvest work of the fruit was done here.

There were five huge eucalyptus trees, several Monterey cypress, a row of California walnuts, and two orange trees at one side. These trees had been planted by an early-day neighbor who, being unfamiliar with the survey lines, thought this pleasant bit of land belonged to him. This planting had been done in 1881, just when the news of President Garfield's assassination hit the papers. This information was given us by a gray-haired little old lady who came to the house one day asking permission to look about the place and see what changes time had made since her childhood when she used to visit with the people who then lived next door. She remembered the time of the planting very clearly.

Below these trees at the edge of another gulley was a hand-dug bricked-in well, topped by a small gasoline engine. This was the ranch water supply. Across from the well at the edge of the adjoining orchard which was a mixture of prunes and apples, stood four small buildings.

The one to the left of the roadway was the one known as the blacksmith shop, equipped with a forge and anvil, workbenches, various hand tools, a supply of nuts, bolts, and washers, repair parts for mowers, hay rakes, plows, harrows, and cultivators as well as numerous odds and ends that might be handy sometime and often were.

The other little houses were occupied by men who worked on the place. There was Bill DeVoe who was busy at whatever task came first in the orchard or hay fields; he fed and looked after the horses and did his own cooking. He went away that summer to take a job in the San Jose Post Office.

The next was Mr. Pruttin, a nice old gentleman who had been in the community a long time cutting wood and odd jobs as they came his way. Woodcutting was becoming too heavy for him, so he went away to look after a neighbor, Mr. Bazata's garden.

The fourth building was a very small rather dilapidated structure; it might have been a Hansel and Gretel witch's home somewhere in an unknown forest instead of on the edge of a California orchard shaded by an old apple tree. The occupant was John Patric with whom I was to become very well acquainted as the years went by.

Leaving this yard and turning west the way led to the barn, home of four horses, Flirt and Cupertino, called Cupie, a light team used only on the road to pull the buggy or the surrey complete with the fringe on top, depending on how many were going to town or church. These rigs were stored in the buggy shed right beside the barn.

R. V. and "Cupie" ready for town

The heavier work team, also bay in color, did the ranch work and hauled the heavy loads in and out of town. They were introduced to me by a young cousin who was part of the household that year, as Kitty, good at working, and Prince, best at stopping, a very realistic description.

Near the barn were a pen for a pig or two and a yard for a flock of chickens that had a house but preferred to roost in a nearby oak tree.

A friendly brown part Chesapeake spaniel had joined us on our tour of inspection; his name was Ford, and he spent most of his time by the kitchen door to which a short walk from the barn returned us.

The Family

That kitchen door led into a long, low lumber farmhouse almost hidden under some great climbing roses; I was told they were double Cherokees.

The occupants were Mr. and Mrs. David Garrod, Fred or "Fritz" Hansen, the sixteen-year-old cousin from Los Angeles, their eldest son Ralph Vince my husband, and now myself.

Mr. Garrod Sr. was a small, gray as to hair and beard, soft-spoken man. As his son R. V. had for years been responsible for the welfare of both the ranch and the household, Mr. Garrod now busied himself with such chores and odd jobs about the nearby yard and orchard as he chose to do. He did not drive and seldom left the place.

The cousin was more a visitor than a worker, spending his time just riding along.

Mrs. Garrod Sr. was very definitely the dominant member of the household. She spoke with what my father called a real cockney dialect. She loved her garden and was always pleased to show and share it. She r sed her young plants instead of raising them, the lady next door was her n bor not neighbor, and every evening at exactly te o'clock she called a friend whose phone number was te te instead of eight eight and every evening the operator professed not to understand her.

She was a kind and well-meaning lady. Although she lived in California many years and her children grew up here living useful happy lives, enjoying opportunities they would not have had if their parents had not moved them to America, Mrs. Garrod never gave up England. Everything was better there; the peaches were juicier, the apples sweeter, the neighbors more friendly, and the schools more thorough.

This was an old story to me except according to my father, it was in Germany where this universal perfection was attained. I have always regretted that neither of these dear people had the opportunity during their declining years to return to their home countries and visit the scenes of their youth. This was something they both dreamed of.

The new house for his parents which Vince had hoped to have finished before we married was slowly nearing completion. George Wilson, a carpenter who lived on the Lawlor place next door, had undertaken the job with what help Vince could give him. John Patric, who worked for the Garrods for many years, built the living room fireplace.

In June, we invited friends and neighbors and held an old-fashioned housewarming. I met many strangers that evening who were to become my friends and neighbors during the succeeding years.

Among those present were the Frank Lawler family; besides the parents, there were a daughter Ethel and three sons Frank, Milton, and Raymond, Mr. and Mrs. Lee Finley, Capt. Alex Ovens, Charles Roecliff, Mr. and Mrs. John Felix, Mr. and Mrs. Hawlish, Mr. and Mrs. I. Bernstine from nearby, Wallace Moody, Bill and Martha Van Lone from the mountains, Vera Pannighetti, George and Robert Pfeffer and their wives from San Jose, also several groups from Saratoga, their individual names I am not sure of. It was an evening worth remembering.

By the first of July, the new house was ready for occupancy, a nice tidy four-room house with a screen porch to the north off the kitchen and a big open porch across the front to the east, which afforded a delightful view of both hills and valley.

Although they had made, I think four moves from house to house and back again always on the ranch, this move to the new house proved to be what they both had wished for, the last and most permanent.

Mrs. Garrod lived in her new house for ten years with her garden, potted plants, and husband to do for. Old friends came to visit; for a year or more, she had a paying guest, Mr. Cross, a very English Englishman, who expected a cup of very black English Gunpowder tea to be served to him every afternoon at four o' clock.

He was a nice old man with set opinions, one of which was that "Children, like snow-capped mountains, should be seen at a distance." As there were at that time, three small Garrods and a friendly bevy of neighbors of like age who were all fond of Mrs. (now Granma) Garrod and the milky puddings she used to make especially for them, somehow Mr. Cross and I sometimes saw things from different angles.

If some small party became too curious and asked "How old are you?" she would tell them, "I am as old as my tongue and a little older than my teeth." That would hush the questions for a time.

It was an accepted fact in her family that she had suffered with a heart ailment from her earliest childhood. I learned to know her after she had passed the three score and ten mark; she was still an active, busy person of remarkable endurance.

During the last several years of her life when spring came and the long winter had taken its toll, she would be tired, all tuckered out, so we would bring her up to our house, put her to bed, and coddle her for a few weeks; this she enjoyed. After about a month, she was rested and ready to return to her own house and manage her own affairs.

At these times, if Vince thought that her condition required the attention of a physician, he would have Dr. Robert Gober of Los Gatos come to see her. This pleased Gramma very much as she liked Dr. Gober and enjoyed visiting and matching wits with him. Her parting shot as he took his leave was something like this: "Don't bother to prescribe any medicine for me, as I shan't take it," nor would she.

Grandmother was very fond of the beach and its surroundings in the Twin Lakes section on Monterey Bay where her brother, Ralph Creffield, had had a cottage for many years, and she had been a regular visitor, learning to know many of the people who lived or summered there.

In time we acquired a lot and built a small one-room house on Twelfth Street near her brother's. Here she spent some weeks every year. In September 1926, she had been there longer than usual. Late on the evening of the seventh, we received an urgent telephone message telling us she was very ill; a doctor had been called and to come at once. This was followed immediately by a second call to say she had left us.

It has always been a comfort to us to know that she was not alone. Besides some nearby neighbors of whom she was fond, a close and very dear friend of many years, Mrs. E. B. North, was with her to the end. Mrs. North had had the messages sent us.

After his wife's death, Grandfather Garrod insisted on staying alone in the house. This he did for almost ten years, going his quiet way with his chores and his books. Except for taking his noonday meal with us, he took care of himself.

After an illness of two days, he died on March 8, 1935, going as he had lived, quietly and undemanding.

After seven years in this country, on September 5, 1899, Mr. Garrod appeared before the Hon. W. A. Lorigan, Judge of the Superior Court of

Santa Clara County, and pledged his allegiance to the United States of America, thereby not only gaining his own citizenship but that of his wife and three children as well.

That November at the general election, both he and his eldest son cast their first votes for William McKinley for president.

THE OLD HOUSE

With the senior Garrods comfortably settled in their new house, we started on the job of renovating the old one for ourselves.

That old house was a new experience to me. There wasn't an inch of level floor or a plumb wall in the entire building. The way this house came into existence is a story I think will bear telling; it was truly a matter of make do with what you have.

To begin at the beginning, in the year 1870, when the acreage now part of the Garrod holdings was still government land, there for the taking by anyone willing to fulfill the requirements set up by Uncle Sam, it so happened that two men came into these hills at that time, liked what they saw, and decided to stay.

One Elisah "Lash" Parks chose the front 160 acres, the other man, August B. Purfurst, settled on the adjoining 120 to the north.

Each built a house; Mr. Purfurst put his on what we know as the flat by the pasture gate. Mr. Parks built his just above the big oak tree still growing behind Vince S. Garrod's barn.

The Parks house was not very big, one main room, twelve by eighteen feet, with a smaller room or building hitched to it. This was the house in which the Garrods lived when they first came to the ranch. The Purfurst house was a similar building; I believe it had only one room.

Mr. Purfurst borrowed money from Alfred E. Penney, an Englishman, and later lost his land to him through foreclosure of the mortgage. Penney purchased the Elisha Parks place and later sold both places to Chipman and Simonds of San Jose who also bought adjoining land and organized the Mt. Eden Orchard and Vineyard Company. They planned to divide these hills into ten-acre parcels, plant these smaller plots to trees and vines, sell them to various buyers on the plan that they would care for these individual holdings for a price, while the owners continued in their established lines of work and every year pocket the profits from their well-kept little farms. Sort of an early day subdivision, only it didn't work.

The same scheme with variations has been tried in other parts of the country; none of these attempts fared any better than the Mt. Eden Orchard and Vineyard Company.

When Chipman and Simonds concluded that their plans would not prove as successful as they had hoped the time coincided with the decision of the Garrod-Creffield partnership to leave the home they had established in the Cambrian District and secure for themselves a larger acreage. This was in the year 1893.

After bargaining and considering trading and mortgaging, David Garrod and Ralph Creffield, brothers-in-law, took possession of seventy acres of the Lash Parks piece and forty adjoining acres from the land once owned by Purfurst, one hundred and ten acres all told.

The Orchard and Vineyard people had moved the Purfurst house from its place on the top of the hill down to the Parks property where it still exists as part of the Vince S. Garrod home.

When the two families moved from the valley to the Mt. Eden Road place, Mr. Creffield, a widower, his three small children and his sister-in-law housekeeper, Miss Groome, occupied the former Purfurst house.

Mr. and Mrs. Garrod, their three children Vince, Mary, and Harold and a young cousin, Archie Creffield, who had accompanied them from England made their home in the Parks house.

After some months, the partnership proved unsatisfactory to all concerned. With Mrs. Garrod's urging, a division of the property was decided on; the result was that the southwest forty-five acres being considered of highest value were designated the Creffield share, the remaining sixty-five acres with less planting and more untillable land went to the Garrods. The mortgage was split fifty-fifty, $2,800 to each.

They now found themselves with sixty-five acres of land and no house. Timon Oldham lived in a house just across the east line but was now in the unhappy position of leaving his place because of mortgage foreclosure. He offered the use of his house till something else could be done; this offer was gladly accepted. Some sort of family agreement gave them ownership of the Parks house; all that had to be done was move it to their own property.

There was an assortment of manpower available; Mr. Garrod, a schoolteacher here in America because of ill health, his fifteen-year-old son, Vince, and somewhat older cousin Archie, Mr. Creffield, a behind-the-counter salesman, all without any knowledge of house moving. Nearby were the Roecliff brothers, young English bachelors ready to give help and advice on any project, and Terence Murphy, a man who had worked hard all his life on many different manual jobs. There may have been others.

All gathered round with their tools and their horses. The house was divided in two and all walls well braced, the sections jacked up by the old-fashioned lever and fulcrum method, probably a tree stump for the fulcrum and a freshly cut sapling for the lever. Blue gum eucalyptus growing close by were cut and fastened under the buildings to serve as skids or runners, a team of horses hitched to each front corner and they were all set to go.

I wish I could have been there, men and horses willing enough but quite unused to working together. The ground to be covered may have been cultivated that year and fairly smooth or it may not, the way led up and over a small ridge for the first part of the journey the ground sloped to the west; after they topped the ridge, the slope was just as bad to the east. By nightfall, they had hauled the first half just to the edge of the gully where I knew it.

Mrs. Garrod, the spark that set this whole effort in motion, always on the alert to better the condition her family happened to be in, had chosen an attractive spot for the house on the other side of the present roadway not far from the spot the house had been left that evening.

As the story was told to me, the next morning the men and the horses ready for work looked the situation over, someone asked, "What's the matter with this spot for a house?" No one came up with a good reason for moving it farther, Mrs. Garrod was evidently not present, Vince was asked for his opinion, kid fashion wanting to be a man among men, agreed that was as good a place as any to put a house. His word was final.

So everyone went along and helped move the second and larger section as near to the first as possible. Terence Murphy took the job of putting the pieces together again and gaining a fair degree of livability.

A huff and a puff job it must have been. There had been no ground leveling or other preparation done. It was a case of lift and push, block and brace with simple manpower and sapling leverage. In the end, it was a job remarkably well done.

At least one tree runner was left in place; I know because some twenty odd years later I had occasion to crawl under the kitchen to rescue some baby chicks a mother hen had deserted. There it was, still sound, efficiently supporting the house even though its one end had been brought to level by setting a forty-pound redwood apple box under it. The apple box was also still in good shape.

With numerous additions and changes during the passing years, there it stood. A house by the side of the road, within six feet of the wheel tracks to be exact, giving shelter to family and friends for almost fifty years.

As soon as the two parts were fastened together, a rough, narrow shed roofed storeroom and kitchen separated by a small entry from which a stairway led to the ground on the east side of the house were added.

During the first years, every effort was made to supply the household needs from the farm: potatoes, green beans, corn, etc., from the garden. A cow supplied milk and butter, there was a pig or two for meat and a flock of chickens could be depended on for fryers and eggs.

There was some fruit of which apples proved the best. In his first business venture, R. V. picked the Johnathans, now an almost forgotten variety; they ripened early, red and sweet, excellent for both cooking and eating, kids loved them. With his mother's help, the apples were sorted, polished, and packed in standard forty-pound boxes. They were then taken to the valley and offered from door to door for twenty-five cents a box.

In later years, men still told the story of that kid selling apples to their wives while better apples were going to waste in their own orchards. Those husbands just neglected to pick their apples and carry them into the kitchen; besides R. V. was always a good salesman.

Mr. Garrod walked the three miles to the vicinity of Highway 85 to work for a Scotchman who lived on the northeast corner of Cox Avenue and the highway at whatever task was put before him at the rate of one dollar for a ten-hour day. In the evening, he walked the three miles home.

Mrs. Garrod did her bit, sewing for other women who had learned of her ability in that line of endeavor.

R. V. became equal to taking a man's responsibilities at an early age. As well as accepting full charge of the family farm, he found time to work for others, mowing and baling hay for Ira Fox, picking the grapes and helping make the wine at Guppy's winery. Both Fox and Guppy were nearby neighbors.

When current bills were paid and mortgage interest taken care of, if there was any ready cash left, some improvement on the house could be made slowly, step by step.

One year, two bedrooms with a hall between leading to a new front door which faced the south and opened on to a nice porch across the entire width with a step way leading into the garden.

With this done, the original smaller building which had been serving as two bedrooms had the partition removed and became the kitchen; from here a door was cut into the storeroom, the small entry done away with and what had been the kitchen became a bedroom.

Anderson, a woodchopper, let it be known that he could lay up bricks, so Vince salvaged some used bricks and for twenty-five dollars a fireplace was built at the north wall of the living room with its back to the kitchen so that the stovepipe could be let into the chimney.

The finished fireplace was not very big, neither level or plumb but without question one of the best burning hearths I have ever had the pleasure of sitting by on a cold and wintry day.

Another time, a screened service porch was added to the kitchen, giving more working room which was needed.

Some years later, a nice big screened porch was built on the east side of one of the two newer bedrooms with an entrance from the front porch; there was enclosed storage space beneath; it was a wonderful place for summer sleeping.

Finally, a bathroom complete with all accessories and hot and cold water was tucked in between the east-side bedrooms. The kitchen walls were covered with tongue and groove redwood and some cupboards built in for dishes and pots and pans.

This was the house when I took possession in 1916. Mrs. Garrod had planted two thrifty white roses one by the steps from the porch to the garden, the other on the roadside of the living room they had spread over the walls and roof till they met on the gable, very picturesque. Strangers were known to drive to other parts of the yard and later ask, "Do you live near here or where is your house?"

With most of the furnishings gone from the sitting or living room, it was a pretty sorry-looking place. George Wilson who had built the new house took the job of putting new floors in the two original rooms. I tackled the rest of the renovating, tearing out the old wallpaper and removing thousands of tacks put there by early-day tenants when it was common practice to tack up newspapers for wall covering.

Along with everything else, I found myself in a state of expectancy suffering all the discomfort and misery of pregnancy. I, who had never really known the meaning of the word "tired," learned its fullest meaning that summer, but the walls got papered, the woodwork painted, and the new floors laid. The fact that the living room was several inches off level from north to south while the kitchen floor following the line of its predecessor was lower in the middle than at the edges like a very shallow bowl. This had one advantage; no matter what was spilled or dropped, everything ran to the center and was easy to clean up.

These drawbacks really didn't matter; I had the promise of a new house next year, didn't I?

The years rolled on, three small people added themselves to the family, the vision of that new house next year was always there, something to look forward to.

A house like this one has one good quality; if you don't like it the way it is, you can take a hammer and saw and change it to please yourself.

One day, Vince cut a door from the bedroom to the screened porch. This proved to be a great help and step saver. Again with the help of George Wilson, a small bedroom was tacked on to the first east-side bedroom to give our little daughter a place of her very own.

Soon, a new roof became a necessity. The old one leaked so badly. For this job, an old acquaintance of R. V.'s was called on: Henry Boosinger.

This project required the removal of the climbing roses, a team of mules, Jim and Nellie, were hitched to the severed trunks, but the load was more than they could move so the bushes were cut into smaller sections, dragged off the roof, and hauled away to be burned. Then we found that the wood rats which all along had known ways of getting into the attic where we could hear them moving things at night, had also made themselves some handy entrances, holes about an inch in diameter, straight through the roof, no wonder it leaked. While about it, we decided to add six feet to the width of the living room on the west or road side. The new section of floor was built to the same slope as the old one.

With the space around the kitchen dinner table becoming more crowded all the time, a young fruit picker, Charlie Hyleman, built a bay window and narrow window seat across the west end of the kitchen, which relieved the congestion noticeably.

Finally, I personally tore out the sink and a rather useless window at one side and rebuilt it with a long window above which allowed me to look into the trees in the nearby gully. This eased the boredom of dishwashing.

Twice I was unintentionally responsible for real danger to the old house, both times by fire.

During the holiday season of our first year, while burning quantities of old paper and other rubbish, I realized that the soot in the chimney was also on fire. Hurrying outside, I found Mr. Garrod Sr. and asked him to bring a ladder; he did and set it against the eaves. By then I had the water flowing through the

The Old House

hose. We both looked up at the flames pouring from the chimney. Mr. Garrod stepped back and asked, "Who is going up there?" There I was, eight months along, but seeing no other solution to the problem said, "I will," and did, up the ladder and the roof to the base of the chimney. The blaze was soon drowned, but the mess in the living room was something to see.

When my husband came in from the field where he had been plowing, he remarked, "Someone in the neighborhood has had a chimney fire. I can smell the burned soot." After lunch, he gave the living room another look and said, "You've got quite a cleanup job ahead," and went back to his plowing. He wanted to get the seed into the ground before it rained again.

The second fire was almost a repetition. My young sons were home this time, and we doused the fire with lots of salt and some water. Then I let the boys go up on the roof to cover the chimney and so smother any fire still glimmering in the soot. The theory was all right, but we didn't allow for the fact that some of the mortar had fallen from between the bricks and these cracks filled with soot.

Late that evening, I heard strange little noises somewhere above the mantle and realized there was trouble ahead.

The boys tumbled out of bed ready to help. One brought the spray rig full of water, the other got into the attic ready to man the hose. Frank Bradley and his son came from next door; young Frank chopped a hole in the roof which didn't help much. After an hour of intense excitement, the danger was over. In the morning, R. V. consulted with Mr. Stelling, representative of the Santa Clara County Mutual Fire, who came and looked and decided on a repair job on the roof and new wallpaper for the room. The work was to be done by professionals.

Lee Renn carpenter and Everett Priest, paper hanger, both from Saratoga came at once and the room was in spic-and-span order for Thanksgiving when our young daughter came home from college accompanied by a special guest, George Cooper, a fellow student and now our son-in-law.

Nothing more happened to the old house for some years, except some makeshift repairs to the floors where the termites had been busy.

Meanwhile, the new house was still somewhere in the future. I dreamed houses and drew dozens of plans, but nothing happened.

Finally, Dick, stationed on the island of Saipan with the armed forces of World War II, wrote to say, "When I get home, we'll build that new house on the gravel pit." After thirty-two years, to everyone's amazement, we did.

Early in 1948, the old house stood empty for a short time when the John Hamiltons rented it for a few months. Soon Frank and Anita Hawkes and their small twins came to live there; they stayed seven years and during their stay, Danny joined the twins, Mike and Ellen. The Hawkes moved to a home of their own a stone's throw down the road.

Not wanting to see it just stand there and disintegrate, the boys dismantled the old house and stored the useable lumber for some future enterprise. I was sincerely sorry to see it go; the old house had served us well.

JOHN PATRIC

That fourth little house, just nine feet square built of split lumber and furnished with a narrow bed, a very small cast-iron cookstove, an equally small table and a chair was the home of John Petrenovich, known as John Patric or Garrod's John, to everyone in the neighborhood.

By the time I became acquainted with him, he had already lived in his little house for nearly fifteen years, earning his living clearing land and general farmwork for the Garrods and occasional short jobs for nearby neighbors. But the little house was his home to which he always returned by evening to prepare his own supper and feed his cats of which he always had a goodly number; in his philosophy, it was as great a crime to kill a cat as to kill a king.

John was without question "a character," a native of Austria, and by his own telling "a man of the world," proudly declaring that he spoke seven languages; if he spoke the other six the way he did English, his knowledge left much to be desired; at that he could certainly make his wishes known.

No longer young, somewhere past seventy, quite tall and thin, a battered specimen of humanity, his face was scarred and blackened by an untimely explosion of blasting powder while engaged with many others in the construction of the Suez Canal. This mishap also destroyed his right eye. His later life had not been an easy one, hard work always of the rough manual variety, along with an unmanageable thirst for alcoholic beverages and the quarrels and fisticuffs that resulted from overindulgence had all taken their toll.

When sober, which was now most of the time, John had a cheerful outlook on life, took a proprietary interest in the welfare of the family and the ranch, and resented anyone but himself imposing on Vince's good nature.

Shortly after I knew him, as we met in the yard one morning, he took the opportunity to explain to me that Vince was a good man and he wished him well, but he was also a fool; he had everything a man needed—a farm, a home, and a mother to keep his house, the freedom to come and go as he pleased, living like a king—what did he do? He spoiled it all by getting married, and life would never again be the same for that young man! John was right; it wasn't.

He was perhaps justified in having a poor opinion of matrimony. When he came away from Austria to try for a better life in America, he left behind a wife and two daughters; twice he sent money for their passage to America, and twice she spent the money for something else, finally writing that the money was welcome, he should continue sending it, but she had no intention of coming to America nor did she want him to come back to her. "Bah women—they are all deceitful."

He and I established a friendship of sorts though I often became terribly aggravated with him. He wanted what he wanted when he wanted it, and somebody better come wait on him right now if they wanted any peace and quiet around there.

His daily needs were simple, for some things he would bring a list to be brought from town, other things he expected to get from the house, 10¢ worth of sugar, a few potatoes or onions, a can of condensed milk, not all at once, and more likely one article a day. These were all entered in his little book, and about once a month he came to settle accounts, so much work against so many supplies. As this was during the time of prohibition, there was always a bottle of Peruna on his grocery list.

This routine went on for years; the trouble was John came at most inopportune times, perhaps I had just gotten the baby down for a much needed nap or I was busy with some task I was especially anxious to finish when that old man would come into the kitchen, stomp his foot on the kitchen floor, and call loudly for someone to get him this or that, till the baby was wide awake and mother—?

During my second summer as a member of the family, in the midst of the prune harvest, being short of help, Vince has asked John to help him bring the fruit from the orchard. I suppose the task was more than he could handle as it meant lifting and carrying numberless boxes of prunes each weighing about sixty pounds to the sled and lifting them again to unload the sled when it reached the dipper; he was too stubborn to admit he couldn't do the job. Among other things, John knew the whereabouts of all the local moonshiners in a radius of miles, so he solved his problem by going off on one grand "high lonesome."

When he staggered home again, sorry and ashamed, his good friend in whom he had such abiding faith fired him, just like that—bang—so John walked away sad and repentant.

It was the best thing he ever did for the Garrod family, for still in need of help, Vince phoned the employment agency to send him a man who wanted to work for a few days. Next morning Ed Jones came and stayed twenty-five years, but that is another story.

When John left he trudged about ten miles into the mountains to the Pfeffer ranch, finding work and shelter there, on our next visit to them, Mrs. Pfeffer, being our aunt Mary, John begged to come back; he was tired and lonely; this was his home, and we were his family. Vince, being softhearted and liking the old man despite his shortcomings, said, "Yes, go get your things, I'll take you home."

So back he was and took up his old routine, climbing the hill to the back eighty every day to cut wood and clear the ground for fresh planting. This he could do at his own pace; working on hillsides, I'm sure he had cleared some years before when the cleared ground was not planted and cultivated the chaparral had grown back again, and John was able to support himself with honest work which he enjoyed.

Little by little, he cut and dug out all the small growth, leaving anything a bit bigger, like a small oak tree or a large red berry bush, and then he would go to Vince and explain all the difficulties connected with removing them and make special contracts at somewhat higher rates for removing them.

As a sideline he set gopher traps; only those working in arms' reach of the roadway were in any danger, still he caught a surprising number. He would save the tails till he had a dozen or two, and then he would come to the house and collect a bounty of ten cents apiece.

In the course of time because of changes to be made in the yard, it was decided to move three little houses which stood at the edge of the orchard. John chose the new location for his on the edge of the ravine in the shade of some native live oaks.

After putting skids under the sills, a team of horses was hitched to the skids and the house moved to its new destination without trouble and looked as though it had always been there.

John lived this independent though somewhat dependent life year after year till July 1927, when he fell ill. The best way to help him seemed hospitalization, so Vince took him to the County Hospital, where he received good care and seemed better, but he was most unhappy, pleading to be taken out of there saying it was no place for him; it was only for old men.

He being, by his own telling, eighty-six years old, his complaint wasn't valid, but the doctors said he might as well go home, so back he came.

When he was again safe in his little house, he said, "The Father is good, here I will wait."

Declaring he could look after himself and refusing most of our offered attention, there he stayed, till early one morning going to his door to be sure he was all right, I found him trying to build a fire in his stove to make coffee, seeing that he was too weak to manage; I urged him to lie back on his bed and wait for me to bring some I had already made.

I hurried away and returned in a few moments as my summer kitchen was only a few steps away; my offer of coffee was useless, I found John Patric was gone, his waiting ended.

Dinnertime

Making hay

MT. EDEN NEIGHBORS

In the Mt. Eden, Pierce Road, Saratoga community, I learned to know an entirely new group of people.

Mr. and Mrs. Lee Finley lived on the adjoining farm, which had once been part of the Garrod-Creffield holdings. Mr. Finley was almost as much a stranger as myself, having only a short time before married Mrs. McLellan who had owned and farmed the place for a number of years.

They were pleasant and friendly people; sad to say, their marriage did not last. Mr. Finley returned to wherever his former life and interests had been, and Mrs. Finley took up the task of managing for herself again, which she did with the usual assortment of more or less efficient help from the employment agency, till Jack Bacigalupi came along. Jack had been befriended by Mrs. Finley, then Mrs. McLellan, when he was a boy in great need of an older person's guidance. He now settled in, becoming a member of her household and the community. Later, Louise, an orphaned granddaughter, came to make her home with her.

In the course of time, Jack met with a hunting accident which cost him his left arm. Louise finished grammar school and tried attending high school, but her grandmother arranged for her to enroll at Fremont, which was somewhat nearer than Los Gatos but not the district where Louise belonged. Mrs. Finley, being afraid to have Louise drive on what was then Highway Nine, insisted that she park their car at Miller's service station and walk the rest of the way. Needless to say, Louise McLellan's high school career was a short one.

The good lady had positive opinions on other matters too, as I learned one day when she found out that a third little Garrod was about to join the family. Where she is living now, she would without doubt give the "pill" her wholehearted support.

As long as I knew her, the mortgage on her property was often the topic of conversation. After her death from pneumonia, Jack returned to his own people in Santa Clara, and Louise married Ivan Cox and lived on Cox Avenue until her own death.

Through legal processes, the mortgagee's estate absorbed the Finley property. When the mortgagee's estate in turn came to be closed and all properties sold, R. V. bid on the Finley place and Garrods still hold it.

Toward the east, the Frank Lawlor family from San Francisco lived, Mr. and Mrs., one daughter Ethel and three sons, Frank, Milton, and Raymond. Ethel married a young World War I soldier, "Duke" Herndon. There were two little daughters, Frances and Vera.

Frank and Milton served in the army and later married. Frank had three sons, and I think there were two daughters for Milton. Raymond, being younger, missed the war. He married Nellie Sporleader of Los Gatos; they had one son.

My earliest knowledge of the Lawlor place is the story that a man named Smith owned it, built a two-story house, and did some planting with easy disregard for property lines. Consequently, the almost ninety-year-old eucalyptus trees, a tired old black walnut or two, and the poor little orange tree in the middle of the yard have always been on Garrod land.

The Smiths developed a summer resort and kept a stage and horses to make daily trips to the Los Gatos Railroad Depot to carry their guests back and forth. Mrs. Smith spent part of each year in the Sierras while the railroad was being built. There she managed eating places for the railroad men.

Whether the Smiths had mortgage trouble I do not know, but I have heard that Timon Oldham who had the place when the Garrods came, did. Oldham lost it to Mrs. North who in turn lost it to a bank from which Lawlor bought it. About 1917, Mr. Lawlor sold half the place to Don McHenry. He struggled with it for a year or two. I think next a doctor, Mrs. Cornnet held it for a while and various men sharecropped it. Then James U. Porter took possession but soon traded it to Bill Hines for property down Morgan Hill way.

The Hines were a nice neighborly family. There were two boys, Wesley and Leslie. When the school bus route came into existence, Wesley was the first driver. There was a younger redheaded daughter, Dorothy, a playmate and school companion of our children.

Bill Hines fought a losing battle for some years but in the end was foreclosed on by the Levys, clothing store people of San Jose.

They held it longer than most; various people were employed to farm it. One young man named Wilson with a wife and two babies soon found himself with a paycheck of $75 a month and time payments on furniture and clothing for a greater amount.

He had made a very favorable impression on everyone. Sad to say, he solved his troubles by bouncing checks on a number of Saratoga merchants and disappearing from sight.

His wife and little ones returned to her family.

They were followed by the Noyers—Frank and Sally, and their pretty little blonde daughter, Alice.

Noyers were good neighbors for a number of years; when they moved away, their place was taken by the Bradley family, Mr. and Mrs. and their three children, Frank, Betty, and Bob, equal in age to our own; they traveled to high school in Los Gatos with our children till the place again changed hands.

This time it was bought by John Alonzo of Sunnyvale, a well-known citizen of that town. He farmed it for a few seasons, decided against becoming an orchardist or making his permanent home in the hills, and dismantled the house and sold the land to a real estate promoter, Oscar Rockledge. He had great plans for its development, after much surveying activity maps were made showing roads and I believe fifty-eight home sites.

Poor man! This was in 1946 or '47, before the subdividers had become so active in the valley or the hill property so very attractive.

Along with everything else, his money problems must have been beyond belief.

He solved all his troubles by committing suicide.

This turned the property back to John Alonzo because of his financial interest in it, as he had no intention of living on it he again put it up for sale, with his eye on the young Garrod brothers as prospective buyers. The deal was tempting, the price reasonable, and its close proximity to the home property made it worth thinking about. When a San Jose bank was approached about a loan, their appraiser came, looked the place over, shook his head, and said it wasn't worthwhile to turn in a report on it. His decision did not deter R. V. from arranging a loan from a private source, a lady who had always had faith in his good judgment.

Though it took thirteen years to pay off that loan, that fifty acres is now an important part of the whole, worth many times what it cost, and not yet subdivided, thank goodness.

Dick now has his home there on a knoll with extensive views of both valley and mountains. The greater part is taken up by the horse enterprise in which the Garrods are now interested. A visiting clergyman one day remarked that "that field yonder would make a beautiful cemetery," so there are still possibilities ahead for this piece of land.

Over the other way, the Bernsteins were nearest; they had only been on their farm a short time, city people, complete strangers to country living or farmwork.

Mrs. Bernstein, unlike her Jewish husband, was a Catholic of Irish lineage, a gentle friendly lady who was working far too hard in her effort to master the many tasks a farm woman is faced with. Nevertheless, she asked the neighbors in and gave a party in my honor shortly after we returned from our honeymoon. There were perhaps twenty present; a very pleasant evening. It was good to meet everyone at once.

Just beyond them lived Vince's old bachelor friend—not so old at that, perhaps fifty odd, but usually spoken of as Old Charlie—Charles Roecliffe, an Englishman who had been here on the hill to welcome the Garrods when they arrived. He lived in a small white house under a huge oak tree and owned a good twenty-acre farm with prune and apricot orchards.

He kept a team of horses and a flock of game chickens of which he was very proud, especially one little hen which every spring made her nest in a hollow branch of the oak tree, ten or fifteen feet above the ground, flying to her chosen spot like any wild bird. When her chicks hatched, she would lift them to the edge of the nest one by one in her beak and drop them to the ground. The fall never seemed to hurt the little ones; she always raised them like any other hen. The next spring back, she went to her nest in the tree.

Charlie also kept a number of deer hounds. Hunting was his favorite pastime. In season, he usually had groups of friends with like interests loosely organized into something known as Company I, who made his place their headquarters for their forays into the hunting field. There were reports that these gatherings developed into very convivial affairs.

During the winter months, some of the men, whose work in the lumber mills was slack at that season of the year, would come and help Charles with his farmwork, of these I knew two. One was Mr. Butler, a slow-spoken elderly man who helped R. V. build the road from the pasture gate along the east side of the hill. The other was Pat Murphy, just as Irish as his name implies; he lived at Roecliffes off and on over the years.

One spring I made the mistake of going into the beekeeping business. Because my brother-in-law wanted out and I had a small monetary interest in his hives, I had them all brought from Alma and set where I thought I could manage them.

Hearing of my venture, Charlie remembered that a friend of his had abandoned several swarms in the farthest corner of his place and made me a present of them. Not knowing what I was getting into, I accepted his gift, and Pat Murphy gallantly volunteered to carry them across the orchard for me. This he did without bothering to shut the bees securely inside. There were bees buzzing all over that man before he had gone ten steps. He assured me that beestings didn't hurt.

In the end I found beekeeping far too big a job for me, too much heavy lifting, too much work in the noontime sun, just too much everything. After a losing battle with the bee moths and foul brood, I gave up in despair.

Another time Pat gave me a beautiful Indian mortar and pestle, which he had dug out of Oil Creek while building a skid road for the Carmichael Mill. It is an unusually fine specimen. The pestle he found with it was either damaged or the stone had a natural flaw in it.

It chanced that our youngest son's birthday fell on the same day as Charlie's so he asked to be allowed to stand as Dick's godfather. We were both willing and pleased. Thereafter, until his death, it was a set thing for him to come to dinner on their birthday.

Charlie was not only an Englishman; he was a Yorkshire man, a native of the county of Yorkshire. He also had a rather wry sense of humor and enjoyed explaining the meaning of the Yorkshire coat of arms, which by his telling pictured a flea, a fly, and a fletch of bacon because: a flea will bite anyone, so will a Yorkshire man; a fly will drink from anyone's glass, so will a Yorkshire man; a fletch of bacon is no good till hung, nor is a Yorkshire man. Not very flattering to his fellow Yorkshire men, but he enjoyed it.

After his death, his place was sold at auction, his debts paid and the balance sent to England to his elderly spinster sisters. Jean Casanova was the purchaser, and with his wife and son, Kelly, came to live in the little house under the big oak tree. Fearing storm damage, Mr. Casanova cut down the oak tree.

At the foot of the hill was the Johnson place being cared for by a retired, somewhat disabled sailor, Alex Ovens, known to everyone as Captain, a nice, responsible, unobtrusive sort of a man, capable and willing to lend a hand whenever needed. His means of transportation was a Petaluma cart drawn by a nice red roan horse.

The property really belonged to Mrs. A. R. Johnson who lived in San Francisco, but came to the Mt. Eden Road place on frequent visits. She was the daughter of a Saratoga pioneer, widowed while very young with five children to rear and educate. She was a person of experience and wisdom, both a comfort and pleasure to have near. Sometimes instead of staying alone in a rather scantily furnished cabin on her own place, she would come to stay at our house. I was always happy to have her with us.

Eventually her son, Harry, retired from the Navy, took over the place and built a nice home there. He and his family were our good neighbors for many years.

There was a stepson, Frank Conway, and a little daughter, Nancy. Nancy went all through school with the Garrod children.

The Louis Bonnets lived a bit farther on the road. He and his wife were both Saratoga natives. Louis farmed and took care of his family like other men and was well liked in the community. His wife Carrie was afflicted with serious deafness and seldom left the house. I did not learn to know her well.

There were three children: Frank, somewhat older than the Garrod kids, and two little girls, Caroline and Marie, of the right age and inclination to be in and out of our house like our own youngsters.

On down the road were other nice, friendly people, but they all seemed to feel that climbing what was known as Garrod's hill was a major undertaking, so they almost never came to our house.

The hill road was steeper then than now, coming up in an almost straight line. It was years before the better grade which now makes a shallow westward pointing angle was put in. Mrs. Johnson generously gave the land to make that improvement, but being a canny old lady, she tied a string to her gift. There had never been an open road to Stevens Creek. Mt. Eden Road ended in Charles Roecliffe's yard; in his mind that was it, no need to go any further. Others felt that the road should go through Roecliffe's land to what had become a county park and on down to the creek.

Mr. Roecliffe was very much in favor of a better grade on the hill, joining with others in the idea that it was Mrs. Johnson's civic duty to further that project. Now she said yes: "the road could be changed by cutting through her land, if Mr. Roecliffe would also grant a right of way for an open road through his land."

He agreed because he could not hold out against his neighbors wanting so much to change the hill. But he gave his promise grudgingly, kept that fence up and discouraged anyone wanting to drive through his orchard, though the way was supposed to be open. It was not until after Charlie's death that the Mt. Eden Road was taken all the way to the creek.

The people who lived on down the road as I knew them were the following: the Stanfords, Bazatas, Hawlishes, Andy Loyst and his wife, the Sanders family, Charles Davis and his wife, Rose, the Corpstein sisters, Misses Annie and Lizzy, Louis Bonnet's elderly aunts, beyond them the Ralph Husteds, and on the corner of Pierce Road and the Saratoga-Sunnyvale Road the Charles Millers, just across the road lived Mr. and Mrs. Allen, going from there toward Saratoga, Dan Reagon was manager of the Blauer Ranch called The Argonaut. That place is now a subdivision and shopping center with the same name and only an occasional fruit tree left in someone's yard.

The McGuire family had long lived on the west side of the road, their one daughter and son-in-law, the Johnson Kerrs, on the other. There was also the Malone family and that of Alan Rice who held the office of Justice of the Peace.

Just on the edge of town on either side of the road stood the attractive homes of the Carmichael brothers, Neil on the west and Dan on the east.

Over the hill to the north, a pleasant walk across the eighty a path through some chaparral and an orchard, led one to the home of Fremont Older, the editor of the *San Francisco Call-Bulletin*. This was a well-kept modern home with extensive gardens which fitted perfectly into the surrounding landscape. Mr. and Mrs. Older were both busy with away from home activities but took time to be neighborly, so the way across the hill was kept open.

The renowned dentist, Painless Parker, had a rather pretentious home on land adjoining that of the Olders.

SARATOGA, 1916

In 1916, Saratoga was much smaller and much less busy than it is now. The business district was confined to about two blocks on Lumber Street, now Big Basin Way, and a house or two on Saratoga-Los Gatos Road.

The most noticeable activity was the Interurban Electric Railway. Its course ran through the valley forming a loop from San Jose to Saratoga on to Los Gatos and Campbell and back to San Jose; I believe the schedule alternated the direction one trip going first to Saratoga, the next coming by way of Campbell and Los Gatos.

Mostly the tracks were laid parallel and very close to the edge of the county roads, but in the towns they were put right in the middle of the main streets.

There was another line to which one could transfer at Congress Junction, now known as Champagne Crossing and travel to Palo Alto. Many local Stanford students were daily commuters.

There was a spur track that went up Big Basin Way, past the County Gravel Quarry, to the point where the water treatment plant is now. At that time the railroad owned the Congress Springs property, and picnic grounds along the creek were open to the public. The San Jose Water Company now owns this land, and picnickers are no longer welcome.

There is a story that one day a car, as was customary, in charge of one man who acted as both motorman and conductor, was returning from the picnic grounds with a number of passengers aboard, gathered more speed than usual as it came down the grade, as it made a rather sharp right-hand turn its momentum threw the motorman off the back platform. The car rolled on down the track with the passengers unaware of what had happened. Fortunately the road leveled off, and Papermill Hill helped to slow it down. As it was told to me, the motorman, running madly, overtook the car, climbed aboard, and took it on its way.

A small ticket and Wells Fargo Express office was located where the Plaza is now. There was also a Y for switching cars and much banging and backing went on while the gravel cars were being shunted about.

Merchandise for the stores came in freight cars and farm produce, especially dried fruit, went out that way.

Lorrain Hanchett was in charge of the office. He had a helper and general roust about, a rather odd individual known as Skibbouch. There were four young Hanchetts, Ned and Billy, Barbara and Hilda. Mrs. Hanchett taught music and for some years had charge of the music classes in the Saratoga School.

Miss Grace Hanchett, aunt to the youngsters, a cheerful little blind lady, was also a member of the household.

I recall two general merchandise or grocery stores, one at the lower end of the street owned by Joe Corpstein and Artus Metzger in the same building where Whitlows Clothing Store is now. Both partners waited on customers, and there was one young clerk, Stanley Johns.

At the upper end of town was Tom Smith's on the northwest corner of Big Basin Way and Fifth Street. This building now houses the Washette and an art gallery upstairs in what was then the Odd Fellows Hall. There was one clerk, Mr. Marshall.

Both stores carried about the same line of merchandise: flour and sugar by the sack, tea mixed to your order from their original containers, coffee beans ground coarse or fine as you wished in a hand-operated mill. Various other staples and canned goods, potatoes, and onions were always available. Other vegetables, unless you grew your own, were to be had from the vegetable man who made regular calls from door to door once or twice a week.

The grocers also carried feed for farm animals and took eggs, butter, some fruit, and wood in trade. There was a counter where men's work clothes and perhaps shoes were on display and a shelf for standard patent medicines.

Next door to Corpstein and Metzger, Stephen Buckley had a drugstore. That building has housed a drugstore ever since.

Dr. Robert Hogg, the only medical man in the community, had his office in one of the buildings just beyond the corner of Big Basin Way on the Saratoga-Los Gatos Road.

Going up the street on the left, there was the telephone office. It was equipped with a switchboard in charge of a woman whose name I never learned, and a counter where bills could be paid and complaints registered.

This was waited on by a schoolgirl scarcely tall enough to look over the top of it, Natalie Boisseranc.

Across the street, the brick building at that time was occupied by a branch of the American Trust Company Bank. One man, Mr. Tuthill, filled all the offices and a few years later the branch was closed, not enough business to keep one employee.

Then for a short distance, I remember only some vacant lots and a few homes. Where the Bank of America is, Frank Hatakiyama, a Japanese, had a busy laundry. He planted the biggest of the ginkgo trees now on the street. At the time of Pearl Harbor, the Japanese people were all rushed away from Saratoga and to the best of my knowledge none returned.

Almost next door to the laundry, Martin Kane owned a blacksmith shop with a hall upstairs. Mr. Kane was no longer active in the shop. Whether Bert Bertelsen was there at that time, I'm not sure. He was the only blacksmith in town for many years after. The hall above the shop was the meeting place of the Foresters Lodge and was also used for public meetings and dances.

Just across the street, shaded by some fine old oak trees, was the Christian Church and Rectory. Mr. J. A. Emerich was the minister and Mrs. Emerich and a son, Wilson, made up the family.

There was a two-story empty building on the corner and across Fifth Street was Smith's Grocery. After that, the street was mostly inhabited by Italian and Swiss people. There were several small hotels with public dining rooms and bars, somewhat frowned upon by those in other parts of the town who supported the long established branch of the WCTU, but on the whole, honest, hardworking, law-abiding citizens. A beautiful white-painted Catholic Church stood in their midst.

The names Marenco, Poncia, Nardi, Matteri, Lotti, Paris, Albini, and others are still familiar to the town.

About a block above the Catholic church at the corner of Sixth and St. Charles Street was St. John's Episcopal Mission which the Garrods had helped to establish. In 1916, Rev. Ralph Bray was the rector. The little building is now a private home. Through changes and additions, it has lost its churchly identity.

St. Charles Street led up to Oak Street where the Saratoga Grammar School took care of all the district children which numbered well under a hundred.

The lot just east of the school was the site of the Congregational Church, the largest of all the Saratoga churches.

Lundblad Lodge, already in the capable hands of Mrs. Joseph Bargas, then as now, was known for its good food, pleasant care, and delightful surroundings.

Turning about and going west on Oak Street, you find the street ends at the cemetery gate. The cemetery dates back to Saratoga's earliest days when a youth drowned in the creek and the Spanish owner of the Land Grant gave permission to his people to bury him there. I doubt whether this first grave is marked.

It is an appealing, tranquil spot, shaded by many native trees as well as other trees and shrubs planted by loving relatives and friends. When I first saw it, there were no lawns and wild oats leaned close to many of the gray and moss grown headstones.

Jim Boyce was the sexton then. To him fell the task of digging a new grave when one was needed and otherwise do what he could to keep the place in order.

The words of a forgotten poet described it then and still do:

Neath the blue of the sky
On the edge of the steep
God has planted a garden
A garden of sleep.

It is pleasant to think of being laid to rest there for that long, long sleep that will come to us all.

Just to the right of the cemetery gate was the beginning of Bohlman Road, practically a continuation of Oak Street. The first entrance off this road was that of the College of Notre Dame, a novitiate for novice nuns. From there the road wandered off up the mountain to the former home of Mrs. John Brown of Civil War note, and the vineyards of Pete Albini and others.

Going back and down Oak Street, opposite the church, there was a line of small rental cottages owned by William Small and all painted green. Farther down on both sides of the street were some nicely kept homes. Los Gatos Road was not far, turning left one came to the Methodist Church which is now the Corinthian Antique Studio.

The Methodist people had a long roofed overshed at one side of their grounds for the shelter of the churchgoing horses on Sunday. During the week, others could tie their horses there if they were perhaps going by electric car to San Jose and would be gone a long time.

Beyond the railroad ticket office and switching place, Lumber Street became Saratoga Avenue. To the right of this avenue, the Foothill Club house had just been built, its garden not yet planted. On the left, almost across the way, the Saratoga Inn had also just been finished, the nearest thing to a real hotel the community had to offer. Mrs. Louise N. Scott was its very efficient manager.

Beyond and below the Inn was a natural amphitheater where the Blossom Festival programs were held.

This was the town; roundabout were thrifty farms and well-kept homes, many of which have already been taken over by the subdividers and the rest, I am sure, will soon follow.

There are those among the Saratoga residents who sigh for the past when Saratoga was truly a small country village, when everyone knew everyone else, their joys and their troubles as well as their family histories. No one has, as of now, devised a way to turn time backward. Change comes despite all the wishing that can be done.

People come, like the place and stay, each one apparently breathing a variation of the prayer which goes something like this:

Thank you, Dear Lord, for leading me to this lovely spot. Now that I'm here, please close the gate and keep all others out.

A Busy Man

Early in my years on Mt. Eden Road, I learned that outside interests and contact with people were matters of the greatest importance to the man I had married.

The Pierce Road Improvement Club was local and dealt only with neighborhood problems, mostly the roads, their upkeep and betterment. The members met at the call of the President, Mr. Bazata, or at the request of a member. The meetings were held in a pleasant room off the Bazata garage and Vince always attended.

Another local interest was his membership and attendance in the Episcopal Church, St. Johns Mission at Sixth and St. Charles streets in Saratoga. As the attendance dwindled, for a few years the remaining members held early morning services in the Federated Church until they moved again, this time to their parent church, St. Luke's of Los Gatos. During this time, R. V. was always a member of the vestry. When St. Andrews of Saratoga was established, he became a faithful attendant there.

There were various political groups and meetings which did not interest me. The Farmers Union, of which I have told in another chapter, was always in the background and a term on the Grand Jury took up one summer.

Fortunately for all concerned, Ed Jones was there to keep the daily work moving. Looking after the children and other members of the ranch family kept me very busy and very tired; I had little time or desire for social contacts.

One organization that pertained entirely to farm products was the California Prune and Apricot Association which had come into existence for the express purpose of marketing the dried fruits of California cooperatively.

During the 1920s, there was much dissatisfaction with the management and complete dissolution seemed the only answer. However, a small group of members, firm believers in the principles of cooperation, R. V.

among them, gave freely of their time and talents to the task of saving that organization. Now under the simpler trade name of Sunsweet, it stands high in the field of farm cooperatives.

At the time of the reorganization, R. V. Garrod became a member of the Board of Directors. Now after the passing of forty years, he still serves in that capacity.

When he met Fred Hart, owner-manager of KQW radio station in San Jose, he was promptly invited to serve on the advisory board of that outfit. Vince knew nothing about radio, but his knowledge of people active in the affairs of the county and state made his name of value on that board. This took much time, although it brought us into contact with people whose friendships we have enjoyed and treasured through the years. Still there were times when I wasn't exactly overjoyed with the prospect of meeting some of these strangers, as their coming might be announced by a 9:00 p.m. phone call that went something like this: "Honey, I've invited Mr. and Mrs. So and So to a chicken dinner tomorrow noon. Hadn't you better get the birds ready tonight?"

Getting the birds ready meant going up to the chicken house by lantern light, catching and beheading a couple of unsuspecting young birds and going on from there. Sometimes that young man skated on awfully thin ice.

There was also the year that R. V. let himself be talked into running for the office of State Senator. For that he really took to the road, out electioneering early and late. I remember the whole summer, the fruit harvest and the campaign, all jumbled together as pretty much of a nightmare. I made my one and only appearance on radio for him, reading an article favoring his election written by one of his staunch supporters, Ben S. Allen of Palo Alto.

R. V. lost the election. Having never fully approved of his candidacy, it probably sounds silly to say I was more disappointed by his defeat than he, but such was the case. The whole campaign seemed such a waste of time and energy.

The next thing of interest that came along was the Farmer's Automobile Inter-Insurance Exchange. This reciprocal company was coming into existence through the imagination and leadership of two men, John Tyler and Tom Leavey. It was planned to be statewide with headquarters in Los Angeles.

These men, both still active in the company's affairs, have seen their modest beginning grow into one of the biggest, most powerful and respected organizations of its kind in the nation.

Mr. A. T. Jones of Morgan Hill had joined the group as an organizer. He drew heavily on his persuasive powers before he secured R. V.'s promise to become an agent and try his hand at selling this particular brand of automobile insurance. Auto insurance, of any kind, was a rather unknown commodity in 1928.

As he took a deeper interest in the work, he was placed on the Board of Governors. Now for many years, he has been president of that advisory body.

This has called for a monthly trip to Los Angeles, of which he has missed only two. He enjoyed making the monthly trip via the Southern Pacific Lark which left San Jose about 9:30 p.m. and arrived in Los Angeles in time to go directly to the office. The return was at about the same hours in reverse, the only drawback to this arrangement being that someone, usually myself, had to turn out early and be at the San Jose railroad depot at 7:00 a.m., rain or shine.

When the Southern Pacific made it known that the Lark was to be discontinued, R. V. turned his energies to trying to persuade the company to change its plans. That was one skirmish he didn't win. He now travels by air.

Early in his association with the insurance people, he found himself representing the company before the legislators in the state capital at Sacramento. This again meant much time away from home, but on the other hand it resulted in very welcome financial gains.

R. V. enjoyed this work enough to make up for the inconveniences. It also left time for him to work on other worthwhile projects that drew his attention.

Such as being appointed on the State Board of Agriculture by Governor Merriam and serving there for ten years. During this time, he was also appointed on the State Commission for the Treasure Island Fair. When Governor Olsen succeeded Governor Merriam, we were all pleased to learn that the appointment had been continued as R. V. Garrod's participation gave us all frequent opportunities to visit the exhibits as well as enjoy many special events taking place in the California building.

No sooner had the 1940 Treasure Island Fair closed its beautiful gates, and then the plans for a yearly fair in Santa Clara County took shape in the minds of a number of citizens already busy in the public affairs of the county, R. V. among them.

In 1941, with agricultural and floral displays and a women's division devoted to needlework and the cooking and preserving of foods all housed in two big tents, these plans came to life.

During the war years, no fair was held, but the dream was not forgotten, the Board of Directors, of which Vince was a member, continued to meet and plan for the future. Slowly but steadily, the fair grew. Now the Santa Clara County Fair ranks third among all California fairs, only surpassed by the State Fair in Sacramento and the Pomona Fair in Los Angeles. R. V. is still a member of the board of directors.

R. V. being on the Board of Agriculture gave me a trip south one year when their president, Mr. Hardison, invited that board to hold its monthly meeting at the San Diego Fair, a delightful affair attuned to the Spanish mission influence, tiled roofs and shaded walkways. We also visited San Diego's world-renowned zoo and spent an afternoon in Mexico as guests of a boyhood friend of R. V.'s, Maurice Essery. As our time was limited, we went only as far as Santa Anita race track, a very colorful place. There were no races being run that day. Our host sniffed snuff, not so good.

One very worthwhile accomplishment while busy in Sacramento, and of which we are all very proud, was the establishment of a School of Veterinary Medicine on the Agricultural College campus at Davis. This school is now considered the best in the nation. Some say, the best in the world. In 1968, at the hundredth anniversary of the founding of the University of California of which the Davis campus is a part, R. V. was presented with a plaque honoring him for his good work.

His efforts and interest in the many projects that promised betterment for agriculture and his equally sincere work to defeat those that would prove harmful led the authorities of the California Polytechnic College of San Luis Obispo to confer upon him the Degree of Master of Public Service.

One trip, sort of semi-business, semi-pleasure, on which I accompanied Vince, was to Merced for the dedication of the Farmers Insurance Group building there. After the festivities, we went to the Yosemite Valley.

We had been there once when the children were small and Ed Jones was with us. Then it was springtime and all the falls were at their best, roaring and splashing. This visit was in August of a very dry year. Not a drop of water in Mirror Lake, the Merced River, all but invisible and the falls just dry granite cliffs, everything hot, dry, and dusty—a far cry from the beautiful fairyland of my first visit, a most convincing example of the extremes reached by nature.

At this time, my husband is still President of the Board of Governors of Farmers Auto Insurance, on the boards of directors of both Sunsweet and Santa Clara County Fair, president of California Farmers Inc., and honorary member of the Saratoga Lions Club, a fifty-year Odd Fellow, a faithful Episcopalian, the husband of one, father of three, and grandfather of ten.

THE FARMERS UNION 2

The farmers' organization, which had served as an inanimate cupid in our behalf, continued to function in Santa Clara County and some other parts of the state.

R. V. took an active interest and did a lot of traveling about the country taking part in the meetings. I, having soon found myself with three small Garrods to care for, became more and more a stay at home.

One little girl and two little boys; they weren't triplets but might as well have been or monkeys as far as the twenty-four-hour task of looking after them was concerned. Besides, someone had to be around to represent authority on the place, even though that authority was pretty wobbly at times.

The yearly picnics were always enjoyable. The children could be present, so we always went. I remember one at the Stevens Creek Park when Mr. LeRoy Anderson of Saratoga was speaker of the day. Twice the gathering was held at Alum Rock Park. The first time, Mr. Charles Barrett, the National Farmers Union President presided; I cannot remember who spoke the second time.

Another year, the Gilroy group arranged to picnic on the Uvas, a very beautiful spot. We also met in the picnic grounds at the IOOF Home in Saratoga. California governor, C. C. Young, addressed the members. My old neighbor, William O. Post, was present. As he left for home, I heard him say to himself, "just the same empty promises that are never kept." Mr. Post was the only one I ever met who seriously studied Esperanto and had faith in it becoming a universal language.

At a state meeting held in Fresno to which Ralph Weaver from Evergreen and R. V. Garrod of Saratoga went as delegates representing Santa Clara County, Vince was chosen to serve as State President, an office he held on and on over the passing years.

One summer we arranged to have the yearly picnic at the Garrod ranch in the yard under the gum trees. This was found to be so convenient for everyone; it became the official gathering place during the succeeding years.

Various people came to address these picnic meetings. One of the first was our neighbor, Mrs. Fremont Older. She took us along the paths of the Padres as they made their way along the Mission Trail northward from the Mexican border, scattering mustard seed as they came so that the growing plants would mark the way for their journey south in the spring. The Padres are gone, but the tall, stalky variety of yellow mustard is still with us. Its tender young leaves in the spring make tasty greens for any table.

Another year, the organization's National President, Mr. Ed Eversen of South Dakota, came to speak at great length on the farmers' problems. It was also the year that the Los Gatos IOOF band came to entertain the gathering. There were about three hundred present.

We also listened to Mr. Rex Goodcell, who wanted to be governor, and Harvey Mydland, whose aim was to save the state from political corruption by getting himself elected to some legislative office.

The Blue Ribbon Coffee Company, represented by Mr. Hussey, would prepare and serve coffee to such a gathering as good advertising. Once when the big efficient electric percolator wouldn't work, someone came up with the idea of using the prune dipper to make a batch of real boiled coffee. After much scrubbing and rinsing of the dipping kettle, the coffee making proceeded. But the scrubbing crew had forgotten about the heating pipes under the kettle, which always retained some of whatever had been heated the time before; so as the coffee came to a boil, there was enough of the dipping water mixed with the coffee to make the most impossible brew ever concocted. Just a cup of water became the order of the day.

Another time while the audience was politely listening to a rather boring speaker, I noticed that everyone seemed to be more interested though the speaker seemed to have made no change. As I looked about for the reason, I discovered my smallest son standing almost directly behind the speaker. He was about two years old, dressed in blue-and-white-striped coveralls into the pocket of which someone had put a tight-fitting orange. The small boy was bending all his energy on getting that orange out of there so he could eat it. He won his battle just as the speaker reached the end of his discourse. Mr. Speaker no doubt found the applause very gratifying.

Once I wrote a parody of the song "Oh My Darling Clementine" and suggested that it be sung at some picnic or meeting just to pep things up a bit. My President husband wasn't poetically inclined, so this is its first public appearance.

Oh, The Farmer

In the county of Santa Clara
 Raising prunes and cots so fine
Dwell the farmers, hardworking farmers
 And their families, like yours and mine.

—Chorus—

Oh the farmer, Oh the farmer
He's a trusting sort of guy
Fills his life with work and worry
But he'll win out bye and bye!

In the springtime bright and early
 Out to work the farmer goes
Sprays his trees with oil and water
 With an engine and a hose.

—Chorus—

Takes his shears and trims the treetops
 Looks for bugs and gophers, too
Burns the brush and chops the weeds off
 Working hard he's never blue.

—Chorus—

Then he plows and disks and harrows
 With a tractor or a team,
And his orchard is like a garden
 Nicest place you've ever seen.

—Chorus—

Trees are blooming, full of promise
 For a record-breaking crop
Comes the frost or comes a rainstorm
 And the crop that was is not.

—Chorus—

Comes the harvest, hopes are soaring
    That the price will reach the top.
But where he looked for ninety dollars
    Twenty-five is what he got.

—Chorus—

So join the union, join the union
    Give it all the help you can
Tho' it can't control the weather
    It will watch the middle man.

—Chorus—

Occasionally, I reaped a bonus from my husband's away-from-home activities.

In 1937, a trip to Oregon was made to attend the annual Farmer's Union convention of that state's members. It was springtime; and the azaleas, rhododendron, and dogwoods were in full bloom. We spent one night with friends near the little town of Gazelle not far from the Oregon border.

Going on through Oregon, we saw all the gardens overflowing with iris of every color imaginable. I have never seen their equal since. From Portland, we followed the Columbia River on its way to the ocean and arrived at Klatskani where the meeting was held.

One special bit of entertainment arranged for the visiting delegates was a short trip to the edge of the river to watch the salmon fishing. If I remember correctly, men in a motorboat took one end of a net out toward the middle of the river, returning shoreward in a big circle. When back in shallow water, I suppose as near shore as it was safe for the boat to go, waiting men drove a team of horses out to meet them and quickly hitched them to one end of the net, the other end was fast on the boat. The horses then drew the net with its captive fish into water shallow enough for the men to unload it.

We were told that sometimes the horses got out where the water was too deep and the current too strong. Then all the men could do to save themselves was cut the tugs and let the poor horses be carried out to sea.

The men seemed more concerned about losing the harness and the fish than the horses. One man said, "We only use old horses that aren't worth much." Poor horses!

The main dish at the convention banquet that evening was baked salmon. It was delicious.

The Santa Clara County membership comparatively speaking was only a small segment of the entire Farmer's Educational and Cooperative Union of America. It was, nevertheless, the motive power that started and pushed to completion a number of enterprises that have proved to be of great value to agriculture and the general public as well.

An early venture was the establishment of a number of cooperative dried fruit marketing plants. These later became the foundation on which the present Sunsweet Cooperative was built.

These were the people who first saw the value of water conservation and worked the hardest to accomplish the formation of the water district and its dams which hold back thousands of acre feet of water every winter to be later percolated into the ground to replenish the fallen water table. The largest of these reservoirs bears the name of the member who headed the campaign for water conservation, LeRoy Anderson.

The well-known commercial center, the Orchard Supply, while not actually built by the Union, was thought of and brought into existence by a loyal member, Stanley B. Smith.

Various pieces of legislation of value to agriculture were given full support, among them the Frazer-Lempke Act which was of federal origin and of immeasurable value to farmers in all parts of the United States.

The Deciduous Fruit Experiment Station near Santa Clara was supported and kept active for many years through the persistence and determination of the Santa Clara County members.

The membership in the organization dwindled. Death took its toll and many early enthusiasts became old men and let the management of their farms go to younger family members whose interests were different. There still remained a dedicated portion of the membership who attended all the meetings and showed their concern in the many problems facing agriculture whether production, finances, or legislation by making their findings known through letters and resolutions.

The years rolled on, the toddlers grew up and went about their own affairs. The national groups began to lean too far in the wrong direction; at least the Californians thought they were wrong, so they canceled their charter and reorganized under the name of California Farmers Inc. Vince was elected to the Presidency and again holds that office year after year.

I attend the quarterly and yearly meetings and often act as secretary. Though small, the meetings are worthwhile and the members good and responsible people quietly striving to do their share toward keeping agriculture in its proper and well-deserved place in the overall scheme of living in California.

BUILDING CONTINUES

After I married and came to Saratoga to live, Father put the home ranch up for sale. He was not a man to live alone; we had arranged for a nice old man to be with him to do the cooking and be a companion and helper, but this plan did not work out as we had hoped.

He told his son-in-law to get busy and sell that place, as the real estate men he had talked to were doing nothing.

Next thing I knew, Vince had a deal going with his brother-in-law and sister the Henry Pfeffers, in November the sale was closed. Father accepted a share in a San Jose livery stable thereby going into partnership with Attilio Picchetti; this was the most unsatisfactory part of the deal as the stable was on the point of dissolution, it being just at the time when all vehicular traffic was changing from horses to motors.

Father lost the full value of that part of the deal.

He also took in part payment the undivided half of eighty acres which Vince and his sister had purchased some years earlier and known to the family as the back eighty or pasture.

Later he deeded that undivided half to me with the understanding that he receives fifty dollars cash from us every year as long as he lived. This promise was kept.

With these two trade items, some cash, and a small mortgage, the place went for $1,600 which was the price that had been set.

Father left the ranch and arranged to board with an old friend, a widow living near Campbell. Before Christmas, all very hush-hush, without a word to any of us, they were married. I learned it through a telephone call from someone in Los Gatos who had seen the announcement in the local paper.

My little stepmother was the widow of a good friend of my father's, Louis Ziegler. We had been well acquainted for many years and had always called her Auntie. All the time I had known her, she had been the victim of severe asthmatic attacks, and she became a semi-invalid. The marriage lasted about two years. After her death, Father moved to Alma to make his home with my sister.

In January 1917, at the height of an unusually cold spell with all the water pipes frozen, someone shouted fire! George Wilson's little house just over the fence from the cow barn was a mass of flames. With no water to use against it, we could only stand by and hope that the burning cinders would not fall on the barn and set that afire too. Luckily, there was no wind and the little house burned to a heap of ashes without doing further harm. An untended kerosene stove had done the mischief.

That evening my sister called to say there had been a fire at what was now the Pfeffer place, and everything but the barn had been burned.

By chance, Father happened to be there that day. Although no longer his, it was heartbreaking to stand by helplessly and watch his work of those many years destroyed. Here too, there was no water because of the extreme cold; all the pipes were frozen.

The Beattys, seeing the fire, rushed down to help and were able to save a little furniture. Unfortunately, the Pfeffers carried no fire insurance. The neighbors were more than generous in giving help, food, clothing, and household goods. As soon as Henry recovered from the shock of so great a loss, he made plans to rebuild the house. Vince was able to be of help in making contacts to secure bank loans and other credits and spent much time with them while the house was being built. The near neighbors came with their teams and wagons one day and hauled all the needed lumber. George Wilson went up and became chief carpenter. Vince's brother, Harold, being between jobs at the time, came from San Francisco to lend a hand.

On March 17, we attended the housewarming for the new home, taking our six-week-old daughter to her first party. She spent the evening fast asleep on a pillow in a fruit box out of harm's way under a workbench. By April, they were established in their new house. The other buildings were never replaced.

George Wilson came back, and Mr. Lawlor supplied the material to build him another little house. This one is still standing. It is known as the Fig Tree House. George made it his home for a number of years, although sometimes taking work in San Francisco as jobs were offered him and sometimes staying away for months. He always showed up again at unexpected moments in need of rest and general recuperation. Soon he would declare his "tools needed exercise. Wasn't there something he could build?"

One spring, he built the summer kitchen which proved to be a lifesaver for me. The kitchen in the house being exposed to every ray of the afternoon sun became unbearably close and hot. The new building on the shady side of the gully with the upper half of the walls screened was always livable and sometimes almost cold.

Early in April, I would move the cooking utensils, pots, pans, dishes, and groceries in and do all the cooking and canning in reasonable comfort until the autumn rain sent me back to the house again.

The next job for George developed because Grandmother Garrod, while staying in her brother's cottage at Twin Lakes near Santa Cruz, learned that a nearby lot forty by eighty feet was on the market to be sold for $150.

As visits to the coast not only afforded his mother great pleasure but benefited her health as well, R. V. decided to buy the lot and have George Wilson build a very simple roughly finished house on it. George and my father set up a tent and camped there while they worked at building a house. Before long, they had the proposed structure completed.

We all enjoyed the place. As the children moved along in school, beach picnics with their young friends were frequent affairs.

The biggest job George undertook was the fruit house. This turned out to be a 20 x 48 foot story and a half building. The cost of any undertaking was always of major importance. This entire building aside from the foundation timbers, some supporting pillars inside for which ranch grown eucalyptus trees were used and the standard hand split three-foot redwood shakes on the roof was all built of secondhand lumber which came from Goldworthy's blacksmith and wagon repair and paint shop in Los Gatos, which was being dismantled just then. Henry Mineo, who was just starting a trucking business with a big noisy motor truck, took the job of hauling the lumber to the ranch. He moved it all in one trip.

The first floor was designed for dried fruit storage, the upper half story to shelter anything that could be moved up there. We found that as soon as the dried fruit was moved out to the Association Plants, it made a fine place for friendly gatherings.

For years, weather permitting, groups which progressed from just nearby neighbors and friends to the high school kids, then the young college people from far and wide as acquaintanceships widened. During World War II, parties were forgotten. After that came the folk dancers followed by the 4H youngsters. Now the social activities in the fruit house are mostly by the people devoted to horses, Castle Rock Horsemen, etc.

The main requirements for a party are still the same: a place to meet, music to dance by and simple refreshments, always coffee and sometimes sandwiches and cake or doughnuts.

The most satisfactory music ever heard in the fruit house was made by Rocco Armento of San Jose on his accordion. A blacksmith by trade, musician by avocation, he would play tirelessly into the early morning hours. His compensation: whatever the passed-hat collected. Now modern phonographs and loudspeakers are used.

That building was almost too much for George. Every now and then he would threaten to quit because he was tired of old lumber full of hidden nails. He really couldn't be blamed; secondhand lumber is not easy to work with. The building couldn't be left standing there half-done of no use to anyone, so we hired young Bill Pfeffer, a husky, good-natured, and very capable teenager to help. He not only took over much of the heavy work; his cheerful optimism lifted George's depressed spirits, and the building was completed.

As the years slipped by, there was always need of more building, mostly help houses. One was located by the oak trees just west of the dry lot; long since it was taken apart and the lumber used elsewhere. That summer a visitor from San Francisco, Mr. Brennan, a Rope Walk workman, was with us. What he lacked in building skill was overbalanced by his eagerness to be of help. He undertook to do the roof. He decided on the easy way to reach the job, starting at the gable instead of the eaves. Someone else took those shakes off and put them on right way round.

Mr. Shumate from Santa Cruz built the first part of the one where the Cendijos family lived for many years and Lawrence Erickson of Los Gatos, the one now used for the office and tack room. This was done during World War II when lumber was scarce so they took the one-by-twelve redwood floor from the hay barn to help build the house. The Gonzales family of Los Angeles was its first tenant.

After the war, when both sons were home, they bought and erected the tin workshop, filled in and cemented the space between the shop and the fruit house, put a corrugated roof overhead, and had a spacious and convenient cutting shed which also comes in handy for other things.

Always the extra help needed to accomplish these changes and improvements, whether paid employees or guests working for fun, found their places at the dining table.

My time seemed all to go toward preparing food, stews, and pot roasts, kettles of beans and bushels of vegetables. For one who never liked to cook, I have worked my way through more groceries than most housekeepers.

APRICOTS

Apricots—that beautiful delicious golden fruit of which California is so proud and which can give the poor trusting farmer so many headaches.

The encyclopedia says that the apricot belongs to the rose family, that the fruit is sweet and juicy; it is a native of Armenia, is also grown in India, China, Egypt, Europe, and the United States of America.

Somewhere the statement has been printed, that it was not the apple but an apricot that made all the trouble in the Garden of Eden.

One thing is certain, apricots grow in California in Santa Clara County, and over the years I have become well-acquainted with them.

When I was a very small child, there was an apricot tree of the Royal variety growing near the yard, and once in a while there were a few not very good apricots to pick. The altitude and cold winters killed that tree in its youth.

Below us in Lakeside district, there were apricot orchards which produced crops well worth harvesting. Mr. Jefts owned such an orchard. In the summer when a favorite city cousin came to spend his vacation, we always found it convenient to take an evening drive on the road that led through Mr. Jefts's orchard, gathering enough fruit from the overhanging branches to eat on the way home, most often because of the dark and our own ignorance we gathered more green inedible fruit than ripe.

When I became acquainted with my husband, he was most enthusiastic about apricots; they were such a worthwhile crop coming as they did before prunes, just when the summer weather was at its best; they were easy to handle, delicious to eat, looked like balls of gold when ripe; when sent to market, they always fetched a fair price, in short a very fine product.

Beside all this, they offered two chances: a grower could sell to the canners, or dry either part or all of the crop; a good optimistic point of view.

Before long I began to learn about apricots in general, and Garrod apricots in particular, and found them not quite as delightful as I had been led to believe.

At the beginning of the Garrod regime, there were a few Moorpark trees on the place, like the Royal an old-fashioned variety, nice big fruit, delicious when ripe but inclined to become nice and ripe on one side and stay green on the other. They were also "shy bearers" perhaps one good crop every three years.

Agriculturists had been busy improving the apricot. There were now three commercial varieties: the Alameda Henskirk, the Tilton, and the Blenheim.

Vince had made several plantings of Blenheims before I joined the family. The first was in 1900: two hundred trees on the face of Knob hill, a very steep and hard to cultivate piece of ground and the first to be abandoned years later when the change from horses to tractors was made.

The next planting was made on the flat by the pasture gate and the third lot he put on the ridge southwest of the old house; some of these came out to make room for the new house.

During the spring of 1918, the north and east sides of Knob hill were planted to Blenheims. All available land on Knob hill was now an apricot orchard, except the very top where a space of about an acre was devoted to grapevines in an effort to preserve a clear view of the surrounding country.

From this point, it was possible to identify part of eight California counties, providing it was a good old-fashioned clear day.

When the Finley place which joined the Garrod land on the south and west became an estate, R. V. bid it in and another lot of apricots was added to the Garrod total, somewhat later when young Vince was in high school, he with the help of a schoolmate, Kelly Casanova, surveyed and planted more cots on that part of the Finley place known as the knobs which had always been used as hay land.

Finally, Vince and Dick took over the orchards to the east then owned by John Alonzo; this gave them another lot of apricots. Now the Garrods had something like fifty acres of the precious things to cope with, a possible 250 tons; this point was not reached till the 1940s.

To return to 1916 the beginning of my working acquaintanceship with apricots, these first plantings Vince had made were in full bearing, the trees still young enough to produce fine quality fruit, big, clean, perfect.

I soon learned that despite their many virtues, apricots, or "cots" as they are known to all who grow or work with them, are a most demanding species of plant life.

From the first year of their life in an orchard, they must be carefully and thoroughly pruned, no lick and a promise this year with the good intention of a better job next time.

In the early years of apricot growing in California, the orchards were free from disease but soon a fungus known as "brown rot" made its appearance, until the growers learned to combat brown rot by spraying the trees with a mixture of lime and bluestone, known as Bordeau, plus a percentage of DDT added to take care of any worms that might show up. This fungus would destroy the new spring growth on the trees, and the crop would be lost.

For a time, it was thought the hill orchards, because of altitude, weather, or perhaps the Grace of God would be immune, but the fungus spores traveled on the air currents which carried them upward. Soon, spraying was just as necessary in the hills as in the valley.

This meant another expensive and difficult job, the time for the application of the spray material is determined by the progress of the blossoms, and the proper time is just when the buds are "in the pink" not shut tight, not wide open.

As bloom time is late February or early March, it follows that the weather will probably be unfavorable or at best the ground so wet the rig cannot be taken off the roadways and hoses must be dragged great distances to reach the trees; or if a tractor is being used and the driver ventures into doubtful places, he stands the chance of finding his equipment settled so deep in mud, it must be left till better weather and sunshine make extricating it possible.

Spray rigs, like everything else, have changed with time, from a hand-operated pump and a barrel of material on a horse-drawn sled with one man to drive the horses and work the pump and another man to handle the hose to which was attached a piece of pipe encased in a bamboo covering with a nozzle at the tip and a valve on the other end with which the man controlled the flow of material.

Now spray rigs are complete units with built-in tanks, motor-driven pumps, and automatic blowers instead of hoses.

Each improvement, although being much more efficient, also resulted in more weight to move and far higher cost.

If nothing happened to the baby cots during the next few weeks, like heavy storms or freezing weather, everyone could relax.

Freezing temperature in the hills in April or May occurred very seldom; if it did, there was nothing to be done but hope that the more sheltered parts of the orchards had escaped.

In the valley where the orchards stood on almost level ground, some precaution against loss by frost could be taken. The growers supplied themselves with portable crude oil burners, commonly called "smudge pots"; these were set in the orchards at frequent intervals fueled and ready to light.

Through the cooperation of the County Agricultural Commissioner's Office, the weather bureau, and the telephone company, they arranged for warnings to be sent out when the mercury fell to the danger point. Most often, the warning calls came in the wee small hours of morning. Mr. Grower would then hurry out into the cold and the dark to light his smudge pots; that done he could hope to still have his apricots come morning.

The heat from the fires warmed the lower strata of the atmosphere, while the heavy smoke from the burning oil formed a protective screen overhead, stopping the fall of the cold air from above.

This smoke hung like a gloomy black pall over the entire valley carrying great quantities of soot. As the huge mass drifted about, it scattered its load of black flakes everywhere calling forth many complaints from housewives with clotheslines and window curtains and businessmen and office people in the cities and towns.

There was talk of legislation to stop the use of smudge pots; I do not recall any such law being enacted. My guess is that the subdividers moved faster than the legislators; now smudge pots are no longer needed.

When the cots were as big as the top of a man's thumb, it was time to thin them. This meant breaking up all the clusters and leaving the fruit so spaced on the twigs each could grow to usable size.

This was first done by hand, a long and tedious task on which much ladder climbing and endless patience were expended. Later bamboo fishing poles were used, these held by the tip or thinner end were tapped against the twigs and clusters thereby knocking off the surplus fruit. With this done, there was a fair chance that the cots would be safe till picking time.

When ripe, again the apricot is fussy, a real "prima donna" in the world of fruit, prunes, grapes, apples, and many others will cling to their parent plants a reasonable length of time after ripening, giving the grower the opportunity to take care of them next day or next week if need be. Not so the apricot. If ripe today, Mr. Grower better get out there and take care of it at once for by tomorrow it will no doubt have fallen off the tree and be nothing but a squashed yellow blob on the ground when the picker gets there.

When the cots were ripe, the grower had those two choices: 1) sell to the canneries; 2) dry.

Cot cutters

The dry lot

Prunes ready for market

HARVEST

When the time of harvest arrived, the grower still had his two choices: sell to the cannery or dry. If he wished, he could split the deal and do both.

Selling to the canners was less work and needed fewer hands, the grower picked, sorted, and delivered his fruit, and his money was soon available.

The biggest drawback to the cannery deal was the fact that the canner set the price. The grower had no opportunity to dicker; it was a simple case of "take it or leave it." In the canner's book the cans, sugar, labels, labor, insurance, and every other item he could think of were of greater importance and outranked the value of the fruit that went into the can.

From the 1920s to the 1960s, the cannery price for apricots dropped from an acceptable $125 per ton to a not so good $75.

In the same time, the grower's costs had been climbing, not only had the price of equipment, repairs, and material as well as labor become greater but more and different taxes were continually being added to his troubles; the whole enterprise was thrown out of balance, and the thought of coming out ahead just a dream.

The canners also set the specifications for the fruit they would accept; they of course wanted the very best, unblemished, just the proper size usually twelve or fourteen to the pound, not too ripe, not too green; perfect.

When a grower dealt only with the cannery, any fruit which did not meet requirements was a complete loss. If the split deal had been decided on much more work had to be done, but the grower could at least market almost the entire crop.

As a rule, the canners furnished the boxes in which the fruit was delivered to them. These boxes known as "orchard lugs" held fifty pounds of fresh fruit each.

Transporting both empty and full boxes to and from the cannery was done by the grower with his own trucks or through arrangements he made with commercial truckers. Some canners added a nominal sum to the agreed price to help defray the hauling expense.

Besides having boxes on hand, other preparations for picking had to be made. The fifty-pound cannery boxes and the smaller forty-pound ranch boxes moved into the orchards, ladders taken from winter storage and put into safe working condition, numerous twelve quart-picking pails each with an extra hook clipped to the handle so they could be easily hung on a branch or on a loop nailed to the side of the ladder, all had to be ready to go.

When the picking began, sorting stands were set up near where the empty boxes had been stacked; it was here that the picker's full pails were checked on their cards, and empty pails ready for them to carry back to the trees.

The cards were only checked when the pickers were doing piecework, each check was worth perhaps seventeen cents with the promise of a three-cent bonus if the picker stayed to the end of the season. These figures varied from year to year.

When the crop was heavy, a good man on piecework could do very well, often filling several hundred pails a day, this fast work of course led to careless selection of fruit by the picker and made more work for the sorters.

A light crop resulted in hour work; this way all pickers received the same amount of money, but the end result for the grower between the fruit gathered by the interested picker who liked to see the boss do well, and that brought in by the one mainly looking for quitting time and payday was unbelievable.

The sorters emptied the fruit from the pails into boxes at the same time removing the fruit which did not meet cannery specifications, setting this aside in the smaller ranch boxes to be brought to the yard for cutting.

Sometimes women and girls worked at the sorting stands a few tried picking, but moving ladders in a hillside orchard is no picnic; as far as possible, the orchard end of the harvest was left to men.

Transportation for the fruit from the orchard to the yard and for the workers to and from had to be taken care of every day, first with horse-drawn sleds and wagons, later with trucks and tractors.

The drying operation was an enterprise by itself, requiring much getting ready before any fruit was brought from the orchard.

A supply of trays, lightweight, shallow containers, eight feet long, three feet wide, about two inches deep, hundreds of them, washed and dried in the sun, repaired when it was needed and made ready for use.

Sulfur houses, almost airtight little buildings just wide, long, and high enough to take twenty of these trays stacked one on top of the other on a low-wheeled car. The loaded car was pushed into and pulled out of the houses on narrow iron tracks, the houses, cars, and tracks were checked and repairs made.

Sawhorses or frames of some sort were needed to place the trays on to bring them to a convenient working height.

A good supply of inexpensive paring knives had to be provided and small boxes to receive the pits as they were removed from the fruit.

According to the expected tonnage, sulfur in hundred-pound sacks was needed.

The dry lot was cleared of its crop of grass and weeds and made as dust free and smooth as possible so that the trays of freshly cut and sulfured fruit could be set there to be dried by the sun.

A dry lot covered by hundreds of trays of drying apricots was a joy to behold.

Beside all this preparation and clutter of equipment, people were needed, preferably women and young girls, with a man or a husky boy to lift the boxes and trays, check the cutter's record cards, and give the cutting shed general supervision.

The process of cutting apricots is really simple, one by one the cots are picked up in one hand, the blade of the knife in the other hand is passed completely around the cot on the suture line, the pit removed with thumb and finger, and the resulting halves placed cut side up on the tray with no wasted space between this last pair and those already there. Sounds easy but try it sometime hour after hour, day after day, you'll be surprised.

About seven tons of fresh fruit must be cut to make one ton dry.

The nucleus of the harvest crew was of course the family, next relatives, often old acquaintances or their children, any one available among the near neighbors or our young people's schoolmates and transients.

A transient family would move into a picker's cabin, of which in time a number were built, or set up camp in some convenient spot with their own gear, they would take care of their own shopping needs. The men would work in the orchards, the women and children in the cutting shed. Children too young to work played about nearby and often right underfoot.

With relatives and friends, it was different; bed and board were taken for granted.

As the upcoming generation reached the age of usefulness, this included cousins from far and near and favorite school friends. There were summers when I found myself with twenty or more hungry people to feed three times a day. This meant work, lots of it; at the same time, it was great fun to have them.

By then the summer kitchen had been built across the gully from the house and quite near the yard where the fruit work was being done.

This building was a real lifesaver to me. The upper half of the walls was screen, and the nearby trees shaded it from the sun; though the cooking was all done on a woodstove, the heat from it was always bearable and on a cool and foggy day very welcome.

I, being blessed or cursed with the inclination to take a hand in any current activity, soon found myself with the doubtful honor of keeping an eye on the cutting shed whenever my good husband had other matters to attend to, which was most of the time. So I spent my days shuttling back and forth between the kitchen and the fruit, either something was boiling over or burning on the stove or my attention was required instantly in the shed.

Every season the shed man or boy was a different person, most often a youngster afraid to exert much authority, and too often it was some older woman who had worked in some shed in her youth who was now the most difficult, always sure that the boy hadn't checked all her boxes as she had certainly cut more than her card showed. Besides, "that moonstruck young idiot was giving all the good fruit to his favorite girlfriends, leaving the little bitty ones for people like her." Then it was my job to be diplomatic and smooth the ruffled feelings; it was difficult to explain that young hands simply moved faster.

These young girls were not above reproach; if allowed to giggle and gossip as they pleased, the amount of fruit cut was noticeably lessened. Teenaged boys, unless accompanied by older members of their families, were just about useless.

I fail to remember a season just when the harvest was at its peak, too much fruit coming off the trees, too much coming into the shed, that someone didn't come in from the orchard, first my husband later a son, saying I must have extra sorters, we are swamped; after dinner I want her and her and her out there, without fail pointing out the best workers in the shed.

This meant a hasty call for more hands in the shed. On one occasion, R. V. went out and recruited a group of housewives from among our friends in town; one day was enough for them, and several declared they were unable to leave their beds for days afterward. One dear lady, who had lived with apricot orchards nearby all her life, sat down by a tray and proceeded to slice apricots as one would apples for a pie. She was very surprised to learn it must be done differently.

Having the orchard crew take away the best cutters was bad, having a neighbor or friend finding himself unable to handle his fruit, because it did not measure up to cannery standards, talk the head of the harvest operation—either husband or son—into promising to dry it for him was worse. It always meant finding more help and made more work at every turn; for twenty dollars a ton, it wasn't worthwhile.

In the early years, it was always an English bachelor neighbor who was first on the scene with his tale of woe. One season, he arrived promptly every morning with a load of little apricots that were not much bigger than cherries; when weighed, they counted sixty to the pound.

One day, I insisted that he stay and help cut them a very short time settled that problem, Charlie admitted no one should be expected to spend time on them. That was the first time we tried drying cots whole, if ripe and full of sugar they are pretty good, but the trade has never really accepted them.

With fruit of the ten or twelve to the pound size at the proper state of ripeness a good cutter working a ten-hour day could do about half a ton or twenty-five ranch boxes. The going price in the Garrod shed was ten cents a box, each box averaged thirty-eight pounds of fruit. There were drying operations in the valley which paid only eight cents per cannery lug.

Small or overripe fruit brought everything down to a slow walk, sometimes to a complete stop.

The overripe fruit and any that had fallen from the trees but could still be salvaged, the kids who picked them up called them "grounders," though more trouble to cut and when dry were flat and shapeless and considered of lesser value by the trade where they were known as slabs, were never the less sweeter and of richer flavor than those known as "extra fancy" in the markets.

Slabs were always kept for home consumption. They furnished the young people with their favorite nibbling material.

The pits were dried by the sun on trays or spread on a special section of black topped yard later to be hauled to cracking plants where the outer shells were removed and the kernels crushed so the oil in them could be extracted. This oil was almost all used by the cosmetic manufacturers. When obtainable, it is a pleasant salad oil. Before the world war, much of what was left of the kernels after they were crushed and the oil removed was exported to France; there it was toasted and used in pastry and candy in place of bitter almonds. I believe this is no longer done.

To finish the process of cot drying; after the filled trays were placed on the cars and pushed into the sulfur houses, a quantity of sulfur was placed in a hole under them which had been dug deep enough to avoid fire danger, the sulfur carefully ignited the doors shut tight and left overnight or at least four hours to be bleached; the sulfur fumes also held the flavor. After the allotted time, it was moved to the dry lot and spread out tray after tray for the sun to finish the job. In favorable weather, two or three days was enough; gloomy or foggy weather of course look longer. If by chance a shower of rain came along night or day, everyone hurried out to stack and cover those cots; a good wetting meant they must be brought in and resulfured or they would be of darker color and lower grade.

When dry the cots were removed from the trays at the same time roughly sorted, slabs and discolored fruit removed, all grades put into boxes and stored in the fruit house ready to be hauled to San Jose to go on the market under the Sunsweet label.

As the years passed, the orchard on the south side of Knob hill was abandoned; it had always been hard to work with horses, when tractors came in to use it was judged far too dangerous for anyone to attempt.

The practice of paying for the cutting by the box continued for many years, until someone figured out that paying according to the weight of the pits each worker collected during the day, at the rate of fifteen or more cents a pound added up to the same total as they might earn by the box, parts of boxes could be taken care of more easily by this method and punch cards were no longer needed, the change was quite satisfactory to everyone.

At the time this change was made, the cutting operation was moved to a cement floored roofed overspace which had been built between the fruit house and the workshop. A grader for sorting fresh apricots was installed, doing away with the need of orchard sorting.

The next move was to try out the value of mechanical cutters; personally, I could see little improvement, the clatter and rattle of the machines was very tiring, the fruit was not as well cut, the waste was much greater, and the end result left much to be desired. More tonnage could be handled, but the cost per ton was about the same.

The sulfur houses were done away with and the full trays stacked in ranks of a hundred or more covered with big sheets of construction plastic and the sulfur burned under them in the usual way; this worked very well.

Now in 1967, most of the orchards have been turned into horse pastures.

By the time the mechanical cutters were tried, common sense told me I shouldn't try to keep pace with my grandchildren, so I retired from active participation in apricot drying. Enough is enough.

APRICOT SEASON

The summer our daughter Louise went away with her soldier husband, George Cooper, I sent her a letter in rhyme which gives a fair picture of the apricot harvest at Garrods in 1941.

Apricot Season, 1941

It's here that annual summer nightmare
Why no one knows or seems to care
We all rush about without rhyme or reason
I'll have you know its apricot season.

Trays to be washed and some to be mended
Dozens and dozens whose life span is ended
Pit boxes found and car wheels oiled
Here is the harvest for which we have toiled.

The breeze in the gum trees softly sighing
Warns that by noon of heat we'll be dying
Or a wisp of fog o'er the hilltop blowing
For sweaters and coats will send us going.

The cutters have come, the Durons, the Kings,
With bundles and bags and various things
Julio and Aligio with spunky new hats
Bertha and Christine all dressed up in slacks.

And from Kelly's Mrs. Tovar comes
Works all day with her three small sons
Brown-eyed cherubs underfoot squealing
Must have fallen from some church ceiling.

The shed man is new, Fred Ryan by name
To his aunt, Mrs. Bordi, from Iowa he came
Pleasant and quick a veritable treasure
When against Clyde or Frank you measure.

Dick does the chores, runs the truck and the tractor
Shouts at the dogs and threatens disaster
Vince in the orchard bosses the picking
To his own job believes in sticking.

R. V. mends trays and supervises
Jollies the cutters and offers them prizes
Then with his usual blithe greeting
Puts on his hat and goes to a meeting.

Mother, on cool days busy as a bee
Mother, on a hot day loafs completely
Aunt Jo's in the kitchen, O my, O my,
All sorts of good things and super, super pie.

We all rush about without rhyme or reason
Darling—I've told you it's apricot season.

Mother

MORE HARVEST

After the apricots came the peaches which grew on trees planted by Mr. Charles Simonds about 1879 or '80 part of the first orchard set out on what is now Garrod land. They were early and late Crawfords both freestones, sweet, and tasty, but not good keepers and not to be handled commercially, so they were used for home canning or sold locally a few boxes at a time and some years those that could not be disposed of otherwise were dried. Peaches are not my favorite dried fruit.

There were also a few tons of Bartlett pears to be taken care of. In the course of time, the peach trees died of old age and the pears taken out to clear the ground for the first water storage dam.

Part of the family felt that peaches and pears were just something to keep people home when it would have been much pleasanter to spend that time at some beach or other vacation spot or gone hunting or fishing.

By late August or early September, the prunes were demanding attention; as prunes were, along with the apricots, a major source of income to the family, there was no question about all hands being home to help harvest them.

The growing of a prune orchard was much the same as any other planting. They all require care, pruning prunes is not as exacting a task as pruning cots, but a moderate amount is needed every spring.

The picking was not begun until the little blue plums began to fall to the ground and a light jarring of the tree caused a worthwhile number to shower down.

Incidentally prunes are plums, but all plums are not prunes. A ripe prune is a completely sweet fruit having none of the sharp tartness in the skin and around the pit which is found in most plums in the fresh fruit markets.

I have heard it said, "that nothing hurts prunes," and the manner in which some people handled them one could almost believe it to be true. Nevertheless, care and cleanliness always paid off in a better finished product.

The prunes in the Garrod orchards were always picked up from the ground at so much a ton by local or transient labor. Of late, mechanical shakers and pickers have been developed. I am not familiar with them. To be economically worthwhile, level acreage and heavy tonnage are needed. I know they are not for hillside orchards such as Garrod's.

The family went through almost the same routine as we had followed at home, aside from the fact that there were more of them and the equipment to handle them bigger. I learned little new about prunes. Instead of grading them before dipping, here they were graded after dipping. When dry and removed from the trays, they were stored in bins or piles in the fruit house; when delivery time came, they were shoveled into standard jute sacks also known as gunny sacks, sewed shut just like grain or other cattle feed, loaded on trucks, and hauled to wherever they were supposed to go.

When the California Prune and Apricot Association was formed about 1917, and in the process absorbed the cooperative packing plants which the California Cooperative and Educational Union locals had established some years before, the Garrod dried fruit, both cots and prunes, were delivered there.

In 1918, the prune harvest was completely disrupted by a very unseasonal storm; eight inches of rain fell one day that September. The ripe fruit on the ground was beaten into the mud and had to be left to mold and rot, as for that out on the trays the force of the rain was so great it was fairly beaten to pieces.

When the storm was over and the orchards and dry lots began to dry out, the valley smelled like huge distilleries so much fruit was fermenting.

One grower, anxious to clean up his trays and boxes, dumped the ruined fruit on a creek bank forgetting that a nearby dairy man's cows had access to the same creek bank. When the dairy cows all came home drunk, their owner insisted that the grower gather up his messy prunes and take them elsewhere.

That storm was a turning point in prune drying; before the next crop was ripe, the Association, as well as many individual growers, built dehydrators. These were really huge ovens in which the freshly washed prunes were dried in hours instead of days or weeks.

ED JONES

It was September and prune-picking time; Vince had had a trying summer suffering from sciatic rheumatism, had in fact, spent the month of August at the Tassahara Hot Springs in Monterey County in an effort to find relief and was now trying to handle the hauling end of the prune harvest with the help of John Patric, an old man who had for many years lived on the place, cutting wood and doing odd jobs at his own slow pace.

This season, no one else being available, John tried but soon found himself unequal to the task. He was no longer young, and time had taken its toll. Unwilling to admit his inability, he went off and got very, very drunk, a condition in which he was absolutely useless, so Vince fired him.

In response to a call to the agricultural employment office in San Jose, Ed Jones came with the understanding that he would stay a few days till the rush was over. This he did, a few days, a week, a month, soon it was a year; when death stepped in and took him from us, he had been a beloved member of the household for twenty-five years.

I met him on the second day of his stay with us. Upon my return from a short visit with my sister, Vince, his mother, and this strange man were at supper.

I saw a spare tall elderly man showing the evidence of years of hard work, quite bald with twinkling blue eyes and a most engaging smile.

Grandmother Garrod had taken my eight-month-old daughter on her lap and shortly said to this stranger, "Mr. Jones, how would you like to hold a baby like this in your arms?" "I would like it fine," said he, and held out his hands to her. Ordinarily, she was shy of strangers, but she transferred herself into those waiting arms so quickly Gramma just couldn't believe it.

We soon learned that all babies held a special place in his heart, human babies, kittens, puppies, chicks, little pigs or calves, were all deserving of special attention and all responded to him in kind.

Ed was a native of Janestown, Wisconsin, the first of a family of eight, his mother Irish, his father Welsh. He was not a talkative man but over the years, bit by bit, we learned much of his past. His age was sixty years when he came. The preceding years had been spent at every type of work expected of a man in those pioneering times. While he was making his way across the northern part of the United States, he worked in the harvest fields of the plains and the timber of the mountains, seeing many attractive and promising locations, but never settling on land of his own as he was often tempted to do. While he was young, the urge to see what lay beyond kept him moving; later, time moved so fast he never got around to it, and now it was too late.

A confirmed bachelor, he would smile and say he supposed he had as much right to starve some woman to death as any other man but had never wanted to do just that. Anyway, the girls he wanted didn't want him, and those that wanted him he didn't want, but you couldn't tell; he might still get married someday. He never did.

Strangers sometimes asked him why he had left home and started his wandering career. He had an answer for them. When about fifteen, the news came that the railroad was finished and the first train would come to their town one certain day. Father Jones put his wife and children in the ox cart and traveled to town to see the excitement. He left the oxen and the cart by the side of the street with young Edward to keep watch over them. When the train came with a great clatter, blowing of whistle, and ringing of bell, the oxen became frightened and started off across lots in a westerly direction at a great rate of speed. Finally, the cart fell apart and the oxen stopped to graze, but Ed continued in that westerly direction and never stopped till he reached California and the Garrod ranch.

When the prune season was finished that year, the matter of his time with us being ended never came up. He took over the day-to-day work, anything that could be done with a team of horses or with hand tools was what he was accustomed to, liked to do, and did very efficiently.

Tree pruning and fruit picking were not in his line of endeavor. As he accepted more and more responsibility for the everyday farmwork, R. V. was able to take greater interest in civic and political affairs which suited him fine and eventually led to an off-the-ranch income which was of the greatest help in our efforts to keep the acres all had worked so hard for, free from debt.

The money agreement with Ed was two dollars a day and board. As soon as practical, a tidy little house was built for him, quite near the barn and in easy calling distance from the house.

Having no outside interests, Ed expended all his time and energy, when not actually engaged in orchard or fieldwork, in fixing things, rehanging a barn door here or a gate there, rebuilding a fence or repairing the road. There was always something else to take his attention.

The workshop was equipped with a portable forge. As Ed liked blacksmithing, he soon installed a full-sized fire bed and regulation bellows which Vince secured for him from a Saratoga smith. The kids had great fun watching the sparks fly from that bed of coals at every puff of the bellows.

Plows and hand tools were sharpened and all sorts of things repaired. The old harness was mended till he could scarcely find room for any more copper rivets.

Ed said keeping the farm equipment patched and in working order put him in the same position as an old lady with all the family socks to darn; there was no end in sight.

To me the masterpiece of all Ed's fixing was the bridge he built to take the place of the one near the bottom of the gully between the house and the service yard. The summer kitchen had been built by then, and I was forever going back and forth from house to kitchen.

On a place like ours, there is always material of some sort salvaged from other enterprises that come in handy if one has the ingenuity to use it. Ingenuity was something Ed had in abundance.

Needing more timbers than were readily available, he went to the back pasture and cut good straight gum trees six and eight inches in diameter to serve as upright supports and proceeded single-handedly to put a new bridge well above the old one. The finished structure was between seventy-five and a hundred feet long and about four feet wide. The flooring for the walkway was purchased from a lumberyard; everything else was scrounged from about the place.

When finished, the bridge reached from a few steps beyond the back porch door to a spot almost level with the summer kitchen steps. There were banisters of blue gum saplings along the sides securely screened with inch mesh chicken wire to make it safe for little people.

That bridge was a joy and comfort to everyone on the ranch, especially me. It served its purpose for many years. After we had moved to the new house and the traffic pattern had changed so the bridge was no longer of great importance, one stormy winter a laurel tree whose roots had been loosened by the rushing water crashed down on the bridge, wrecking it beyond repair. It was never rebuilt.

When our little daughter, who never relinquished her hold on him, reached the run about age heard me call Ed to come to meals, she would hurry out to meet him, knowing she would ride back on his shoulder. This one evening Ed came in without her; when asked, he looked surprised and said he hadn't seen her. Supper was quickly pushed to the back of the stove, and we all hurried out to find her as it was fast growing dark. Her daddy thought she might have gone to Granma's and went in that direction. I started up through the orchard trying for a shortcut to the pasture road. I might as well have stayed in the kitchen. I found myself knee deep in a tangled growth of bur clover and alfilleree, a splendid cover crop but impossible to hurry in.

Ed meanwhile had moved off on the established roadway, reached the top of the hill in short order, and soon called to say she was safe. She had missed the turn to his house and accompanied by Pollo, the collie, had gone out of hearing distance when she caught her knitted jacket on the barbed wire fence and couldn't untangle herself. When Ed found her, she was crying bitterly, the dog sitting beside her barking. When he brought her to me, he remarked in a matter-of-fact way, "Mama, it's always best to take a slow step but a long one."

After a time, young Vince was added to the family and little sister looked a bit put out when Ed paid attention to the new baby whom she herself welcomed most happily. But when the second brother arrived, and a woebegone little specimen he was for the first few weeks of his life, they declared in perfect accord, "The baby can't have him. Ed belongs to us."

Dick got him nevertheless. They were partners; before he could walk, the determined little guy would make his way on hands and knees, out the door, up to the barn or blacksmith shop, anywhere he heard Ed at work. There he stayed till I or someone else brought him back to the house. At fourteen months, he straightened up and began to walk; after that he had it made, he could follow Ed to the farthest corners of the ranch and often did.

When I heard a Pied Piper sort of whistling in the springtime, I knew that Dick and his partner had been to the far end of the pasture for a supply of whistle timber from the willows just turning green with the first push of the spring sap.

The Garrod children had two perfectly good grandfathers: Granpa Garrod, who never scolded them no matter what mischief they got into;

and Gramp Stolte, a firm believer in the theory that the younger generation needed firm guidance and supervision.

One of his favorite mottos was "Honor they father and thy mother." When his grandsons were grown men, they would tease him by saying he had changed the motto to read, "Honor they grandfather," he didn't mind and still enjoyed trying to guide them in the direction he thought they should go.

It was Ed whom they loved, honored, and believed from earliest infancy. If he said no or do this or that, the question was settled without argument or hesitation.

There are still times when my now middle-aged sons will remark, Ed would do it this way, or in forming an opinion of someone's workmanship will decide he is a good man, he reminds me of Ed.

Ed's little house now stands in Dick's dooryard serving as a general purpose shop and work room. To him, I am sure it still holds an aura of his beloved partner.

Once, a gray goose adopted him. One of his self-appointed chores was the care and feeding of the poultry. This goose would leave the flock and follow wherever he went even out into the orchards or hay fields, always when he came to the house at mealtime along came Mrs. Goose talking to him all the way. She would take her station by a low window where she could watch the progress of the meal. When Ed left the table, she quickly moved to the door, knowing he would have a slice of bread for her which she ate, bite by bite, from his hand.

Sometimes in the summer, we would entertain groups like the Farmers Union members or the Farmer's Insurance Agents at basket picnics for which tables and benches were set up under the trees in the service yard. At such times, Ed would shut Mrs. Goose in a coop to keep her out of mischief and guard against her becoming a traffic casualty.

This day, as usual, the guests who had come a long distance left for home about five in the afternoon; the nearby members of the group decided to stay for supper and enjoy the evening. This being feeding time for the farm animals, Ed went about his chores and in the process let Mrs. Goose out of her coop and both came to the supper tables.

During the day, a guest of one of the picnicking families had found Ed an interesting person so she settled herself beside him at the table. She was somewhat overweight, dressed in a snug white dress with a floral pattern of big red roses and green leaves. Mrs. Goose had taken her place nearby; after eyeing that luscious-looking red and green design for a while, she decided it was edible, waddled closer, and tried for a bite. A wild shriek startled the assembled diners. When the goose made a second try, the lady screamed again and left the table in great haste. Ed tried to explain that the goose didn't know any better. It was no use; the lady wanted no more of his or his pet's company.

In the end, that bird became so jealous of Ed it was unsafe to work beside him or even stop for a moment's conversation. She would sneak up very quietly, seize a bit of a woman's skirt or a man's pants for anchorage, and beat the offender with her wings. The blows from a goose's wing elbows feel just like hammer strokes and leave the victim black and blue.

As no one in the family wanted that particular goose roasted, Ed gave her to a neighbor who thought she would be such fun to have. In new surroundings and away from Ed, she behaved just like any other goose.

As the children moved along in school, Ed took a deep interest in their progress. A man of little schooling himself, he enjoyed the daily paper, but books did not interest him. I never knew him to write more than his name, but he knew the value of education and would urge the youngsters to get all the schooling they could as it was costing them nothing or at most very little. What they had in their heads was no trouble to carry with them, and no one could take it away from them.

Money as such was of little importance to him. He did not smoke or indulge in liquor, a suit of clothes lasted him almost forever, as for his overalls and work shirts, their cost was not much, and he found real pleasure in mending and patching them.

Although he often joined us on a family excursion to the beach or the mountains, the Fourth of July was his own personal holiday. For this, he would draw a moderate sum against his wages and go away. He never said where he was going nor upon his return, after a few days, where he had been. In the last years of his life, he gave up these trips, saying he was satisfied at home.

When the change was made from horses to tractors and trucks, Ed relinquished much of the work he had been doing so cheerfully and so well. Time was overtaking him, and he was content to busy himself with the lighter tasks. His health began to fail badly, and he accepted the support of a cane.

This was the point where his partnership with a demanding small boy paid off to some degree, for Dick was there always ready to do his bidding, and he in turn did not mind sending his partner about on his few personal needs. Ed was under the care of Dr. Kilbourne Sr., his heart growing weaker day by day, but any mention of hospital care was met with stern resistance. At last a morning came when he said, "Tell Vince I am ready to go to that hospital." There were twenty-four hours under an oxygen tent, and Ed was gone.

We laid him for his eternal sleep in the shadow of a friendly oak tree in the old part of Madronia Cemetery in Saratoga, a resting place I am sure he would have liked had he chosen it himself.

To my knowledge, Ed who had never attended Sunday church services would solemnly declare I am an Episcopalian; I am sure of it because I have always done that which I should not have done and have failed to do that which I should have done. Then with a twinkle in his eyes, he would enjoy a private chuckle and go on with his work leaving his questioner, who should have had better manners and less curiosity, somewhat dumbfounded.

Now when I go to church on a Sunday morning and the congregation repeats the General Confession in unison, I see Ed in memory and am thankful that the Garrods had the privilege of knowing that good old man, Ed Jones.

PEOPLE

The people that came to work at Garrods over the years were many and varied, some I did not learn to know and others I have forgotten, many became valued friends and of others I can only say, "They worked for us one year, remember?"

They came from different parts of the United States and some from foreign countries.

A well-remembered early family was the deGregorios of San Jose, the parents' natives of Sicily, the children first-generation Americans, four boys and one little sister Annie. They came with bedding and provisions and themselves plus a lot of camp gear in a light spring wagon drawn by a small bay horse. They set up camp near the yard, stayed all summer, and made a good job of their share of the harvest work.

This is one of the families that have kept in touch, the third son, Bennie, now an exceptionally good machinist stops by now and then to check on the welfare of the Garrods and give a report on all the deGregorios.

The oldest son, Joe, has long been owner of a metal working shop in the Cottage Grove district of San Jose.

In contrast, there were the Willises who moved into a newly built and partly furnished help house, after about a week, declaring themselves dissatisfied with everything, departed early one morning, taking with them all the cooking utensils and dishes as well as a very good woodstove leaving in its place a burned-out wreck of no use to anyone.

As automobiles became more available, young boys in their late teens would come adventuring, usually two in a stripped-down Ford Model T. Stripped down meant they had two axles, four wheels, the bare chassis members, an engine and steering wheel, a gas tank and a makeshift seat; there was a battery and lights too. In such a contrivance, these kids would travel hundreds of miles, stopping now and then to earn money for food and gas.

Some were excellent workers, especially those with country backgrounds. Ingve Erickson and Charlie Hyleman from Kingsburg, California, stayed on for some months, among other things helping to make the cement blocks and build the P. M. Pike home on its hill above Saratoga.

Another group of three from Missouri, their names I've forgotten, came in one day when help was needed, saying they wanted to work and the butcher in Saratoga had told them if they worked here Mrs. Garrod would feed them. She did. They were good kids and stayed till no longer needed.

There was young Mr. Brown, a student from Berkeley out to gain firsthand information on the hard lot of the agricultural worker so he might write that important paper all college students seem to write before they graduate.

Poor chap; he was sadly out of place and had only a vague idea of what he was researching. There seemed to be no country experience of any kind in his perhaps twenty-two years of life.

The noisy meals in the summer kitchen with their mixture of family, relatives, hired hands, transients, grandparents, and babies all gathered around one long table were an unsolvable puzzle to him; out in the orchard, he could not grasp the idea of staying on his assigned tree or row wandering off looking for easier picking elsewhere, never learning that apricots just never grew on prune trees and green peaches not what he was supposed to gather. As the job was being done on a piecework basis, the poor fellow didn't fare very well financially, but he furnished a great deal of amusement to a young Mexican picker who had been detailed to keep a watchful eye on him. After a week, he went away; whether his paper, if written, met with approval I did not learn. Young Julio had no idea that he was one of the overworked downtrodden humans Mr. Brown had come to write about.

We learned to know Jesse Funderburg, an Arizonan, when he came to help one of his daughters, Josie Barnes and her husband Alex, move into a help house one evening. They came for the apricots in 1943 and stayed almost ten years doing general farmwork. A few days after the daughter settled in, Mr. Funderburg, commonly known as Pappy, came to work in the fruit bringing with him as many of his children as happened to be home. He was the proud father of eight sons and four daughters; several of the sons were at that time in the army. The mother was, I believe, of American Indian lineage, a quiet, much imposed-upon person.

Since their first appearance, seldom a year passed without showing one or more Funderburgs listed among the employees, some good, some not so good.

The parents made their home in the Saratoga community. The young people drifted hither and yon and back again. I had the pleasure of attending their golden wedding, a happy affair with all twelve children present. On being asked to say something in the way of an after-dinner speech, Pappy said, in all the years of their married life, he and Virgie had had only one quarrel which had started on their wedding day and was still going good.

At the time of his death in the spring of 1967, he left eleven living children, one son, Tommy, having preceded him in death, fifty-seven grandchildren, and a goodly number of great-grands.

As friends of Pappy, the Hudson family joined the ranks; they came from Louisiana where they had lived behind the levee while the father, R. J., worked on the highways for Hughie Long. They had six children, four daughters and two sons. Two of these children where what some people call child minded; this state of mind however was not serious enough to keep them from embarking on the matrimonial sea. Three Hudsons married three Funderburgs. These two families are now very much one.

There was "Shug" something or other, a husky seventeen-year-old from Oklahoma, making his way alone. He spent one season with us then dropped from sight until ten years later with a wife and a number of children, identifying him with the statement, "You know me. I'm Shug. I'm the guy that butted his head into the hornet's nest and fell off the ladder." After that explanation, several remembered, and Shug was made welcome to help harvest more apricots.

The Bowers family came one summer with all their children and worldly belongings in a truck and a smaller car. They were literally refugees from the Midwest Dust Bowl. They had really abandoned their farm there unable to face another year of dust and disappointment. Had they stayed near, they would have been excellent neighbors; they chose to make their new home in the San Joaquin Valley, all but one son, "Bud," who married a neighbor's daughter, Jean Clark, and has been employed by Permanente Cement Company ever since.

One of my favorite families was that of Reynoldo Duron. The parents and some of the older children were natives of Mexico, the rest Americans. My introduction to them came one day in 1939 when a young boy rapped on the summer kitchen door and asked for fruit work for his family.

Knowing the cots would be ready in two weeks, I promised him work if they would come back then.

My family was sure they would never be seen again. Other orchards would be ready earlier, and we would be forgotten. Not so; on the appointed day, there they were coming by truck from their temporary home in Gonzales in the Salinas Valley. There were five girls and three boys, the two youngest, a boy and a girl, were mere babies. The oldest boy had been left behind in a hospital because of a traffic injury.

They made camp under some walnut trees and proved to be good and conscientious workers with the exception perhaps of the boy who had asked for the work. Again and again, one heard his patient mother say, "Come Julio—hurry—there is work to do." Julio and work just didn't see eye to eye.

They came back to us year after year; the girls became capable and very attractive young ladies.

The eldest daughter, Christina, married in her early twenties, later held responsible positions as liaison between Spanish workers and non-Spanish-speaking growers. Bertha trained for nursing at St. Joseph's Hospital in San Francisco. I attended her graduation at St. Mary's Cathedral on Van Ness in San Francisco. She passed the State Board exams becoming a full-fledged RN and next entered an Order of Nursing Sisters, is now head surgical nurse in a hospital in Southern California. We correspond, but because of the distance, seldom see her, my little Bertha who always wanted to run and hide from the sight of a cut finger.

Alice worked in the drafting department of the telephone company, Ramona, an office secretary, Ida, a beauty operator. The girls are all married now and raising happy families.

We went to Salinas which became the parent's home, for Alice and Ramona's weddings, also to Mr. and Mrs. Duron's golden one. In turn we had a good representation of the family, both old and young at our own golden anniversary, May 1, 1966.

Some of the grandchildren have spent summer vacations with us working in the fruit. A wonderful family we are very fond of them and proud to call them friends.

Another family stemming from old Mexico is the Gonzales. Mr. Gonzales says that way, way back, they were Aztec Indians; they are all small of stature and very good workers.

They first came through the agricultural employment office, the father, two sons, and a friend to pick prunes. They were from Los Angeles; our hills pleased them. The father said they were just like the hills where he lived as a child.

The next year due to World War II, help was very difficult to find. Young Vince had been struggling along with some most unsatisfactory Oklahomans, Messrs. Shrum and Couch and their equally undependable wives. Following some hasty correspondence, he took a truck to Los Angeles and brought back the Gonzales family, bag and baggage, minus one daughter who worked in someone's office and wanted to keep her job. They set up housekeeping in the then empty Finley house, stayed through the apricot and prune harvest, and returned to Los Angeles as they had come via the Garrod truck, promising to return the next year, which they did.

By the following summer, the older boys in the family—there were eight boys and three girls—had acquired a used pickup truck so part of them came in that, the rest in the truck as before, plus a big police dog named Lobo and a pet quail which used to ride about on the dog's head or shoulders. Seems to me there was a pet jack rabbit too.

The youngsters, down to the smallest toddler, were all willing and anxious to work. Having been here previous years, they knew how to take advantage of every opportunity and wasted no time doing so. After the apricots, they went to the valley to pick pears; finding cull pears could be had for nothing, they brought home pickup loads for the mother and girls to cut and dry using Garrod trays and sulfur on a share basis. They also harvested a field of potatoes which the owner could not market because of some weed which sent its wirelike roots into the potatoes. With a little trimming, they were edible and of good flavor. The owner of the field plowed them up glad to have someone willing to haul them away. We had an abundance of potatoes that winter.

After taking care of the Garrod prunes, they picked grapes for nearby neighbors. The mother and small children gleaned the orchard for overlooked prunes finding enough for their winter use; the children also gathered armloads of good corn husks for Christmas tamales.

It was a happy family that left us that fall with several thousand dollars in earnings and a truckload of goodies for the winter pantry, even a small keg of wine given by the man whose grapes they picked.

They paid off the debt on the house they lived in, put it up for rent, moving into a bigger and better one. We learn that they are now all more or less involved in nurseries, landscape gardening in Hollywood, and flower shops in Los Angeles. Several of the boys have been back to introduce their wives or show off their children, the third daughter, Rose Virginia, writes to us every Christmas.

It is people such as these who restore one's faith in humanity; just a little of the spirit of "I can do it myself" goes so much farther than the cry of "give me, give me."

The story of their start in flowers and gardens shows the same spirit of self-reliance.

One year our son, through the blandishments of a very black, very personable labor contractor who wasn't as honest as he looked, tried to harvest the fruit with colored help; unfortunately, these people knew nothing of country living or fruit work. It was a most frustrating season.

And the summer of the secretaries! During World War II, the papers had much to say about the shortage of agricultural labor, and a drive was started in San Francisco to encourage office workers to spend their weekends in the country to help save the crops. R. V. was invited to address groups to explain just what was needed to help the poor farmer. Willing as always to help a good cause, he made such weekends look ever so attractive.

The result was numbers of young women arriving Friday evening all set for a pleasant and entertaining stay, beds had to be found for them and space to prepare their own meals if they wished, or a place at the family table if they didn't.

At that time, it was disconcerting to say the least to have a young lady appear for work dressed in white short shorts and bra. The sun was of course too hot or the breeze too cold calling for frequent changes of her station at the trays to the great exasperation of an already rushed shed man. And the nasty little black gnats, "the no see ems" which plague us every year had a ball.

These young women meant well and some continued to come to work in the prunes; here they soon learned that it was much pleasanter to pick prunes on the shady side of the tree, and some patient Mexican kid would have to be sent to pick the sunny side.

Young Vince scolded about half-filled boxes and boxes hidden in unhandy places, but in the end most of the prunes were picked and delivered to the dehydrator.

The last people who came to offer help were a middle-aged couple from San Francisco, determined to do their bit. I tried to discourage them, but they wouldn't listen. The man expressed some rather strong convictions about misrepresentations and the ingratitude of farmers in particular so I said OK; you can go pick prunes if you like.

They wished to dine first as it was almost midday, would I kindly direct them to the nearest restaurant. I explained that restaurants just weren't nearby and made room for them at the table.

They went off to work in our nearest orchard in the company of Alice and Bertha Duron who were house guests and prune pickers that year.

When the man found that prunes must be picked up off the ground, he returned to the house sadly disillusioned and spent the rest of the afternoon on the fruit house platform learning of the trials and tribulations of the fruit farmer from R. V.

Well, not quite all afternoon. That was the day I heard a strange flutter-flutter from my station at the kitchen sink and realized an unsupervised fire was making its way through fallen leaves and trash onto Garrod land from Barney Levy's dipping kettle just across the line fence.

There's nothing like a fire to shatter the peace and quiet of a summer afternoon. After much running about dragging out hoses and telephoning, the Saratoga Fire Department came to our aid. The fire was soon taken care of with little harm done. After sharing our supper, the strangers returned to their city home. That evening, Bertha said, "That lady would never learn to pick prunes. She was afraid to get her hands dirty."

It was a very interesting, sometimes entertaining, and often aggravating procession of people that came and went year after year, like the Oklahomans who said Garrod was the only man they had ever worked for who set his land up on edge so he could plant both sides of it. These men were very tall, all inches over six feet and very slender, excellent cot pickers, having little need of ladders.

Then there was the lumber man from Boulder Creek whose wife and older daughter indulged in hip-reducing exercises, rolling back and forth on the hillside while the man and the younger fourteen-year-old daughter picked up the prunes.

Frank Noda, a young Japanese veteran, spent an arduous summer redesigning and rebuilding the farm machinery as well as helping bale the hay and take care of the fruit. Frank is now in charge of the agricultural holdings and processing plants of Spice Islands at Dixon, California.

Through a good friend, Mr. N. M. Parsons of Oakdale, contact was made with two families: Bill Schlapkohl, his wife Minnie, and four children; and Otto (last name forgotten), his wife Louise, and one little boy. This group too, came by means of the Garrod truck, good people to have around; Otto and his family soon moved on to the shipyards as he was an experienced mechanic. The others stayed until winter. Minnie saved things, as she put it, before someone took them, like the oranges from my garden, the apples on a special tree, or the eggs the hens had laid in the horses' mangers.

Sylman Manners and his strangely assorted family were something of a problem. He could not or would not stay away from liquor, came home late at night, and sometimes beat his womenfolk. Their stay was short; when they left, he knew he was doing so in disgrace; however, sometime later, R. V. met someone who had also employed them. This man reported that Sylman said, "Garrod was a good old boy, the best he had ever worked for."

Pas Cendijos, an Arizona Mexican with his little wife Annie and baby daughter Linda, came to thin apricots one spring; when they moved away again, there were six little Cendijos. As Pas was a good cement finisher, there are several cement jobs like the garage floor and the one in the cutting shed to testify to his efficiency.

Through his friendship with Pas, we added Nick Orloff, an elderly Russian. A retired fruit worker, he settled in a small house, stayed several years, and became a self-appointed watchman for the yard. He now lives in San Jose very well taken care of by state aid.

The story of these people could go on endlessly. To list them all would count into the hundreds.

By the time the years brought the grandchildren into the working ranks, autos were common and workers came from their homes every day and with subdivisions nearby in the valley often groups of young people were called for every morning and returned to their homes in the evening by some member of the family.

An apricot shed was still an apricot shed. Some of these youngsters were a joy to know; for others, we were just good-natured babysitters.

This era also brought in the portable radio. I declare we worked one whole season to the tune of "The freight train goes slow, goes slow," the work kept time to the music, slow, so slow.

It did no good to turn the radio off, in a gang of thirty or forty young people. There was always some busy little elf that turned it right on again.

Vince, Dick, and Louise

On the beach with Ed

HITCHHIKERS

When the Garrods made the change from horses for transportation to motor-driven vehicles, their first purchase was a Ford Model T for six hundred and some odd dollars.

Being able to go farther faster soon involved R. V. in contact work for various causes and enterprises; this in turn drew him into the newly organized Farmers Insurance Exchange, the name has since been changed to Farmers Insurance Group. It is now one of the strongest reciprocal insurance companies in the United States. Vince has been and still is president of their Board of Governors. This work took all his time and interest and the monetary return was of the greatest help.

This was also the era of the hitchhiker. The dictionary says to hitchhike is to travel by begging rides in stranger's automobiles; that is still correct, but in those early days no one questioned the honesty or good intentions of these roadside suppliants. Most often they were men with their blanket rolls on their shoulders really trying to reach some other part of the country in the hope of employment, or boys in their teens farther from home than they should be, out to see the world.

R. V., being a sympathetic person, would pick them up and carry them on their way, often driving many miles out of his way to take them nearer their chosen destination. At other times, he would bring them home promising food and employment.

Among the first was a teenager from New England, Lester Yurich. Lester, unlike most, was not penniless. He had money coming from home. Unfortunately, Fourth of July was a long weekend holiday that year, and he could not claim his money till Tuesday; he was hungry, having lived on fruit from roadside orchards for two days.

R. V. was headed in the opposite direction but changed his course and brought him within easy walking distance of the ranch, gave him a note to me which said, "Feed this boy and put him to work." Lester stayed with us and others in the community for over a year, unused to farmwork but very willing to learn.

When not at work, liking athletics he took part in boxing tournaments, holding membership in the Golden Gloves.

Letters have been exchanged over the years and several short visits enjoyed when the Yurich family have flown out to the West Coast on business or vacation. His business is in the building field; his hobby is still boxing and has patented a guard to protect the face and head of young amateurs.

Another nice youngster was Loris Roed from the Middle West. Vince overtook him one day marching down the road from Sacramento bound for Campbell where he had relatives. He was handy at many things and liked carpentry and cement work. There are still a motor bed and a cement culvert head in the yard to testify to his industriousness. Shortly after his arrival, he purchased a very secondhand Ford Coupe for the sum total of twenty-five dollars. He and our youngest, son both enthusiastic hunters, had great fun together. They conceived the idea of building a boat and going after ducks in the Alviso sloughs. The boat was a flat-bottomed contrivance of old redwood lumber and makeshift paddles; this they tied on top of the Coupe and took off in great glee. They returned with a collection of funny-looking birds which they dressed and asked me to cook. I did the best I could with them; they were the worst ever, quite inedible. Why some game warden didn't confiscate the lot—boat, birds and boys—I will never know.

Loris enjoyed his winter with us; several years later, he stopped while on his honeymoon to introduce his bride and since has never missed sending a card or letter at Christmas.

There were also men in real need of work. This was before welfare held such a high place in the lives of our indigent citizens. Often whatever type of work R. V. mentioned in the course of conversation that was the very thing his passenger was proficient in. Like one elderly man who came to thin apricots. He did not know an apricot tree from any other nor know the meaning of the word "thin" as applied to fruit. He was, however, eager to please and other workers lent him help. I am sure he needed employment desperately. I learned that by profession, he was an upholsterer. I hired him to redo the living room couch; he did an excellent job and was just as pleased with his work as I.

Late one evening, Vince brought home three dirty, neglected-looking, young fellows he had seen by the roadside and felt sorry for. I found them some supper then handed them soap and towels and headed them for the bathroom while I made up beds. Next morning, after a good breakfast, they looked over the surroundings. Soon the spokesman for the trio announced that they had no desire to do ranch work and asked which way was San Francisco. On being told it was fifty miles north, they walked away to look for the next easy mark with an automobile.

Then there was the man who said he was a cook. He was brought on the theory he would take over the kitchen, leaving me free to

Louise and Vince waiting for a ride

spend more time in the cutting shed which that season was buzzing like a beehive. That poor soul was no more a cook than I am an astronaut.

After the first meal, my children began to ask, "Mom, do we have to eat this?" The out-of-family ones wanted to know, "How long do you have to keep him? Aren't you ever going to do the cooking again?" Ed sized him up as a "hop head"—drug addict.

One youngster was sure he had seen the cigarette ashes drop into the stew. Fortunately, it wasn't long before he asked for time off, saying the work was pretty hard, intimating he needed a helper. I paid him what Vince had promised and advised him to find work more to his liking. I heaved a sigh of relief when he disappeared across the bridge, returned to the kitchen, scrubbed up some pots and pans, and prepared dinner for a jubilant gang of fruit workers.

There were others, but the memory of their coming and going has faded. There seems no point in trying to revive it.

Now the habit of picking up strangers on the highways, and carrying them toward their destination is not always a safe thing to do and sometimes ends in disaster.

Good Samaritans beware!

EDUCATION

In September 1923, my little daughter ventured out on her first day of school; Saratoga had no kindergarten at that time, little people stepped right into first grade and got along nicely there. Our nearby community had, by cooperation and determination, established school bus service for children in this part of the district the year before. Louise had only to go as far as her grandmother's house to reach the bus.

The main building at the present Saratoga School on Oak Street had been built that summer. Louise was a member of the first first-grade class to begin its school life in that building. Mr. Robertson was the principal that year, and Miss Gladys Hooker who became Mrs. Mills Pash, was first—and second-grade teacher.

Some of her classmates were Herman Deurell, Wayne Atkinson, Fred Bartlome, Margaret Kent, Joan deHaviland, Evelyn Stamper, and "Billie" Young.

There was an active PTA, and I soon joined its ranks; this helped me to become acquainted with the teachers as well as other mothers.

The following year saw young Vince enrolled. Mrs. Bertha Seely became principal, a position she held for many years, and I was elected secretary of the PTA.

In 1925, my youngest son Richard ("Dick") entered the first grade, really too young according to school laws and regulations, but the district needed one more child in the class to be able to have a first-grade teacher. Having entered the first grade myself at four and a half, I agreed that Dick should be that one needed child.

These were the years when the PTAs really worked for their schools, like buying curtains for the windows in the principal's office or some needed article for a classroom. In Saratoga, the PTA managed the children's lunchroom.

In this new building, a lunchroom had been arranged for in the basement; there were tables and stools for the children, a gas stove, refrigerator, sink, and counter for food preparation. The children paid a nominal sum for the food; I believe the sum total covered the supplies purchased and compensation for the women who took over the job of preparing the food. There was certainly never enough in the treasury to meet any set monthly bill. The cook lady was supposed to have daily volunteer help from the mothers. Often this expected help failed to report; on the whole a very unsatisfactory setup.

I became president of the PTA for the 1925-26 year. In making my plans for that coming term of office, I knew it would be impossible for me to give the needed time and supervision to that lunchroom. I had also learned that many school boards throughout the county were incorporating the management of a lunchroom in the school budget just as they would meet the addition of another classroom and finding it worked out well. I thought to myself, "Why not do the same in Saratoga?"

Mrs. J. A. Emerich was a member of the school board. She was also Saratoga's librarian and a very understanding lady. I took my problem to her. She thought such a move might be the solution and promised to present the idea to the board at their next meeting. Whether others on the board knew of this trend I do not know, but to my delight by September a school managed lunchroom was an established fact.

Little incidents like once appointing a committee of two, choosing two young women known to be bosom pals and on the day for their report learning they had had a slam bang fight and weren't speaking, were, to say the least, embarrassing, but one lives and learns.

A community like Saratoga should not have had children who were driven to plundering other children's lunch boxes because they were hungry; unfortunately, a few such children did exist.

Learning that the town's share of the United Fund was giving aid to the Boy Scouts and like groups, I made the suggestion that the United Fund extend its good work so far as to make it possible for the teachers to single out the needy children and the Fund allot the necessary amount to the lunchroom to take care of them. I am glad to remember that this was done; there were no more rifled lunch boxes, and the teachers reported schoolwork improved as well.

The next year, there was dissatisfaction in the school. Some people liked and some didn't like some of the trustees. I never did get the strait of it. Mrs. Paul Nerell was president at the time. At one of the monthly meetings it was moved, voted, and carried the PTA should support Mrs. C. Kennedy, a very estimable lady, for a place on the school board.

To take part in an election, local or otherwise, is about the worst mistake a PTA can make. The fact that the mistake had been made became known at once, and the entire board of dignified grown-up men, their names I cannot recall, resigned! "Those women could just forget about trying to tell them how to run the school; furthermore, they would see that the PTA was abolished or know the reason why."

The president of Paradiso Council, Mrs. Alexander, presided at a meeting to arbitrate the difficulty. The County Superintendent of Schools did all he could to smooth matters.

The disturbance died of its own accord as such things usually do. The men returned to their nonpaying jobs on the school board and continued to administer a school that both pupils and parents were proud of.

When that year's PTA nominating committee, which had been appointed before the fuss began, tried to find candidates for the coming year's officers, they met with complete indifference. As a last resort, they centered on me, because I had had a year's experience, knew everyone, etc., and easy me took the job.

The charming little lady, a Mrs. Smith, who had been most persistent in her efforts to persuade me, promised oh so sincerely that she would attend the meetings and support the organization in every way possible. As I might have known, at all future meetings, the lady was very conspicuous by her absence. The monthly attendance dropped to eight or nine; enthusiasm was unknown, but the PTA stayed alive and is still active in the Saratoga schools.

The year Louise graduated from the eighth grade, the ritual of the graduates marching to their places under the flower-decked arches held by the seventh graders was established and is still being used. It has progressed from fresh flowers which were sometimes hard to come by and often faded by evening, to artificial flowers which always look fresh and can be used again and again. A very pretty custom.

As my children moved on to Los Gatos High School, I lost interest in the Saratoga PTA and no longer attended the meetings. I was very surprised one day when a pleasant voice on the telephone asked me to be sure and attend that month's meeting. As refreshments were to be prepared would I please bring cream for the coffee, the request struck me as odd, as it seemed to be important to the speaker. I told her I would be happy to bring cream.

Imagine my surprise to learn the cream was just a ruse to assure my presence. The members had chosen me to be the first person in the history of Saratoga PTA to be presented with a life membership.

I was pleased, of course, and rendered quite speechless. I managed a few stumbling words of appreciation and thanks; everyone seemed pleased, perhaps as much with themselves as with me.

By the time Louise graduated from grammar school, I had taught her all I knew about driving a car. We had a canvas topped Buick touring car then. One of the most difficult things I ever did was to let my little fourteen-year-old daughter take that car to Saratoga all by herself.

When we bought our first car, I think it was in 1920; all one had to do was write to the Motor Vehicle Department in Sacramento requesting a license and giving some data as to the name and address of yourself and make and type of car and a license was sent you by mail. Although I never learned to drive that Ford, I always had a license.

In 1931, when Louise got her license, a little more attention was being given. I went with her to the office of a Highway Patrol officer, John Sansone. He asked her a few questions, turned to me, and asked whether I thought she should have one. I explained that if she was to attend high school, she must take herself. He then cautioned her always to be careful when approaching Austin corner at the beginning of Quito Road and that was that. She had her first license and has been driving ever since.

The boys took to driving at fourteen as naturally as they had learned to walk.

As a license was of little use without a car to drive, we bought a Ford roadster to serve as school transportation. It was painted bright yellow, and the kids loved it. The roadster had a rumble seat so five, even six, could ride in it comfortably. Soon she was carrying neighbor's children to and from school every day.

It was the practice then for high school districts to budget money to help pay the transportation of students having to travel five or more miles to school. From our neighborhood to Los Gatos High was ten and a fraction miles, so these youngsters were all eligible for this help. These allotments took care of the gas, tires, and general upkeep of the yellow Ford and its successor, a black model B during the six and a half years of high school.

Some of the passengers were Frank and Betty Bradley, Caroline and Marie Bonnet, Phil Olavarri and his sisters, Nancy Johnson, Helen Brussi, Barbara Bowie, Mary Dodge, and perhaps a few more.

Looking back, it seems the children were no sooner enrolled in high school than the four years were past and one, two, three they graduated.

There had been no PTA in Los Gatos High while Mr. Ayers was principal. In 1931 when Mr. Prentis Brown took charge, he was more receptive to the idea, and the officers of Paradiso Council organized a PTA unit there which still functions. I was present at the organizational meeting. The plan decided on was to hold their monthly meetings evenings, this made it difficult for me to attend regularly.

In her senior year, Louise served as president of the Girl's League. Vince Jr. was an orchestra member all his four years, and Dick's extracurricular interest lay in biology trips. Neither of my sons broke any athletic records.

After high school, Louise chose University of California at Berkeley as her college, living for the first year in a boardinghouse, after that in apartments with other girls which was better, graduating in 1939 with a Bachelor of Science degree.

Young Vince attended California Polytechnic College at San Luis Obispo for two years then to Berkeley for two, graduating as an Agricultural Economist.

When Dick finished high school, World War II was in progress. The draft boards were watching all young men. With his brother nearly through college and not eligible for the draft, the board agreed to let him stay and farm until his brother graduated. On August 12, 1942, he boarded a bus bound for the Monterey induction center, remaining in the service until December 1945.

School Transportation
To Shf—1-16-67

We have all read and been told stories of children going to school, walking long miles through sleet and snow or terrible summer heat for unbelievable distances; after all, it takes twenty minutes to walk a mile under favorable and pleasant conditions; I sometimes wonder whether memory has been as reliable as one's memory is supposed to be.

I can personally vouch for the fact that at the age of four years and six months, I walked a mile and a half to and from school, night and morning to a newly established school on the summit of the Santa Cruz Mountains. Our way to school at that time followed very closely what is now known as the Skyline Boulevard.

The way led through open fields and shady woods where all the neighborhood cows and horses were allowed to roam. We children gave the animals little thought but our young lady teacher, new to both country life and school teaching was terrified, if the gentlest old Bossy lifted her head and looked our way. As for me, nothing could have pleased me more than that daily jaunt, rain or shine, to and from school.

The year before this school, Central was established; my parents had tried to send my older sister, then six years old, to Lakeside, the nearest established school; this meant a daily journey of about six miles each way.

For this, my father secured a gentle little Palomino called Joe for her to ride. This was fine in theory, but when Joe decided he had gone far enough along that lonely road, he would turn about and carry his little rider home again, so this effort toward education had to be abandoned.

The next step was the establishment of Central School District, which functioned for nearly eighty years and has now become part of Lakeside.

Now to come to Saratoga; let me say, as compared to the life of Saratoga School which I believe is something over a hundred years, I am a newcomer; my personal knowledge runs back only about fifty years.

In that time, I am sure the school has undergone many more changes than it ever dreamed of in its first fifty.

When the Board of Directors of this organization decided on using the past years of Saratoga School as the subject for the program of the January membership meeting, I said, "I'll tell them about the buses." That's why you are stuck with having to listen to me. Now I will try to concentrate on transportation and the story of the first school bus way back in 1922.

At that time, most of the children walked to school; the school district was not as big then as it is now. A mile was about the greatest distance any youngster had to go, and even very young first graders could go that far, usually there were somewhat older children going the same way willing to lend them company.

If an older child drove or rode a horse to school, he or she was no doubt allowed to keep the horse for the day under the horse shed, on the grounds of the Congregational Church which joined the yard of the only school in Saratoga School District located then as now on the same spot on Oak Street.

Failing the privilege of the use of the church shed, the horse was tied to any handy tree or fence.

About the time that I became school conscious because our children were fast approaching school age was also the time that there was a movement among Santa Clara County Schools to unite groups of small country districts into larger units. This was to give the children better housing, better teachers, more books; in fact all the arguments you heard then you hear now in favor of unification. As far as I know, it worked then, why not now?

The people on Pierce and Mt. Eden Roads had, geographically, always been part of the Lincoln District with the schoolhouse at the corner of Prospect and Sunnyvale Road, but the children of this section had always attended Saratoga School. Saratoga also gave these people their post office, business center, churches, and lodges.

So when it was put to a vote, whether or not all of Lincoln District should be annexed to Cupertino, these hill people voted to go into Saratoga and have been there ever since.

The children from this section had always gotten to school somehow, either by horse-drawn cart or wagon, driven by an older child or an adult member of the family, along the same roads we know now, or they walked, making their way down one mountain, up and over the next and up again to the schoolhouse.

Often these youngsters took shortcuts through neighboring fields or orchards, these same shortcuts were often longer than the approved path but far more interesting. If someone's dog happened to be attending school that day and stopped en route to settle some disagreement with a stray skunk, he was most likely forbidden admission to the schoolroom, and perhaps his master suffered the same fate.

Just before I joined the community, a young family on the Mt. Eden Road sold their property and moved away, because they could see no possible way of getting their two small children to school. That solution did not appeal to the more pioneering spirit of those who remained.

By 1921, there were a number of little people about ready for the first grade, kindergarten was unheard of, all living in the farthest corner of the district on Mt. Eden Road.

There were consultations and meetings led by Hines, Bonnett, and Garrod; a new district was considered, but the idea was given up as not practical in view of all the uniting being done. Local cooperative transportation was decided on.

There were three older children in the Crader family living near the corner of Mt. Eden and Pierce Roads. They had a horse and wagon and every day they picked up the children next door and drove to the railroad crossing at Azule Station on the Sunnyvale Road, tied their horse to a handy prune tree in a nearby orchard, boarded the Interurban Electric Car as it came from Palo Alto, made the transfer onto Saratoga Avenue at Congress Junction and proceeded to where the Plaza is now and from there walked up to the school on Oak Street; the school is now and always has been in that same location. In the afternoon, the same trip was taken in reverse.

The interesting point in all this was the information offered by the Craders, that the school trustees subsidized this performance to the amount of $2.20 a month per child which covered the fare on the electric cars.

As everyone knows any new enterprise and most old ones need finances, so a committee was formed to interview the trustees in an effort to persuade them to transfer that $2.20 per month per child from the railroad to the prospective bus line. The first interview was not successful; in truth they were given the "Merry Ha-Ha." One member of the board whose school days had been spent within a stone's throw of the schoolhouse stated that he had always had to walk to school and other people's kids could jolly well do the same.

However, the hill people were a tenacious lot and finally got the promise of the $2.20 per child per month. Next, the committee set up a schedule for the prospective patrons of the line.

The greater distance a child would ride, the higher the charge. I am not clear on the various rates; I have some recollection of the family living nearest to the Sunnyvale Road paying one dollar a month per child—they had two boys—those at the far end of the Mt. Eden Road either two and a half or three dollars.

Now being sure of some money to meet running expenses of a car, gas, tires, etc., and some compensation for the driver, all they needed was a car, someone to drive it, and the school term to start, and the Pierce Mt. Eden bus line would be in business.

Mr. Hines came forward with the offer of his car and his sixteen-year-old son, Wesley, to drive it night and morning.

The car was a canvas-topped, eight-passenger Kissel touring car; if it rained there were plastic side curtains to be buttoned into place. Though designed for eight passengers, there were usually more to be carried, so the big kids held the little kids on their laps.

The time schedule wasn't too good, depending somewhat on the need of the car or the driver in the Hines household. Most of the time the children were delivered at school by nine o'clock.

When Wesley Hine found a full-time job, Mrs. Severence, wishing to buy a car for herself and figuring that the compensation would make the monthly payments, took over the responsibility and did well with it. Her car was always badly overcrowded, so Mr. Bonnett found someone who would gladly drive a second car if assured of enough money to make the monthly payments on a Ford Model T.

As long as Mrs. Gough drove everything was fine, but sometimes her husband took her place. He unfortunately had some cronies in Saratoga with whom he would loiter, till reminded to take his charges home. One evening he missed the entrance to the Pierce Road, tried for the next driveway, hit a pepper tree, and one little girl went head first through the windshield. Luckily, she was not seriously hurt and suffered no scars. On that day, the second car on the bus line idea was abandoned.

The next step was a deal with Mr. Burt Varner of the Varner & Ruddell Garage of Saratoga to take the job, furnish the car, and keep it running and do the driving—all this for $75 a month.

Varner and Ruddell kept the line going for some years. Finding old passenger cars unsatisfactory, they changed to a small bus. Somewhere on the outskirts of San Jose, there was an amusement place known as Luna Park. The small buses servicing this part of San Jose had their destination painted on the side; it was one of these which became school transportation.

The early riders, now graying men and women, tell me this bus was a Reo. This was a great improvement over the cars in use before, the children were all delighted.

The garage owners would relieve each other on the driving, but Mr. Varner was the official busman; he was also something of a disciplinarian. When the boys got too rambunctious, he would carry them to within a reasonable distance of their homes, there set them afoot so they had to walk the rest of the way. Among others, my irrepressible youngest son was left to climb that last long hill on his own two feet more than once.

Finally, despite all the good work done at the garage to keep the Reo, on the road, the poor thing got tired. One day with all the Mt. Eden Roaders aboard, fortunately not on the steepest part of the hill, that bus began to disintegrate; all the mechanical parts tumbled to the road, drive shaft, transmission, engine, the whole works, just like some comic strip. The kids of course enjoyed it immensely.

So Varner and Ruddell bought another somewhat bigger and better Luna Park bus. These vehicles were both of the type where the seats were long benches on either side parallel to the body of the bus.

This brings us, if I am right, to September 1931 when the officers of the bus line were informed by Mr. Varner that the school district was taking over the bus. Because there had been so much pressure brought to bear by people living in other outlying districts for transportation for their children, the trustees had finally agreed to do something about it. So they assumed the responsibility for the Pierce-Mt. Eden route and also sent the bus up Big Basin Way as far as Long Bridge, now Fisher's Resort, to take care of the former Booker District children.

That was fine, and everyone was pleased; although the schedule was somewhat revised, and for a while the Mt. Eden children had to walk to the foot of the hill to catch the bus in the morning and walk home from there in the afternoon. No one complained. Till one day, the Highway Patrol came along and said to the school authorities, "This bus is not safe and not legal. It does not measure up to the required specifications you must have a vehicle with seats crosswise and an aisle in the middle and only two passengers to a seat." It was then that the Saratoga School purchased its first yellow bus.

When young Vince graduated from the eighth grade in 1932, there was one school building in the district, the one on Oak Street. This building housed all eight classes. Some teachers taught two grades on one room, like first and second, third, and fourth, etc. There were then one hundred and twenty-seven pupils in the school, six teachers, and the graduates numbered twelve.

Now there are five separate school buildings: Saratoga, Redwood, Foothill, Argonaut, and Congress Springs, with a total of 97 teachers and 2,956 students. The district owns 6 big yellow buses with a capacity of 70 passengers each and leases 4 more the same size. This gives them 8 active every day and 2 standing by ready to take care of any emergency that may arise.

They carry 1,600 children to and from school every day, gathering them from all parts of the district and in the process they travel 549 miles every day and cost the district $66,000 a year.

By law, they must carry all children from the first through the third grade who live more than three-fourths of a mile from school. Older children can be expected to walk as far as one mile.

For safety, the trustees keep the buses off difficult and unpaved roads, as well as any with more than 18 percent grade. The bus drivers, some of them are also on the teaching staff, are chosen for both ability and reliability.

Mrs. Isabel Priest Mavio, now Mrs. Richard Marquez, was an exceptionally good driver. She drove the Pierce-Mt. Eden route, which is known as the most difficult in the district, for twenty years without mishap and a record of low overhaul bills.

We had a neighbor for many years who had a delightful way with words. This is what he said about the yellow bus.

CARGO OF THE YELLOW BUS

Precious cargo of the yellow bus,
    Children of the neighbors, near and far;
    Does the busy driver know they are
Dearest of the very dear to us?

Rough, impatient, noisy boys they seem,
    Shy girls budding in their awkward way,
    Each the pattern of the modern day,
Each the treasure of an ancient dream.

Here are still Gone Ages living now;
    Nectar from the valiant Past gives tongue
    To the eager beings of the young,
Waiting thus the future to endow.

We say good-bye. Deep from our deepest heart
    Pray them happy—home again unhurt.
    Love's most sturdy angels stand alert,
Guard the yellow bus about to start.

E. L. Poor

WATER

Water, next to air is, I believe, nature's most wonderful gift to all living things on this earth—be they animal or vegetable.

The search for water in the surrounding hills has been never ending and very disappointing.

The story of water on the Garrod ranch must go back to the time of the family's arrival in the spring of 1893. At that time, so I've been told, there was a small stream on the surface of the ground flowing southward about where the workshop now stands. This stream was led into a wooden gutter, which emptied into a half barrel from which it was dipped into a bucket and carried to the house or wherever it was needed. As time passed, this little stream became a trickle, then vanished completely.

The Garrods' first effort toward a new and better supply was a well just north of the sugar gum. Terrance Murphy, a neighbor, did the work. At twenty-five feet, what appeared to be a generous stream of water was uncovered, and the well was cribbed or lined with new redwood lumber. This was a poor choice, for fresh-cut redwood, still loaded with sap, will taint a water supply for a long time before all the sap and coloring matter is leached out. Otherwise, this well was fine for a number of years. Then the flow became less and less till there was no more.

Hydro-engineers say that the water in these hills is gathered by gravity into underground gravel pockets, walled in by masses of nonporous clay. When such a pocket is tapped by a well or other means, the stored supply lasts only for a limited time. In our case, ten years use invariably brought us to the point where something else had to be done.

For the second try, they went back to the course of the original little water run. There John Prutton dug a pit about fifteen feet square and ten feet deep, which gave promise of enough water for everyday use. The sides were lined with concrete, the top covered, and a windmill installed, which Vince bought from a Scotchman name of Graham who farmed on the northeast corner of Highway Eighty-five and Cox Avenue for $25. The windmill had either been blown down during a storm or toppled by the 1906 earthquake.

True to form, this supply gave out, and someone whose name is forgotten dug a well about twenty feet deep through the bottom of the pit and again reached water. Three-thousand clinker bricks were used to line it.

The water was now down too far for the windmill suction pump, so a small gas engine and force pump were installed. This pushed the water into a tank on the hill west of the house from which it flowed down to the house and yard. This was the setup when I joined the family. Right on schedule, this well began to give less and less every time the pump was started.

The next try was a well at the edge of a spot west of the barn that was spoken of as "the swamp." It stayed wet late into spring and always slowed down cultivation in that part of the orchard.

Charlie Laird of Saratoga dug this one, when down twenty-five feet the water rushed in and overflowed. Everyone thought the long looked-for source had at last been located. But to be doubly sure, with a well man ready to do the work, another thirty-two-foot well was sunk at the other end of that wet spot. Laird bricked both, a windmill was installed over the first and some other type of pump on the second. The story was the same; both wells began to fail in the usual time.

Someone volunteered to witch the place and find a location for a well that would never fail. None of the family felt any confidence in the chosen spot; it was above the yard in what the folks called "Gold Gulch" and is now covered by the upper dam.

R. V. decided to give it a try. He engaged Bill Williams, a native Saratogan and an excellent well man, to come and with the help of Ed Jones dug a well in the chosen spot.

They went down to a depth of seventy-five feet, a standard well about three feet in diameter. The soil was just as dry there as it had been on the surface. To be sure, beyond any shadow of doubt, with a miner's drill and pipe extensions, they bored twenty-five feet deeper, all to no avail.

Casting about for another location, R. V. decided on a spot on the line of that first little surface stream, at a lower elevation. In fact, the chosen starting point was about level with the bottom of the well which had gone dry years before. This placed the work just over the bank from the summer kitchen and gave me the opportunity to watch the progress of the work and be a busy sidewalk engineer.

The men who undertook these well digging jobs were in a class by themselves. The work was hard and dangerous, not to be undertaken by anyone just because he could use a pick and shovel. A well digger will cheerfully tell you that his business is the only one in which a man always starts at the top.

Work began on what became known as the summer kitchen well. Early one morning, Bill Williams and Ed Jones slid the needed tools and lumber over the bank, scrambled after it, and were ready to go. The important items were a good pick and shovel, their handles sawed off at the halfway point, several very heavy metal buckets of about twenty-five gallons or half a barrel capacity with equally heavy handles with loops at the top so there was no danger of slips or wobbles while being hauled up or let down. A plumb bob and line were part of the gear, for a well that wasn't plumb was considered no well at all. Lumber to build supports for a windlass which would be needed as the work went along, a pulley block and a long rope, in this case the three-quarter-inch manila rope on the Jackson fork used in the barn when the hay was being brought in.

After they had cleared away the dry leaves and twigs, Bill looked up and down the gully, considered the California laurel just above him and the oak trees nearby, turned to Ed and remarked, "This is a H—of a place to dig a well, but if Vince wants it here, here we put it." So he began to dig from under his feet a circle three and a half or perhaps four feet in diameter throwing the loosened dirt aside as he dug, while Ed went about other preparations, building the windlass, etc.

When the hole Bill was digging got too deep to throw the dirt over the side, a bucket was let down, Bill would fill it with dirt, with the help of the pulley Ed would bring it to the top, swing it to one side, dump it, and return the empty bucket to Bill. This went on day after day. When the pull became more than Ed could manage by hand, he brought black Dolly from the barn, fixed a little path for her to follow, and hitched her to the end of the rope. She would go ahead to bring the bucket up and patiently walk backward to let it down again. Sometimes, out of school hours, one of the boys would lead Dolly out and urge her back again. Most of the time, she did it by herself.

As the well deepened, lumber in about six foot lengths was used as cribbing. In this work, there is always danger of a cave in which must be guarded against. To hold this cribbing circular iron bands were nailed in place; these bands were usually discarded wagon wheel tires which were cut so that they could be stretched or tightened depending on the size wanted.

As Bill went about his work, he traveled up and down by means of the buckets. The man working the bottom of the well needed to know that there was a good man at the top, for any carelessness on his part could mean disaster for the man on the bottom; working in such a small space, he could not dodge even the smallest article falling from above.

They finally reached a depth of eighty feet; there Bill struck some rock too hard to break with his pick. He decided to use dynamite to break it into movable chunks. He did the drilling, placed the dynamite and fuse, came up and persuaded young Vince, then twelve years old and not very heavy, to ride the bucket down and light that fuse, which he did. Needless to say, I was not consulted. He says now if he had known what it would feel like down at the bottom of the black hole, he would have refused to go. The men were not taking any chances. They knew they could bring that little boy up out of the well safely and more quickly than a grown man could be, even with the help of black Dolly.

After clearing away the broken rock which the blast had loosened, another day's digging exposed a very promising flow of water. As the incoming water complicated the already difficult work and Bill found trouble in lighting an occasional cigarette because of lack of oxygen in the air, they decided eighty-two feet was deep enough.

Now they were faced with the job of putting a brick lining in that long black cylinder from the bottom to the top. The bricks had been purchased, hauled home, and stacked near the top of the well. When ready, Ed loaded bricks into the bucket and sent them down. Bill, standing in the accumulated water, having cleared the circular edge so it was smooth and level, laid the first layer of bricks so they keyed into an even and complete circle. Layer followed layer. No mortar was used. Each layer was placed so that the bricks joined in the center of the bricks in the preceding layer. As the climb progressed, the cribbing boards were removed and sent to the top, each section as they came to it.

When Bill could no longer place the bricks while standing on the bottom, he improvised a bridge from a piece of two-by-eight plank just the right length to span the center of the circle the ends resting on the bricks. On this, he would stand and place the bricks till he had to move higher. Standing in the bucket, he would remove the plank, insert bricks in the vacancies left by the plank ends, and start again at his next station.

Finally, they built a concrete curbing around the top and covered the opening with planks. Enough two-inch pipes coupled together to reach almost to the bottom, with a brass suction cylinder on the end, was lowered into place, a pump connected at the top on the well cover and an electric motor with a driving belt set nearby.

The well was finished after weeks of hard work. It supplied all water needs for almost fifteen years. There are five thousand good bricks, some pipe, and two good brass cylinders still in that now useless well.

When this well began to fail just as the others had done, our sons decided to build a basin or pond to catch the run off from the winter rains and in that way be assured of an ample supply.

Water conservation was a matter of great public interest just then. A farmer could call on the Conservation Department engineers for help in choosing a location, and they would do any surveying that was required. They settled on a spot occupied by a small pear orchard. The natural contour of the ground there formed a shallow basin.

With tractor and blade, they scooped the basin deeper using the loosened earth to form a well-tamped wall on the south side and soon had a pond of about five-acre feet capacity. Brimful, I believe it figured close to one million gallons. Pipes were laid and connected to the original system, and everything worked nicely.

Our neighbor, Mr. Poor, who had never had enough water, suggested a dam to the west where the properties met, a partnership deal.

The work on this job was done by Dick and his cousin, George Beatty. Pipes were laid and a small reservoir built on the top of the hill so Mr. Poor's share of the water would flow to his house by gravity. The boys also laid pipe all the way to our pond, pump and motor installed, and everyone was happy.

When the boys bought the fifty acres from John Alonzo, they found there was a perfect place for a dam on the lower part of that piece. Again with much hot and dusty work, using three tractors driven by Dick Garrod, George Beatty, and Peter Garrod, they fashioned another pond of eight acres capacity. They installed pumps and pipe, this time using plastic pipe, to bring this water to the upper dam when needed.

Water-wise, everything was now fine, except for the fact that by the end of summer, the water was not as springtime fresh as we would like it.

In 1961, the rainfall was very short, only 15.44 inches falling in such light showers; it was all quickly absorbed by the soil leaving no runoff to fill the ponds. This presented a very serious problem which young Vince solved by arranging to buy water from the San Jose Water Company. This meant the purchase and laying of a mile of iron pipe to bring the water to the last built dam where they could connect with the established ranch water system.

So far so good, unless the water company goes out of business or the Garrods go flat broke, we will have water during the coming years.

THAT NEW HOUSE

All through the years I had dreamed and hoped that the honeymoon promise of a new house next year would come true. The plans I drew and the clippings I saved would have filled several fat scrapbooks.

When my youngest son, Richard, then a soldier in World War II, onboard an army transport in the harbor of Eniwetok, en route to the South Sea Island of Saipan, wrote and said, "Mom, when I get home, we will build that house on the gravel pit," this rather faded dream came to life again.

The gravel pit was a spot on the brow of the hill west of the house from which the family had for years taken gravel for the repair of farm roads. This material, a combination of shale and conglomerate rock, is found all through these hills, anatomically serving as ribs to keep the hills in shape.

Dick returned home in December 1945; it was 1947 before our ideas became feasible. At that time, a cousin of our son-in-law, George Cooper, Wayne Ware—just back from a tour of duty with the Seabees—came to visit the Coopers. He was a carpenter by profession and a very good one, but sadly at odds with life having been the recipient of a "Dear John" letter while overseas.

I found he had a great desire to build a house from the foundation to the rooftop, preferably of man-made blocks of some sort. He had always worked with lumber and was eager to learn the technique of using other types of building material. In fact, he said he would willingly do the work for free if someone would furnish the material.

After much discussion and our young people's steady support, I announced to the world in general and my husband in particular, "We are going to build a house." While my husband, poor man, had listened to all this talk, I think he thought if he just kept quiet, it would all be forgotten. Maybe he thought his wife's mind had slipped a bit, I don't know for sure, but when the decision was finally reached, like the good sport he always is, he turned to and helped push the project to completion.

There were a number of things I now was sure of: (1) the house would be built on the ridge to the west; (2) I knew a man who would build it; (3) most of the material would be some type of blocks; (4) my family had pledged support; and (5) there were about five thousand dollars available to work with.

Against the things I knew, there were dozens I didn't know. Where ignorance is bliss, it is wise to be foolish.

Wayne Ware had secured work with a contractor on a job to last to the end of July. We made a verbal agreement to the effect that from the May 1, 1947, to the completion of the job, he should have room and board. For the month of August, his five-year-old son would be with him and he would collect cash to cover his incidental needs: gas, cigarettes, etc.

Naturally, none of the plans I had drawn nor the clippings I had saved over the years would fit on the chosen site. So I put together a series of large and small rectangles, the end result to be a long narrow ridge hugging house, with kitchen and dining room in one, three bedrooms, a den or office, the necessary service rooms and a twenty-two by twenty-eight-foot living room over a three-car garage with a fourth bedroom and unfinished basement storage space on the garage level.

Having always admired Spanish balconies, I planned to have one on the east side of the living room to shelter the garage entrance.

When I thought my plans were in working order, upon R. V.'s urging, I sent a copy to a cousin, Ferdinand Stolte, a successful architect and builder, asking him to express an opinion as to its workability.

He took the time to come and look over the location, of which he approved, voted against the Spanish balcony as being of little use except to hang some old rugs on, said where I wanted to put the basement stairs wouldn't give headroom enough and explained very gently that five thousand dollars wouldn't go very far.

We left off the Spanish balcony but by fudging on the hall closet and raising the bottom the required amount above the floor level, we gained the needed headroom for the stairway from the basement or garage to the hallway.

Basalite blocks were decided on. These blocks are made of cement and cinders eight by eight by eighteen inches, fashioned in such a way that when put in place, reinforcement steel and cement can be placed in their hollow cores to stabilize the finished wall. No one told us they were not waterproof or that waterproofing material should be added to the cement needed to lay them. The inner side of the west walls still gets damp in winter.

When we had some idea of the dimensions, we found about 2,500 blocks would be needed. The basalite company delivered them direct from Stockton for twenty-five cents a block, bringing the whole lot in one huge load.

Vince, whose work took him to Sacramento, found a lumber company there running a special on cedar shingles and pine sheathing; their prices were very reasonable, and they promised delivery anywhere. Saratoga was, of course, out of bounds even on an "anywhere" delivery from Sacramento. The man wanted to make his word good and refused payment for hauling. When Vince learned that the man's insurance policy did not cover so great a distance, he was able to have that difficulty adjusted. The shingles and sheathing for the roof was the first of many loads of material we needed that season.

Lloyd Rodoni came with his big tractor one morning and proceeded to push apricot trees and gravel in all directions. By nightfall, he had the building site leveled and a road roughed in from what became the yard down to the old barn and the main road.

To make the footings for the block walls and to stabilize them, great quantities of cement would be needed. Proof of the old adage, "One man's misfortune is often another's gain," came one day when Aldo, one of the Picchetti boys, told Dick a cement truck with its load of four hundred sacks had gone through a bridge up in Stevens Creek Canyon and the company would sell all or part of the load at fifty cents a sack. As the regular price was twice that, Dick went at once and bought the lot.

We learned that a new truck driver, a stranger in the community, upon leaving Permanente Cement Works in the hills west of Cupertino with a load destined for Davenport on the coast north of Santa Cruz, was directed to turn right on the first black top road. The dispatcher either forgot Stevens Creek Canyon road was black or didn't consider it enough of a road to mention.

The driver made the turn as directed. By the time he realized something was wrong, he was so far on this narrow road it was impossible to turn his rig and go back, so he went on in the hope of reaching a highway. There was no way out; the road ended just beyond where the weight of the rig crushed the last bridge and put an end to his hopes. The man's boss said any driver who could take a rig of that size up that road was too good a man to lose, so he was not discharged as he had feared.

That cement was a real windfall for us. We soon found that all building material was expensive and a great deal of it hard to find.

In August, Wayne began to dig trenches and set up baffle boards for the foundations. Between times Dick, with his smaller tractor, had improved the road and cleaned up the edges of the building site.

August is the month between apricot and prune harvest so there are usually men staying on from one to the other, glad to work at any job that comes along. Because of this, there was always someone available when help was needed.

J. R. Hudson, Ovie Funderburg, and Bud Bowers were pleased to take part in building that house. Working under Wayne's directions, they hustled and bustled, moving blocks, mixing and pouring cement, nailing this and leveling that as cheerfully as if it was one continuous picnic and the house their own.

Young Vince, busy with the orchard and ranch work, still found time to help when needed.

Dick too was always on call. Much of his time went toward locating and hauling whatever was needed for the rest of the building, pine two by fours and two by tens subflooring and four-inch tongue and groove finish flooring. We had settled on redwood boards and battens for the outer walls of the den, living room, and one bedroom. For these and other redwood, he went to Boulder Creek and Loccattli's Mill. The twenty-nine-foot ridge beam in the living room was brought over the mountain by a mill truck as the ranch truck was too short to carry it on the highway. It was left at the junction of Big Basin and Pierce Roads. There, Dick balanced it on his jeep and carried it home.

Of course, anything not nailed down and in use on the farm was fair game if it could be used on the house. The summer before Dick had used his GI privilege to purchase a still-crated, never-used sheet iron building to serve as a workshop. This came with four-by-ten-foot sheets of pine plywood for the floor. As the boys wanted a concrete floor in their shop, the plywood was set aside. It became the ceiling of the living room.

Corner windows were being advised just then so, as the block walls went up, corner windows were allowed for, and steel sash cemented into place. Corner windows give no better ventilation than any others.

I put in the glass, a hundred and some odd panes. Mr. LeDeit, from whom we purchased the glass, jokingly offered me steady employment. In the end, we decided that if I were to be paid by the hour, he would go broke; on the other hand, if he paid me by the piece, I would no doubt starve to death. We called the deal off.

H. R. Garrod, a cousin from Oklahoma, came to make a long-promised visit and promptly joined in the work, he having had building experience. His help was most welcome.

When the inside walls began to take shape, we found that only a few pieces of sheet rock could be secured at a time. Williams and Russo of San Jose were most helpful. Whenever a supply came to them, they would phone us so Dick could go at once and get our allotment.

As standard red bricks were in short supply, cement bricks were used for both fireplaces. Having known fireplaces that smoked and were almost useless because of faulty construction, we installed ready-built metal forms and terracotta flues; it was no great trick to build the brick facing. The one in the dining room has a raised hearth which has proven to be a great improvement over one at floor level.

Jay Hudson, a redheaded Indian, not related to J. R. Hudson, joined Wayne as a steady helper; he preferred building to prune picking. Jay was a very calm, quiet man, a good foil for some of Wayne's impatience. They worked well together.

When it came to the kitchen cabinets, of which I had planned many, I found a good friend, Steve Richardson, willing to come and build them. He did other things too, like hanging doors and setting the supporting beams for the living room ceiling.

After the redwood plank front door was in place, Robert Pfeffer decided some ornamental iron hinges were needed. He went home, hammered out a set, and there they are.

Young Vince put in all the plumbing and did most of the electric wiring. George Cooper lent a hand with the wiring. Those block walls presented some problems, but we have ample light for all our needs.

There are some heavy pine timbers supporting the living room and other places where special strength seemed to be called for, and the ceiling beams in the dining room which attract attention.

Before Wayne became a Seabee, he had been employed at Mare Island Navy Base. These timbers had been used as supports for ships' hulls. During construction, great numbers of such timbers were stacked for future use or disposal.

The word went out that they could be had for removal; any still on the base at a certain date would be burned. Having hopes of someday building a home in Marysville, he hired a truck and driver and moved these timbers to a lot in that city. There they stayed while Wayne went to war, came back, and began to build our house. Now he was sure he could do a much better job if he just had those timbers to work with. He also learned that they were again being threatened by fire as the man on whose lot they were stacked wanted it for another purpose and said he would burn them next week.

When he set a price of seventy-five dollars on them, which must have been about what he had paid to have them hauled up there, Dick took the ranch truck and brought those timbers here where they will be part of the Garrod home as long as the house stands. Those used in the dining room were taken to Cushman's Mill near Los Gatos to be cut in two to bring them down to usable dimensions.

In the meantime, the question of money was always hovering over us. Some years before, Dick and I had invested some funds, about $2,500, inherited from my father, in a piece of Skyline property. We now decided to let part of it go if R. V. could find us a buyer.

Being a good salesman, he soon found an acquaintance who thought a piece of Skyline property was just what he wanted. L. R. Moore not only wanted that wooded hillside, he had the cash to pay for it. $4,500 gave him all the entire Gamble place that lay in Santa Clara County leaving us a little house, a good spring, and ten acres of accessible land. Next R. V. sold a small triangle, about an acre, cut away from the rest of the place by roads, to John Fahey of Sunnyvale.

With that much actual cash in hand, we splurged and had a hot air furnace from the Atlas Furnace Company of San Francisco installed in the basement by professionals for $1,000.

In November, Louise had asked whether I thought the Saratoga group of University Women might have their February meeting in the new house. At the moment, February looked a long way off, so I said of course they could.

Now we had a due date and really began to push. As soon as the sheet rock was in place, Ovie Funderburg turned painter, by his own word, he was willing to try anything once. The paint job, like many other things in the construction of this house, was purely amateur, but the end result was acceptable.

The morning of February 11, 1948, found the floors still littered with sawdust and scraps of lumber, the skill saw in place in the dining room and confusion everywhere. Everyone joined the cleanup crew. By ten o'clock, Dick and Wayne began to move things up from the old house. By three o'clock, the kitchen stove was in place and the needed dining and living room furniture arranged for the evening's festivities.

The job was done; the new house an accomplished fact, thanks to many willing workers who had certainly labored far beyond the call of duty or union rules.

Of course there were still bills to be paid. After sacrificing some treasured oil stock, there was still almost three thousand dollars' worth to meet. This sum R. V. borrowed on an open note from Miss Alice Turel of San Jose. It took several years to clear the note. No one was disturbed by that.

Since then as we found it financially possible, we put a cement floor in the basement and sealed it with plywood to discourage the linnets which were determined to build their nests on the electric wire. In place of the Spanish balcony that wasn't built, we had Jack Hamilton put a ten-foot-wide roofed deck, a wonderful place to spend summer afternoons.

One year, I laid asphalt tile over all but the living room floor. When waxed, these tiles make floor care easy.

After twenty years, we still call it the new house. The floors are level, the walls are plumb, the views from the windows to all points of the compass are soul satisfying; we enjoy every nook and corner. Though it's a pretty big house for just one pair of grandparents, here we mean to stay just as long as the good Lord will let us.

CUPERTINO DE ORO

Almost twenty years ago, through the kind thoughtfulness of my friend, Mrs. A. E. Rae, I was invited to become a member of the Cupertino de Oro Club. This became a pleasant and happy contact with a group of charming women.

De Oro was organized about 1923 to keep an attractive piece of public school property from becoming a roadhouse of possible questionable character. By the time it was my good fortune to become a member, they had passed the money raising stage of the club's existence. Early day records show that there were many affairs carried through for the express purpose of paying off the mortgage that had come with the effort to save the building and grounds of the Collins School.

Now it is a nonprofit corporation. The building has been moved toward the back of the property, and Standard Oil has a lease for an oil station on the northwest corner facing Highway 85.

Sometimes, the house is rented to a church planning a building of its own and needing a temporary meeting place. Occasionally it is rented for a wedding reception, brand new or golden. Beside these sources of revenue, there are of course yearly dues and new members pay initiation fees. So being assured of something of a steady income, the members enjoy their good fortune, hold twice-a-month meetings with good speakers or other enjoyable programs that make no claim to anything but entertainment. Always the committees of the day serve most unusual and delicious teas, dressed up with flower arrangements of outstanding beauty and variety.

During my years of membership, I have served on various committees, but I fear I did nothing of great value to the organization.

Most important to me was my year as President. President is as high as one can go in almost any gathering, and I did truly appreciate the honor my associates had bestowed on me. My predecessor, Beatrice Stocklmier, and her committees had just finished the major task of helping with the moving and renovation of the building. When it came my turn to be the presiding officer, everyone was ready to relax and enjoy the fruits of their labor, so I relaxed and enjoyed my year along with everyone else.

The office of President leads one right into membership in the Past President's Group which is really the cream on the cake. Their four luncheon meetings a year are just the best ever, filled with fun and congenial companionship.

May de Oro continue to give others as much pleasure as it has given to me.

ABOUT CHARLEY

Charlie was a bird, a big coal black raven. No one in the family knew anything about ravens. Blue jays, quail, flickers, chickadees, mockingbirds, and others were all interesting and aside from the damage they did to ripening fruit, rather nice to have about.

So when a friend of Louise's told her of a neighbor who had a raven for whom she was trying to find more free and open space, what was more natural for the friend to do than ask that Charlie the raven be given a welcome to the ranch and freedom, what could be nicer for him than all those acres of orchard and pasture.

Louise, loving all feathered creatures, said yes, the raven would be welcome.

So Charlie came to the Coopers, was fed and allowed to hop about as he pleased, but the next day he made his way to a neighbor's, his wings were clipped so he couldn't fly much. Here he promptly attacked a young pigeon. Next he took up a position on the house roof from which no one could dislodge him.

These young people knew nothing about ravens either and decided he was some dangerous sort of eagle and should be destroyed. Tony went next door to borrow some ammunition for his twenty-two; there Jane, who had heard about the raven, persuaded Tony to give up the idea of shooting the bird, instead to call the Coopers and have them come and get him. Easier said than done; Charlie had no intention of letting himself be caught, even corn soaked in whiskey didn't befuddle him enough so the boys could pick him up.

Next he showed up at my house, which being at the highest elevation, suited him fine. R. V. and I foolishly thought he would be kind of nice to have around, so we fed him bits of meat and servings of dog food, all of which he would take from our fingers. He had no desire to enjoy the wide open spaces; the window ledges of the house suited him fine. There he could look in and watch what was going on and would hammer on the windowpane with his beak to make sure we knew he was there.

Of all the inquisitive creatures I ever knew, he was the worst. Busy all day long turning over flowerpots, pulling up plants to look at the roots, anything small enough for him to lift, he lifted, dropped, and probably broke. His strength was surprising, and everything was done with that big black beak.

Hopping from this to that to reach the roof, he could then hop down to the clothesline, and balancing carefully, move along the line pulling the pins from the freshly hung washing and watch it fall to the ground.

Charlie couldn't bluff Gyp, the collie, but poor old Black Dog, blind in one eye would run and hide the minute Charlie came near. It reached the point where he would only eat after dark when Charlie had retired for the night in the top of a nearby oak tree.

Visitors found Charlie most entertaining, but after a time of putting up with his monkey shines and tired of cleaning up after him, I arranged with Mr. Louis Moitozo who has charge of the Junior Museum at Alum Rock Park, to give him a home there. I understand there are other ravens there, so I trust he will be happy.

Quoted Gramma Garrod, "Nevermore."

AN EASTER VACATION

In March 1964, as the children were looking forward to Easter vacation, young Vince invited me to join them on a camping trip to visit some Indian cliff dwelling in the neighborhood of Flagstaff, Arizona. I of course accepted with pleasure, and the Monday after school closed away we went.

Vince and Jane, their three daughters—Victoria, thirteen; Emma, six; and Chrissie nine months—plus the two high school boys, Tim and Jan, were all in a camper truck. We met the Koch family of Glenwood at the head of Scotts Valley near Santa Cruz. Mr. and Mrs. Ed and Margaret, with their teenaged children, Kathleen and Tom in another camper and Mrs. Koch's mother, Mrs. Dake driving an Oldsmobile which allowed for rearranging of passengers from time to time.

The first part of the trip was through country familiar to all of us, Highway 101, Watsonville, Salinas, King City, Paso Robles where we changed directions and headed for Wasco, Bakersfield, and Mojave. To this point, I had once driven when my sister and I were en route to Lancaster to visit her son Will who was raising fryers there.

As the campers were equipped with cooking facilities, finding a place to dine was no problem; any convenient parking space beside the road answered nicely.

That first day, I learned Jan had set out on this expedition with a sore throat. Poor youngster; the farther we went, the worse it got.

From Mojave eastward was all new to me, really not a very friendly landscape, sand and rocks, cactus and palms with a scattering of cultivated sections where I presume the soil was somewhat more tillable and water available. Now and then there was a rest station, part of the highway system, and an occasional oil station. Toward evening, we reached Barstow, a fair-sized city. Here the girls shopped for groceries at a Safeway store. I walked about a bit, but the wind was blowing such a gale I was glad to return to the shelter of the camper.

319

Leaving Barstow, we continued on 66 till dusk when our drivers turned into an uncared-for road wandering off into the desert and chose a spot to spend the night. A tent was put up for the three boys who had all brought sleeping bags. The rest of the group were taken care of in the campers and Mrs. Dake's car.

There was an army camp not far from us where they were evidently training the soldiers in night flying. All night long those planes left the ground with thunderlike roars. In fact, I thought it was thunder and wondered about the absence of lightning till the young people set me straight in the morning.

The wind blew all night; before morning the boys' tent collapsed. After some commotion and noisy expressions of opinions, they decided to sleep right where they were since there was no danger of suffocation.

The next day took us through many more miles of sand, rocks, and thorny cactuses. The views of the distant mountains were beautiful even though stark and forbidding because of lack of forest growth. The atmosphere was clear and free of smog, so the mountains stood out in blue and purple silhouettes with masses of white cloud arrangements above them.

The peaks that form a backdrop for the town of Needles give a silent explanation of its name.

With the passing of the day, we came to Kingman and then we reached Williams. Meanwhile it grew colder and colder, though not actually snowing there were puddles in the streets and the weather looked stormy.

Mrs. Dake's car had a radio, and she was the official weather and road monitor. She reported that the road to Flagstaff was closed to all traffic because of heavy snow. As there was a good restaurant beside the highway, we gathered in a nice warm dining room for a ready prepared hot dinner and consultation. It was decided to change directions and go to the Grand Canyon.

We arrived there in time to make camp for the night. There were trees all about, various conifers and oaks and low-growing shrubs, either spaced by nature or thinned by man to form as lovely a park as one could ever hope to see. Next morning we found that the night had added even greater beauty. A coat of soft, fluffy snow had been spread over everything.

After breakfast, with a great showing of energy and know-how by all the male members of the party, the wheels were all dressed in chains.

The day was spent in seeing the park and the extensive and well-catalogued museum. There we met the chief ranger, son of our good friends the Don McHenrys of Saratoga.

Another point of interest was the observation hall with its many windows and their pinpointed views of the canyon with its crumpled silver ribbon in the bottom, in reality, the Colorado River winding its way along a mile or more below us. A pleasant young ranger gave an informative talk on the geological history of the canyon and the surrounding country.

As we stood and watched, one snow squall after another would blot out the view as the wind drove them north or south, I'm not sure which. Between squalls, the sun came out and we could see for miles. It's an incomprehensible place.

The second night the boys rolled out their sleeping bags on the floor of the heated comfort station near which we had made camp.

More snow fell during the night. It was a unanimous wish that we go look for warmer weather farther south.

Before leaving the park, it was agreed to visit the Indian Trading Post. This was located at the lower edge of a rather steep parking lot. To avoid difficulties when ready to leave, the cars were parked at the top where the ground was fairly level, and everyone walked. To prevent the soft snow from getting into the tops of my plastic overshoes, I chose a wheel track to walk in, but on turning to leave the track, I sat down awfully hard. A stranger came quickly to help me up. I found I could walk so I thanked the nice man and joined the rest already in the post.

Our interest was centered on the Indian merchandise: hand-woven robes and saddle blankets and silver jewelry, rings, bracelets and necklaces, really beautiful. My choice was a bracelet set with three green turquoise squares.

By midmorning, we took the road leading back to Williams. As Vince had the heaviest rig, he took the lead. It was his job to break a track for the others to follow. I was riding in Mrs. Dake's car as were Kathleen and her mother.

As the cars moved along, the snow caught on the undergear of the cars. Soon they carried solid chunks of ice which made the driver's job very difficult. I'm sure if anything had caused us to stop the wheels, they would have frozen fast and we would have been there for the duration. Not the kind of road to choose for a pleasant, relaxing drive.

My memory is somewhat confused as to just when we got where. I think we were pretty well out of the snow when we again reached Williams.

That night camp was decided on after dark. It was somewhere on an abandoned road in the desert. In the morning, we learned it was on a peninsula with a railroad line serving many freight trains on the right and a very busy highway on the left. No wonder that night was not as quiet as it might have been.

Our course led steadily southward. There was Prescott and Wickenburg and miles and miles of rocks, cactus, creosote bushes, and smoke trees with now and then a tiny settlement. At Ajo, we stopped to look down into a great open-cut copper mine, with its roadways, railroads, tractors, trucks, and utility buildings all spread out on the walls and bottom of that unbelievable excavation—an animated map.

That evening we reached the Organ Pipe Cactus National Monument and settled on spending the rest of the vacation there.

That fall I had taken near the Indian Trading Post grew steadily worse till every step I took was pure misery. I with my back and Jan with his throat were far from being the life of the party. Fortunately, sitting did not cause too much discomfort, so I could sort of grin and bear it. But I was unable to do any exploring though I would have liked very much to follow to its end, anyone of the interesting paths that led away from camp.

This park or government monument covers many miles of very rough territory. We spent most of one day on a well-marked tour, enjoying the legends of early day bandits and cattle thieves. Judging by the waterless, boulder-strewn terrain, they had to travel, one almost reached the conclusion that they earned whatever it was they made off with.

Mrs. Dake took all the womenfolk to visit an Indian village some fifty miles outside the park. It was the home of the Papagos. They offered handmade baskets woven of native fibers in white and black patterns. Jane and Margaret invested.

The older girls, returning from a hike one afternoon, brought me a fern leaf, small, very dark, and leathery, which they had found growing among those endless rocks and cacti, which, without doubt, belonged to the same family as the fragile Goldback fern of the Santa Cruz Mountains.

We also had a quick trip to a border town in Mexico for no special purpose except to say we had been there.

Sunday saw us on the road home. We back tracked to Gila Bend and turned west to the neighborhood of Yuma and northward parallel but not in sight of the Colorado River. Late that afternoon, we came to Blythe. Here the Garrods made a hasty visit to an emergency hospital. Jan's throat had all but closed, and he was on the point of smothering to death. The doctors were able to give him the needed relief. His sore throat had progressed to a very bad case of quinsy. I shall always be thankful that we reached Blythe just when we did.

That evening we gathered for the last night on the road, just inside the entrance to the Joshua Tree Monument. The next morning the Kochs and Mrs. Dake bade us good-bye and headed for home by the most direct route. We Garrods followed a road that passed through this vast reserve of more rocks and thorns plus the odd Joshua trees. All along the way were outcroppings and tumbled piles of tan-colored boulders which Vince said were composed of rotten granite.

At noontime, we reached a really tremendous pile of these same boulders, a perfect place for someone looking for a hideout, all piled together by some prehistoric force leaving tunnels and caves of amazing dimensions.

Sometime in the afternoon, we reached Twenty-nine Palms, still in the desert country. From there the route was familiar to Vince, first San Bernardino and Mojave, from there on to Bakersfield and home the way we had come, with no more loitering along the way.

It was late Monday when the young people wished me good night at my kitchen door. I was tired but happy with a wonderful time to remember. Aside from the physical discomfort I had suffered and which stayed with me for many weeks, the trip had been wonderful and for me a very unusual experience.

In that short space of time, we had traveled about three thousand miles, seeing a part of this country I could never have imagined. It has to be seen to be believed, so very different from what I had always been accustomed to and which I feel sure I shall never again visit.

Truly a time to be remembered.

The Saratoga Historical Foundation

The spring of 1960 saw the beginning of an organization which has given me a great deal of pleasure. All about there was the stir of an idea in the minds of many people, that there was much worthwhile early-day history being lost because no one was collecting artifacts of historical value nor pictures and records which were so easily consigned to the flames after the passing of some old-timer. Neither were enough people troubling to listen to the reminiscences of the older members of the community who had lived the pleasures as well as the hardships of pioneer days.

Historical Societies became the order of the day. In Saratoga, I think the credit belongs to Miss Florence Cunningham with Mr. Don McHenry a close second. A meeting was called on May 23, 1960, in the Foothill Clubhouse, arrangements having been made by a committee of three, Mrs. Ralph Eaton, Miss Cunningham, and Mrs. Tina Miner; Mr. McHenry presided as President Pro Tem, and Mrs. L. B. Peck served as secretary.

This meeting was well attended. A committee was chosen, namely Arnold Loe, Clarence Neale, Harry Maynard, Robert Mason, Mrs. N. Thompson, and myself, to interview other groups to learn about suitable rules and bylaws to guide our prospective organization. We found the bylaws of the Palo Alto society most suitable to our situation and used them as a pattern.

Still under Mr. McHenry's leadership, Dr. A. Glass, Robert Ryder and Willys Peck were appointed as a nominating committee to select a list of nine people to act as a Board of Directors. They presented the names of Arnold Loe, C. W. Neale, Mrs. Melita Oden, Harry Maynard, Robert A. Mason, Mrs. R. F. Nylander, Miss Florence Cunningham, Don E. McHenry, and E. S. Garrod. This slate of nominees was unanimously accepted.

At the first Directors' meeting, Arnold Loe became president, Mrs. Nylander, secretary, and Robert Mason, treasurer. After some discussion as to a suitable name for the organization, Saratoga Historical Foundation was decided on, and dues were set at $5 per year per family. Directors' meetings and membership' meetings to be held on alternate months.

In September 1961, Mrs. Nylander tendered her resignation, and I was appointed to fill her place, a position I have held ever since.

Mr. Loe was President until June 1963 when the Loe family moved to the east coast and Willys Peck, a native Saratogan, was chosen to take his place, and still holds that office. His interest in the past as well as the future of his hometown makes him the ideal man for the job.

The Director's meetings consist of much discussion on many topics. Deciding on programs for the membership meetings is a major accomplishment. When an out-of-town person known to be versed in some historical topic has been asked to come and speak to the group, we have seldom been disappointed. When a local program and speaker was decided on, the response has been equally good.

A problem always before us is how, where, and when will the foundation find a permanent home for the really excellent collection of historical artifacts, records, and pictures it is so busy collecting.

A contractor who wished to use the lot on which it stood to erect some specialty shops some years ago offered to give us the building if the foundation would pay the cost of moving. The little house had been built by a well-known, early-day Saratogan, Mr. Marsh. It was located on Big Basin Way beyond the Plumed Horse restaurant. It seems historical people will accept anything offered them as long as it is old. We did.

This gift turned out to be an expensive headache. It took money to move it, money to insure it, and work to repair it after it was badly vandalized. It was impossible to find a suitable spot for its permanent location. Now I hear that the City Fathers have offered to dismantle it so that the flood control people can build a lake in Wild Wood Park where the little house now stands still balanced on the moving man's jacks and blocks.

My personal opinion is that the sensible thing to do is to accept the offer and charge the whole deal to experience.

In the spring of 1965, Miss Cunningham died. The Historical Foundation was not alone in the loss of a loyal and enthusiastic friend and worker. The entire community misses her interest and ever ready willingness to work for the good of Saratoga.

At the time of her death, Miss Cunningham left a bequest of $2,500 to a Saratoga Museum, if and when it materializes. Many of her household goods were turned over to the foundation; their sale netted the organization an equal amount. Some articles she had written and other papers and records she had collected over the years were edited by Mrs. Theron Fox and gathered into one volume titled *Saratoga's First One Hundred Years* by Florence Cunningham, a fitting memorial for a Saratoga lady.

Beside offering programs for the bimonthly membership meetings, which have always been well attended and I am sure have done a great deal toward informing newcomers of the efforts and aims of past generations and offered them visions of the possibilities of the future; every spring, members are also given the opportunity of joining a one-day bus tour to some place of historical interest under the leadership of Clyde Arbuckle, Santa Clara County historian. I have enjoyed these tours very much. Through them I have seen parts of California I should never have seen otherwise.

The year of our golden wedding party, many friends old and young, knowing that gifts were not to be sent, joined in making one gift to Gran'ma G's pet project. Consequently, a sum of over $450 was quietly added to the treasury of the Historical Foundation.

When I learned of this more than generous gift, I was very, very proud and also somewhat embarrassed.

The Saratoga Historical Foundation is, without question, my favorite outside the family activity.

Saratoga's Beginning

As told at the Honor Banquet
Saratoga High, June 1968

To begin at the very beginning, Indians lived in the Santa Clara Valley. Some were known to have lived on the western side of the valley in this vicinity, but whether they had a name for this location, I do not know.

The Indians were known as Costanoans and were not credited with neither intelligence nor ambition. They lived much like the wild animals, letting each day take care of itself. It is believed that they made occasional excursions to the coast for shellfish. They are said to have followed the local streams to their head waters near the Skyline, crossed the summit in the neighborhood of Castle Rock, and then followed some westward flowing stream to the ocean.

A group of Saratoga Explorer Scouts are now making an effort to trace this trail by searching for seashells scattered by the Indians as they returned to the valley.

When the Spanish Padres and soldiers came to California, they tried to civilize the Indians, to teach them to work, and to live like white men. The poor things had no desire for change of any kind, least of all to learn to work.

The white man did the Indians no good, just crowded them together near the missions where they contracted all manner of diseases they had never known and for which they had no resistance. Before many years passed, they had become a vanished race.

Along with the soldiers, land grants became part of history. The soldiers claimed the country for the Spanish King or the Mexican Emperor, depending on which one they were serving at the time. In turn these leaders would reward outstanding officers and sometimes civilians of importance with gifts of great tracts of land encompassing thousands of acres.

It so happens that what we know as Saratoga was part of the Quito grant given to Jose Noriega, Alcalde of San Jose in 1839. By 1841, Manuel Alviso had purchased the Quito grant from Jose Noriega.

By then the Americans from the eastern states were coming to California. One William Campbell, exploring the nearby hills, saw the potential value of the redwoods and decided to build a lumber mill.

He bargained with Alviso for permission and put his mill on the creek somewhere above the Saratoga Springs Resort. Later he learned that his mill was beyond the boundary of the Quito grant; there had been no need of his bargain with Manuel Alviso.

However, he built his mill and gave his name, Campbell, to the creek. What is now known as Saratoga was then known as Campbell's Gap.

About the time gold was discovered in California, men had begun to farm the valley land, growing wheat and other grains and raising cattle.

Grainfields stretched for miles. To furnish the growing population with flour, Mr. Campbell built a flour mill just beyond where the Hakoni gate now stands. A few of the foundation stones are still there in the bank of the road.

There was also a paper mill nearby which made brown butcher paper from wheat straw, much of which was hauled from the Murphy holdings at Sunnyvale. About three years ago I met an old man, Jim Blackwell, who told me he drove one of the straw wagons when a young man, and stacked the straw on the flat where the Catholic Church used to be and where the University Preschool is now.

Mr. Campbell sold his holdings here and moved across the valley where he established the town of Campbell. For a short time, Campbells Gap became Bank Mills.

Next along came Martin McCarty. He felt sure that someday a town would develop where the creek reached the valley. He decided a good road up the canyon as far as the lumber mill was the community's greatest need. He and some friends raised the money and built the road. To get their money back, they put a gate about where Third Street is now; everyone passing through the gate paid toll to the gatekeeper and the place became known as Toll Gate.

With a better road, he felt sure of available lumber and proceeded to lay out his town, the first subdivision of the west valley which he called

McCartysville. Although he did not carry out all his plans, the numbered streets off Big Basin Way are just where Mr. McCarty put them.

The name McCartysville held until 1865. By then someone had discovered that the contents of the water from some mineral springs on a branch of Campbell Creek were the same as those found in the water of the famous Saratoga Springs in the state of New York.

Some wealthy men became interested, acquired the property, made plans to develop the springs, and market the water as well as build a hotel, all of which they did.

The Congress Springs Hotel and its adjoining cottages had ninety-two rooms and catered to a wealthy and sophisticated clientele until June 1903, when it was destroyed by fire. The hotel was not rebuilt, nor was the sale of the water continued.

At the beginning of the resort era, the people of the town took a vote and changed the name to Saratoga as being more elegant and in harmony with the nearby Congress Springs Hotel. Saratoga it has been ever since.

For some years after the hotel was burned, the Peninsular Railroad Company owned the resort property. It was then open to the public for picnics or hikers. Now it belongs to the San Jose Water Company and you see no trespassing signs on the fences.

An important event in 1854, 104 years ago, was the formation of the Saratoga Branch of the Sons of Temperance. The members built a meeting house of split redwood on Oak Street just where the grammar school cafeteria stands today. This building was used for community gatherings. It was also the first schoolhouse. In 1860, the average daily attendance was eight boys and twelve girls.

When this building became too small and, I suppose, too rickety for school purposes, a two-room building took its place. When this one also became overcrowded, it was decided to add another story. This was done by raising the original building and putting the second story under the first. There are still people in Saratoga who attended classes in that rebuilt schoolhouse. Mr. Garrod is one.

Eventually this building was sold and moved down the hill to Third and Big Basin Way, part of it then became the Post Office. When this building was out of the way, a bigger and better two-story building was put in its place in 1897; this served until 1923 when the tile-roofed part of Saratoga School on Oak Street was built.

This was the time when the Santa Clara County school districts were being consolidated and Saratoga annexed Austin and Booker Districts and part of Lincoln. It was this annexation that made the residents of Mr. Eden Road, including the Garrods, legal citizens of Saratoga School District. With all these annexations, there was only one school building, the tile-roofed one on Oak Street.

I think there were five teachers and about a hundred children. Now there are five grammar schools with ninety teachers and three thousand or more pupils. There are also two church schools with three or four hundred pupils each.

Once upon a time, Saratoga had its own rapid transit service, an electric car line which circled the valley from San Jose to Saratoga onto Los Gatos, from there to Campbell and back to San Jose, or the same trip in reverse according to the hour.

I think the trips were scheduled on the hour, alternating directions. The Electric Company also hauled freight to and from town and much gravel from the gravel pit.

The electric line operated from 1904 to 1933; by then most people owned automobiles and no longer made use of the railroad. There was a ticket and express office about where the fire department now keeps its engines and a switching yard where you now have the park or plaza.

The streets were not black topped, so they were dusty in summer and muddy in winter.

People often express the wish that the town had stayed just as it was in the old days.

Now I very much doubt whether the people of today, with their shiny autos, oil stations, and other modern innovations, would be pleased to find the town suddenly returned to its early country village condition.

Thank you for listening.

THE TWENTY-SEVEN-MILE
DRIVE

After the road along the summit of the Santa Cruz Mountains, which almost followed the survey line between Santa Cruz and Santa Clara Counties, had been completed and was being kept in fair condition, and as more and more people came to summer in the west valley and nearby mountains, sightseeing drives along the country roads became a popular pastime. It was then that the Twenty-Seven-Mile Drive came into being. It was, without doubt, the most attractive and frequently enjoyed drive in the western foothills.

With Los Gatos as the starting point, one followed the Los Gatos Canyon southward on a well-kept county road with its chaparral-covered hills on the right and the Southern Pacific Railroad just below it on the left and still farther down, the creek itself made its rippling splashing way to the bay. Above the creek on the far side of the canyon was a narrow man-made ledge on which the San Jose Water Works' wooden flume carried a supply of good mountain water to the city of San Jose.

Above and beyond the flume were the vineyards and buildings of the Jesuit Novitiate. Farther on, the mountains were covered with more chaparral which at first glance is a low-growing mass of brush.

A closer look shows an unbelievable number of shades of green composed of chemise, greasewood, manzanita, lilac, clematis, and poison oak with occasional oaks, laurels, buckeyes, and maples scattered about. Many blossomed in the springtime; others turned gold and scarlet in the fall.

A sharp change of direction came when the travelers turned into the reservoir now better known as the Black Road and the five-mile westward climb was begun. This road led past well-kept orchards and pleasant homes except for the last mile where the road was overhung by the reaching branches of black and tanbark oaks, hazel brush, and briars. Finally, the road came out on top displaying a surprising view of the tree-covered ridges and canyons of Santa Cruz County with the long blue line of Ben Lomond Ridge on the western horizon.

The next eight miles offered a series of panoramic views, westward toward the ocean, at one point an occasional steamer might be glimpsed as it made its way up or down the coast. Toward the east, the views were of the Santa Clara Valley with its geometric patterns of grain fields and orchards ending at the base of the Mt. Hamilton range crowned by the white dome of Lick Observatory.

The road was narrow but ample and safe for horse-drawn vehicles. The forest growth along the way was luxurious, shadowing the road and forming protected nooks and corners where the dainty wildflowers flourished, groves of black oaks, stands of Douglas firs, maples, and madrones in profusion, as well as the less common Valparaiso oak.

There was another oak, an evergreen much like the common Live Oak. Its exact species I never learned and I knew of only one, though Fred Herring said there were others. The acorns from this tree were edible with a pleasant nutlike flavor.

At its junction with the Saratoga Turnpike, now Big Basin Road, just beyond the Valley View School, the route turned abruptly east and dropped rapidly down to the valley. Some distance down in a shady bend of the road stood a redwood water trough always brimful of clear, cold water led to it by a V flume from a stream that passed under the road through a culvert, a very welcome sight to both horses and humans. The overflow from the trough drained back into the creek, passed under the road, and went chuckling down the canyon as though happy to escape.

At the edge of the valley the road passed through the town of Saratoga, a quiet little village that served the needs of the surrounding community with its two general merchandise stores, a blacksmith shop, one drugstore and one doctor, the telephone office, the Interurban railroad's ticket and express office, several small family-type hotels and bars in the western French and Italian part of town, and a more pretentious inn with no bar near the eastern boundary.

Five or ten minutes' drive took one the full length of the town to the right-hand turn and beginning of the last five miles of the twenty-seven through beautiful orchards and past prosperous, well-kept homes to the starting point in Los Gatos.

When this drive was popular, even a fast-stepping livery team needed five or six hours to make the trip. If the party stopped to explore Castle Rock or some other point of interest, the whole day would slip by.

It is different now; the entire road has been improved, or has it? It is now a four-lane highway to Lexington and the Black Road, and two-lane black top the rest of it. The steep pitches have been reduced and the sharp corners eased. Along the top, it is an almost entirely different road, still swinging east and west from Santa Clara to Santa Cruz County and back again.

The ridges and canyons of Santa Cruz seem unchanged, but Santa Clara Valley has become one great city, roofs and more roofs are all one sees in the daytime. At night, it is one great sea of electric lights.

The road builders were thoughtful and built a few safe turnouts from which the views can be enjoyed. Sad to say, the few hardy shrubs that venture close the roadside are trampled and broken. The obnoxious beer cans and cigarette stubs are always in evidence.

The Twenty-Seven-Mile Drive is a thing of the past.

Now there is a nice open road with little traffic. The modern autos go whizzing along "full speed ahead." I doubt whether their passengers see much of the roadside beauty.

Back To Horses

When the boys were in high school, which is thirty odd years ago, the Garrods made the change from horses to tractors for doing the ranch work.

Some of our neighbors had tried wheeled tractors, but it was soon proven that the wheel-type machine was not the answer to hillside cultivation. They lacked climbing power as well as presenting very serious safety hazards to their drivers because of the ease with which they could be turned over.

When Charles Krieger, a new neighbor, acquired the Cletrac Agency which offered a crawler-type machine supposed to be able to go anywhere with perfect safety, the Garrods succumbed.

Our sons were, of course, delighted with the tractor. Ed Jones had reached that point in life where it was too much for him to follow a team up and down the orchard rows hour after hour, nor had he any desire to learn to manage that newfangled contraption.

Ted Nickels, who had come to substitute for Ed during several seasons, was an excellent horseman; he also drove his own automobile. When invited to learn to drive the tractor, he shook his head and said, "Uh uh."

So the boys became tractor men and went rumbling happily about, first where the going was pretty good and then where it was anything but good, with Mother in the kitchen hoping and praying nothing bad would happen. Well, nothing really bad ever happened, but they both came close enough at various times so that it wasn't funny.

Tractors, of course, needed heavier implements to do the work. In one way, that was fine, so much more could be accomplished. What used to take days could now be done in hours. In many respects, the change was a good one. There were also drawbacks; the heavier tools were harder to hold in place on the hillsides, and many a much-needed chunk of bark was ruthlessly torn from the trunks of the trees by the sliding disc or harrow. This loss, no doubt, shortened the life of many a good tree.

Soon, to justify greater investment in equipment, more orchards were taken on to be cared for on shares. Either the owner was getting on in years and no longer able to do the work himself, or someone new had acquired the land, had income from other sources, and had no intention of tackling the orchard work under any circumstances.

Next, the Garrod brothers were working all the neighboring orchards and several as far away as Los Altos.

At this time, there was still a team of horses in the barn, kept to do one special job, to pull the mower to cut the hay to feed themselves and a cow. Working the ground, harrowing in the seed and bringing the cured hay to the barn was all done with the tractor.

They were nice horses, Nell and Johnny, and we were fond of them. But at last they had to go; no one could justify keeping them as pets.

Dick still managed to keep a horse he could ride, even though this failed to meet with his father's or brother's approval. They were through with horses.

However, points of view and conditions change. The orchards grew older and for various reasons trees died and replanting was seldom successful. Taxes and all other expenses climbed higher while the money return seemed always to fall lower in comparison; besides, riding a tractor in the hills at forty-five is not the thrilling adventure it was at sixteen.

I notice the next generation of enthusiastic adventurers is told in no uncertain terms to keep off such and such hillsides and not to be such foolhardy idiots.

In seeking for some other means to meet the running expenses, educate his children, pay the taxes, insurance, and all the other obligations that come with a place like this, young Vince turned to recreation and horses. Now there are horses all over the place, big, small, and in between, from aristocratic Arabians to lowly Mustangs, horses for children to learn to ride on and horses for people to ride over the newly built bridle paths on the back eighty. And horses whose owners pay their board and pamper them beyond belief and love them dearly. I think a hundred and fifty all told.

The old fruit yard is very different from what it was in the old days. With the exception of the fruit house, the cutting shed, the workshop, and the summer kitchen, now turned into a small apartment, all the old structures, Ed's house, the original shop, chicken yard, and small help houses are gone, displaced by two new stables and a huge, well-lighted roofed arena usable in all weathers.

The old barn is a mere shell is whose interior new box stalls have been built. It is no longer a place to store hay. The buggy shed is now a tack room.

There are many strangers about from early morning to late at night. They seem to enjoy the place immensely.

Young Vince is satisfied with the venture and looks forward to a profitable future. The change was without doubt a good one.

Soldiers in Saratoga . . .

Some in the Foothill Club

Some in Weavers Barn

THE NEXT GENERATION

January 1920 found me with an almost around-the-clock job, three small people to do for: Louise, Vince, and Dick. Luckily they were all happy, healthy youngsters with all outdoors to grow up in which helped.

Louise and Vince were blue eyed and blond, real "cotton tops." Louise was always a responsible little person, looking after those about her. Vince was quiet and content to mind his own affairs, while Dick, also blue eyed, had hair that just missed being black and a restless disposition that was inclined to lead him into trouble. I'm sure the words he heard most often in his baby days were "No" and "Don't."

They grew up as babies do; we were proud of them then and still are, now that they are graying adults, active and respected members of the community.

I remember no generation gap between us, nor were we worried by teenage rebellions. Everyone connected with our household knew that we had a "One for all, all for one" system of living and accepted it without question.

I am sure they were happy and carefree youngsters with all outdoors to roam about in and an assortment of grown-ups to watch over them and incidentally help to guide them in the way they should go, each one sure that the way they had been taught in their long-gone childhood was the proper way.

They survived nicely. I am sure, if asked today, they would all declare that the varied advice of their senior mentors left them only pleasant memories.

I am firmly convinced that there is no better home environment for children to be born into than one with members of all ages, grandparents, or other elderly members who need and demand special consideration, parents who represent authority and younger members down to babies to be loved and taken care of. If there are out of family people of other ethnicities and nationalities about, all the better.

As the children moved along in school, the various childhood ailments caught up with them—chicken pox, measles, whooping cough, and the most serious, scarlet fever, in which I joined my sons. Fortunately, Louise was immune and made a good job of keeping house while we were in quarantine.

There were other things to worry us, like Dick and his cousin Bud falling from gentle old Kitty and Dick coming out with a badly broken elbow which took a very long time to heal.

Another frightening episode occurred when both boys were bent on becoming great hunters with just one ambition—to have the use of a .22 rifle. As I had wandered about the mountains at home at the age of nine with a single-shot .22 over my shoulder and my three-year-old sister by the hand, I thought it perfectly safe to let them go hunting in the orchards one at a time.

A favorite, visiting uncle had taken the two boys on a tour of the orchard; not knowing about the rule of using the repeater as a single shot, he had left a number of shells in the magazine. Next day, as the gun was passed from brother to brother and Dick was about to have his turn as a "heap big hunter," the gun fired and young Vince felt the sting of the bullet on his posterior. Fortunately the injury was not serious, but he still carries that leaden pellet just under the skin of his thigh. I must say, Dick was more frightened and distressed than his victim.

The summer young Vince got his driving license, he and I took a trip north. We traveled up the coast past Crescent City and Eureka into Oregon and then down on the other side of the state by Ukiah and McCloud. We planned to stop at motels as we went along. Motels have come a long way since then. At that time, the accommodations were very simple. They provided beds with springs and mattresses, but you brought your own linen, blankets, and towels. There was usually a basin with cold water and a standard toilet and perhaps a tiny kitchenette with a two-burner gas or electric plate and a few utensils. The charge, of course, was moderate too, something like a dollar or a dollar and a half a night.

It was a lovely trip; though the car suffered from the "chimmies," it gave no further trouble.

We took many pictures of which I still have excellent prints, enjoyed a side trip to the Oregon Caves and another to Crater Lake.

Our journey ended in Sacramento at the State Fair where we met the rest of our family, inspected the exhibits, and reached home that evening—a wonderful week.

With all three in high school in Los Gatos, their circle of acquaintances kept pace with their other activities and beach picnics, and fruit house dances became the order of the day for this younger group.

It is not at all unusual to meet some sedate and apparent stranger who says, "Don't you remember me? I came to dances in your barn with So and So when we were in high school."

With Louise and Vince away at college and World War II taking away so many young people, social affairs like dances and parties were forgotten.

Dick who was at home busy looking after the home ranch and several neighbors' orchards as well, and I, gave our spare time to Red Cross and Civil Defense.

It was at this time that Cecily Fisher, a very dear childhood friend of Louise's, who for the past several years had been fighting a gallant battle against illness, came to make her home with us. She has, all through the ensuing years, by mutual adoption, filled the place of a beloved second daughter in our hearts. She won her battle for good health with flying colors.

In January 1941, Louise married George Cooper, a fine young man she met while attending Cal. The wedding took place in the Federated Church that being the meeting place of the Saratoga Episcopalians just then. A reception for friends and relatives was held in the nearby Foothill Club. It was a rainy day.

George, having been an ROTC man while at college and graduated as a Second Lieutenant, by April of '41 was called to active duty and for the next three years they moved about the eastern states wherever George's orders took them. When the order came that would send him overseas, Louise wrote that she planned to come home by auto and suggested I should come and make the trip with her.

This suggestion met with the family's approval as well as my own, so I went to Dover, Delaware, by train, arriving some days before George was to leave.

The prune orchards on Cox Avenue were in full bloom the morning I left; it was the first of April. The farther east I went, the more wintery it seemed. In Dover, the first daffodils were coming out.

In Chicago, my ticket called for a change of trains from one railroad line to another in a different part of the city. Mr. E. L. Poor had told me this change would give me time to visit Newman Bros., the biggest department store anywhere and to see it was an absolute must for all visiting strangers. On leaving the train, I asked a nearby policeman for directions. He waved his arm and said, "Right there, can't you see that sign?" Sure enough, there was that great big building with its great big sign, not a stone's throw away.

I went into the store, found the up escalator, and made my way to the top, floor by floor, moved to the down side and descended to the street. I had seen Newman Bros. store.

I took the official taxi to the other railroad station to reach the train to Philadelphia. Never before, nor since, have I experienced anything like that taxi ride. Woosh!

In Philadelphia, my ticket called for more than an hour's wait for the train to Dover. Upon asking about the direction in which to go, I was advised to take a local which was just about to start. I followed that bit of advice and reached my destination well ahead of schedule.

I spent several days with my young people in Dover before George's orders took him to Richmond, Virginia. While in Richmond, Louise and I went by train to New York, visited the shopping district where I bought a dress, dark blue with white polka dots, saw the Catholic and Episcopalian Cathedrals, made a short tour along the Hudson, took a quick look at Central Park, and went to the top of the Empire Building. The following day, being Easter Sunday, we joined the people on Fifth Avenue. Because of the war, the Easter parade was not very well attended that year.

I walked in the Civil War Cemetery in Richmond one day, beautifully kept but a sad and depressing place, especially so with the thought of the current war always in mind. Acres and acres of white crosses, many without names, some lettered ten, some fifteen "Union Soldiers," beside them the same numbers and the words "Confederate Soldiers."

We also made a quick and pleasant trip to Washington DC. As it was Sunday, most everything was closed; there was still much of interest to see. Just the buildings and the gardens should be given much more time than we were able to in that one day.

George's orders for Europe were for the following Tuesday. That morning we drove out to the field to bid him goodbye and offer silent prayers for his safe return.

Before starting homeward, we went to Williamsburg, spending several hours there trying to realize what life was like in Colonial days. I bought a handmade pewter egg cup in the Paul Revere shop. By evening, we had started on the long drive home.

We took a somewhat southerly route. I recall views of the Charles River and skirting the city of Memphis, traveling for miles through a state park in West Virginia, off on some distant mountainside glimpsing splashes of white, lone pear trees blooming in some forsaken dooryard.

Traveling by day and staying nights in motels proved a very satisfactory way to go. We made a side trip to Lone Wolf, Oklahoma, to look up a relative, R. H. Garrod, "Oklahoma Dick," who grows cotton and grain on some very flat, dry, sandy soil, a continual battle between himself and wind and weather.

We also had a quick look at the Grand Canyon. My green turquoise ring comes from an Indian shop there. Our road led past Boulder City, and we crossed the dam under escort; because of wartime regulations, no one was allowed to stop on or near the dam. Our way continued for some time along the shore of Lake Mead. With one more night on the road, we reached the Senior Cooper's home late in the evening, having had more difficulties finding the way through Los Angeles and out to Van Nuys than we had all the many miles across the continent.

Another day on the road brought us home, where everything was very much as I had left it. My month's absence had left no noticeable mark.

George flew with the American Forces on D-Day and served in Europe the following year. Shortly after his return, he joined the Aeronautic Research people of Ames Laboratory at Mt. View. They established their home on the ranch and have added a daughter and three sons to the family.

When young Vince finished high school in 1936, he took over the ranch work for the next year and a half until his brother Dick reached the end of his school days and was free to take his turn at farm management.

In the meantime, arrangements had been made for his enrollment as a student in the California Polytechnic College at San Luis Obispo.

I remember calling at the college one day to arrange for his admittance. After showing us the learning facilities as well as the dining room and dormitories and assuring us that there was housing available for any number of boys, the elderly gentleman escorting us remarked in a rather dubious tone of voice, "You must understand that your son must have reasonably good high school grades to be accepted here." I later learned from the mother of one of the teachers, Mr. Howes of Los Gatos, who served on their Admissions Board, that our son entered "Cal Poly" with the highest grade average of any student admitted up to that date.

After two years at Cal Poly, which I believe he thoroughly enjoyed, except for a stay in the hospital recuperating from an emergency appendectomy, he transferred to the University of California at Berkeley where he continued his studies in agricultural Economics.

On May 17, 1941, he married his grammar school sweetheart, Jane Whiteman. They were married in the Saratoga Federated Church with the Rev. John Collins, a former pastor of St. Luke's of Los Gatos, officiating. The church service was followed by a reception in the Whiteman home.

For his last year of college, they returned to Berkeley. As Jane was a Graduate Nurse from the Stanford Hospital in San Francisco, she filled her year in the study of Public Health while Vince completed his agricultural courses.

They had no sooner established themselves in a home near Saratoga and Vince had again taken up the work of managing our own as well as the neighbors' orchards when the draft board put its finger on Dick and sent him off to Fort Benning.

On August 12, 1943, Peter Vince, our first grandson, was born. In the course of time, six brothers and sisters joined him. Christian, the second one, was not meant to meet the trials and troubles of this world. After a few short months, he died leaving us with only a gentle memory of his presence.

The rest of them—Tim, Jan, Victoria, Emma, and Chrissie—are a happy, busy lot. They, with the four Coopers, add up to ten wonderful grandchildren of which we are inordinately proud.

With the passing of time and the supposed to be progress that has been taking place in the State of California, with climbing taxes, endless rules and regulations, and unavoidable insurance, the young people found themselves fighting a losing battle, in casting about for an enterprise that would allow family members to keep their homes and the land we had all worked so hard for. After much thought and consideration, they reached the conclusion that a recreational setup centered on horses was the most logical turn to take.

Now we have horses and more horses of every size, color, and description.

Vince and his family seem satisfied with this venture; it is on their shoulders that the responsibility rests. To be happy in the work that gains one's livelihood is proof of a battle won.

Dick received his high school diploma in June 1938. His school courses had been completed in February, but Los Gatos High had only one graduation ceremony a year and that takes place in June. Richard, Dick for short, is the type of person who enjoys meeting and matching wits with other people, so his contact with the teachers and other students was a continual pleasure to him, although at that time he thought many of the books unnecessary.

Even though Dick was not one of Los Gatos High's best-known bookworms, his four and a half years there were far from wasted. His membership in the very active Biology Club was one of his favorite activities. His out-of-school knowledge of the surrounding country and where and when desired specimens could be found was a welcome asset to the club.

Mrs. Nelson, the biology teacher, said when on biology trips, she always managed to put the Garrod car first, confident that Dick would not lead them into any place they would have trouble getting out of.

When he finished the required courses and was no longer expected to appear in class, he took over the farmwork, making it possible for his brother Vince to enroll as a student in the California State Polytechnic College as San Luis Obispo.

Dick carried on the ranch work with transient help. By 1941, young men were beginning to answer the draft. George Cooper, our son-in-law, had been called to the service because of his ROTC background and Louise had gone East with him. One heard the oft-repeated statement, "The United States of America is not at war," but things began to look awfully suspicious.

Civil Defense and Red Cross groups were being organized as well as others to handle the care, cooking, and distribution of large quantities of food for, if and when they might be needed. In all these gatherings, there was much advice and counter advice, one defeating the other.

I remember listening one evening to a long talk by a leader in the community, a Mr. James Bacigalupi, a San Jose banker. His topic was "Preparedness and Evacuation." If anything like an attack happened, everyone was to be ready to leave instantly. Where to was not made clear, but we were assured there would be leaders standing ready to guide us. All were urged to have their automobiles in shape for long and hard trips, and above all, everyone should have plenty of extra gasoline ready to take with them.

Next morning, the radios and newspapers spread the word that, beginning that day, gasoline would be strictly rationed and asked people before starting out to ask themselves, "Is this trip really necessary?"

The year ran by and nothing had happened until December 7, 1941. That Sunday morning as I was returning from Saratoga, our neighbor, Harry Johnson, a retired Navy officer, called to me from his gateway and told of the bombing of Pearl Harbor, a report which was almost beyond belief but how well we learned its truth.

Soon soldiers from Fort Ord began arriving in Saratoga, sent to this valley, we were told, because Moffet Field would no doubt be the next target; fortunately that did not happen.

The unit with which George Beatty was serving was housed in the Foothill Club House. Others, Phil Oliveri among them, took over Weaver's barn which stood where the Plumed Horse restaurant is now. A third group was located in an abandoned dance hall on the Congress Springs property that was the least livable of the three. Dick was able to improve matters a bit by presenting them with a sort of portable furnace which he made from a fifty-gallon oil barrel. Crude as it was, the men said, "It took the edge off the weather." The soldiers stayed for some weeks, and then they all went away again.

Vince finished his studies at Berkeley the summer of '42 and again took up a share of the ranch work, as we all knew that sooner or later the draft would take Dick.

This was a time of change for us, not only were our children being drawn away from close home ties but in October 1941, our good Ed Jones left us forever after a twenty-four-hour hospitalization. The following April, Grandpa Stolte, who some years earlier had moved himself to the Odd Fellows Home in Saratoga, to have as he put it "smooth pavements under his feet and someone his own age to talk to," fell ill. After three weeks in the infirmary at the home, he passed away in his ninety-fourth year.

Then in July 1942, Henry Pfeffer, the children's favorite uncle, died. He was comparatively young—sixty-eight or nine but had lived for many years with an ailing heart.

It was through Uncle Henry that Dick had become interested in a piece of Skyline property known as the Gamble Place. As a child, it had been Mr. Monroe Richardson's place to me, now it was part of the Gamble Estate, Mr. Gamble having been the Senior Gamble of Procter and Gamble. Dick and I pooled our resources and purchased the fifty-seven acres more or less for $2,500. At this time, we still hold the most available ten acres.

In August 1942, he answered the draft, leaving Los Gatos by bus for Monterey. From there, he was sent east to Camp Taccoa, Georgia, to become a paratrooper. During training, he suffered a serious back injury because of a faulty parachute. After months in hospitals, he was transferred, first to a medical unit and then to Ordinance, finishing his army service in the South Pacific. December 1945 brought the welcome news that he would soon come home. He did arrive in time for Christmas which made me one of the happiest mothers anywhere.

I was thankful to find the years of Army life had made little change in my young son, older of course, but still the same restless and impulsive, yet at the same time, thoughtful and dependable individual he had always been.

Besides helping with the farmwork when needed, he tried his hand at various ventures. Grinding alfalfa into meal in the field, in partnership with Jack Hamilton, was not a success. Construction work as an independent operator was followed by a specialty enterprise traveling around the country with a jeep and a Beskill sprayer exterminating oak moths. This proved quite profitable while the epidemic lasted.

In between times, every available member of the family helped build the house Dick had mentally located on the ranch gravel pit while he was stationed on the Island of Saipan.

Then the opportunity came to work in Sacramento with his father, who for many years had represented the Farmers Insurance Group before the legislature. The idea being that when the time came for R. V.'s retirement, Dick would be prepared to take his place. This plan has worked out beautifully. He has been busy and happy in this work for almost twenty years.

In August 1954, he married Edna May Duddy, a young lady from Indiana. Although they spend most of their time in Sacramento, their real home is here on the ranch, and we are able to keep in close touch. No babies have come to bless or complicate their lives, so they take a generous and vicarious interest in the nieces and nephews from both families.

So much for the new generations. Perhaps they will write their own stories someday for their own grand and great-grandchildren.

How It Was Done

Someone asked me how was cheddar type cheese made at home. "You said your mother used to do it." As in the old-fashioned recipe for rabbit stew, which began with the statement "First catch the rabbit"; to make any kind of cheese, you must first have some cows.

Stoltes had the cows which gave quantities of milk, and one spring, there was the man who knew how. This was "Louie," a Swiss, not long in this country, working at any job he came upon. At the moment, it was cutting oak stovewood for my father. I can still see his happy smile when Mother asked him to teach her how.

The main requirement in cheese making is milk, five or six gallons of it for a four-or five-pound cheese.

Cheese rings were purchased from Mr. Lewis, the Los Gatos tinsmith. These rings were metal bands about five inches wide made into circles perhaps eight inches in diameter; one soldered securely, its mate left free so it might be compressed to fit inside the other to increase the depth while the curd was fresh and moist. The rings were fitted with loose wooden tops and bottoms to fit snugly inside. A large container of six-gallon capacity with a faucet near the bottom was scrubbed and ready for use.

Beside the utensils there was another important item that must be acquired: rennet, the substance which coagulates milk. This came from the fourth stomach of a calf which had lived all its short life on its mother's milk, one that hadn't yet progressed to grass or hay. Rennet, in a very refined state, in liquid or tablet form, can now be purchased at most drug stores. Its source now may be completely artificial; at that time some nice little calf was sacrificed to supply cheese makers with that needed ingredient.

As veal was much used in farm kitchens during spring and early summer, such a one was easy to come by. I remember Louie removing that fourth stomach from the rest of the innards, cleaning it with great care and hanging it up to dry.

The day the cheese was to be made the morning milk was brought to the kitchen and strained into the big container on the back of the stove where a temperature of about 85° could be maintained. The night before a small piece of the rennet had been put to soak in a tea cupful of warm water. This liquid was now added to the milk and the whole well stirred and the container covered. After a half hour or about that, during which breakfast was eaten, the milk would have thickened and now looked like a beautiful white custard. Louie then took a long slender wooden blade which he had whittled for this purpose and cut the curd this way and that forming inch-square columns. Then with his hands, he pushed the curd down very gently causing the whey to separate from the more solid substance. Gradually the whey was drawn off and a ball of soft rubbery white curd was left to be transferred into the cheese rings, set on a firm board or table, a lever and weights arranged so all the remaining whey was pressed out. This took several days. When done, the cheese was removed from the ring, rubbed with salt, wrapped in cheese cloth, and set aside to cure. The curing time varied according to taste.

Schmierkase or cottage cheese was much simpler to make. Always, as the milk came from the barn, it was strained into flat tin pans holding about a gallon and a half each and set on a rack in the milk cellar for the cream to rise for butter. When the weather was warm, the milk would have thickened or curdled of its own accord. "Dicke milch" in German, "Clabber milk" in English. We would roll off the cream and pour the thick milk into a well-washed still wet flour sack, tie the top with a strong string, and hang it in the sun on the clothesline or a handy post. The next day, there was a bowl full of nice sweet curd to be broken up and salt and lots of sweet cream added. Good! Some added caraway seed, others chopped chives or parsley.

In later years I warmed the clabber milk over very low heat till the mass of curd floated in the whey, turned in into a colander to drain, salted and creamed it; the result was the same.

A favorite summer-day luncheon in our house was nice cold clabber milk sprinkled with sugar and crumbled rye bread and eaten with a spoon, accompanied by homemade bread with homemade butter and pink slices of well-smoked home-cured ham.

Sometimes I helped Mother make a great bowl of fresh schmierkase into balls about the size of biscuits, place them on boards, and carry them up to the attic to dry to a firm consistency. When dry enough, the little balls were packed into clean white wood boxes, such as we used to ship cherries to market, the boxes sealed up tight and set aside in a warm dry place to ripen. The end result was a creamy substance whose aroma outlimburgered limburger.

There were those among our neighbors who counted it a privilege to be able to buy an occasional box of Mrs. Stolte's Stinkin Cheese. No one ever persuaded me to taste it.

Cheese and butter, butter and cheese, whichever way you put it, I think butter is the queen of dairy products.

In the long gone days of my youth, the milk was brought from the barn where the cows were fed and milked every morning and evening, strained into the shallow tin pans, set on the rack to cool, and wait for the cream to come up. This took twenty-four hours or longer depending on the temperature, but must not be left too long or the cream became bitter and poor butter resulted.

The cream was skimmed off with a special skimmer, really just a piece of tin shaped to convenience with a pattern of small holes in the center for drainage. The cream was collected in a large crock till there was enough for churning; about four gallons was the limit of our churn's capacity.

The milk that was left went to the farm animals. For the calves, it must be sweet and therefore did not yield quite so much cream, and for the new baby calves, it had to be warmed on the kitchen stove before they would take it.

The pigs, chickens, dogs, and cats enjoyed it sour or sweet, thick or thin.

Cream, to be turned into butter, must be agitated; that is the whole principle of churning. It must be stirred or shaken by some means until the tiny fat particles separate from the buttermilk and cling together until they form lumps of pure butter. These must then be washed in cold water to remove all traces of milk. A short-handled wooden tool with a broad, slightly concave bowl with which to cut and press the butter was used for this and also to work in the salt of which we allowed an ounce to a pound.

This cutting and pressing was called kneading and called for both patience and muscle, very different from kneading a ball of bread dough. The next day, the kneading process was gone through again, for no matter how thoroughly it was done the first time, the next day it would have a mottled or streaked appearance and must be again cut and pressed till an even color was gained and any remaining salt brine pressed out.

To prepare it for market, it was formed into one-or two-pound blocks or two-pound rolls, by pushing it firmly into hinged wooden molds. There were also pound and half-pound molds shaped like upside-down cups with a plunger in the top to push the butter out at the same time forming an ornamental design on the top. This type of mold came in so small a size hostesses made individual servings which were set at each guest's place on tiny china plates known as butter chips.

All these wooden utensils must be very wet before using, else the butter sticks to them.

At first the market butter was wrapped in a flimsy material called butter-cloth. When wax paper was invented, it was a great improvement and is still used by commercial creameries.

As the pastures turned brown in the summertime, butter lost its rich yellow color and looked pretty sad, so we would add a few drops of dandelion extract to cheer it up again.

When I came to Saratoga, the cows were pastured in the orchard where they stood knee deep in bur clover and alfillarie and got chlorophyll wholesale; the butter from their cream was orange color. A Saratoga family which we supplied for a time said it tasted all right, but Mrs. Garrod should learn not to use so much coloring. Now there is no market for homemade butter regardless of how good it may be.

While on the subject of early-day food preparation and preservation, we might as well salt down a winter's supply of green beans and make some sauerkraut.

When the pole beans in the garden are at the peak of the season's production, gather the best: those that are not overripe but have reached full growth. After stringing and stemming, wash well in cold water and with a sharp knife cut them into thin slices with a slanting stroke. Then pack the cut beans firmly into a large crock or small barrel depending on the total quantity desired. When a layer about an inch thick is in place, it must be well salted before the next is added, which can be done from day to day as the beans in the garden mature.

When the desired amount is reached, a close-fitting wooden disk wrapped in a cloth to form a handhold for removal is put in place. This in turn is weighed down with a fair-sized clean, smooth, water-washed rock which had been carried home for this purpose from some nearby stream. After a day or two, the beans and the salt formed their own brine, the best preservative known at that time.

When stored in a cool corner of the cellar, a supply of green beans was assured for all winter. There was just one drawback; they had to be thoroughly freshened in cold water overnight or longer before cooking.

Sauerkraut was another winter standby. This took plenty of fresh, firm cabbages; after discarding the outer leaves, the rest was sliced very fine on a special cabbage board. This was an oblong board about six by eighteen inches with a sharp steel blade set at an angle across the middle. There was a set screw so the thickness of the slices could be controlled. There was a vacant section under the blade, so the cut cabbage would fall into the container on which the board was placed while the section of cabbage head was pushed back and forth on the board.

The method of storing was the same as that used for beans. The finished kraut was never as salty as the beans and needed less, if any freshening.

If you have an olive tree, you can prepare a supply of home-cured olives. In our house, the ripe black ones were preferred.

This recipe came from the Pfeffer family, pioneers in the old Lincoln School District. Their ranch was located at the western end of Prospect Road.

About seven gallons, two well-filled picking pails of olives, is a workable quantity. A wooden container, like a half barrel with an outlet near the bottom over which a bit of screen has been tacked on the inside and a cork on the outside makes it water tight, is needed.

Fill the half barrel half full of cold water, put in a pound (one can) of Babbit's lye. When the lye is dissolved, add the olives and let them stand in a shaded place for three days. It is well to stir them gently night and morning with a smooth round stick like a broom handle, so as to be sure they are all exposed to the lye solution.

After three days' draw off the lye, discard it, wash the olives thoroughly by letting water from a hose run over them till it comes away clear, replace cork, and cover with water. Repeat washing every day. On the third day, add a cupful of salt and a tablespoonful of alum, lump or powdered, to the covering water.

By the fourth day, the olives are ready to be put in jars or crocks and covered with salt brine, the kind strong enough to float an egg.

These olives should not be kept too long. They are best to enjoy and share while fresh with the texture crisp and the flavor nut like. They should be freshened in cold water a short time to remove the salt brine before serving.

ODDS AND ENDS

Everyone's memory stores up fragments of things read or heard repeated by others of no great cultural value but nice to recall now and then to bring back times, people, and places long gone. I will set down a few that seem to come first to my mind.

The child's "Christmas Hymn," sung to the accompaniment of Great Grampa Stolte's accordion.

Otannen baum, Otannen baum,
Wie grum sind deine blatter.
Du grunst nicht nur in sommer zeit
Nein auch im winter wenn es schneidt.

A LOVE SONG

Du, Du, liegst mir in herzen
Du, Du, liegst mir in sinn
Du, Du, machts mir viel schmerzen
Weist micht wie gut ich dir bin.
  Ja, Ja, Ja, Ja weist nicht wie gut ich dir bin.

AN OLD GERMAN NONSENSE SONG

Ich bin der Doctor Eisenbart
    Quidder, widder wit wat bum
Kurier die Leut auf meiner art
    Quidder, widder wit wat bum
Kann machen das die blinden gehen
    Und die lahmen wieder sehen
    Quidder, widder wit yuch heiresah
    Quidder, widder wit wat bum.

From my early school days, when Miss Sobey, an English lady, presided over Central, I, a mature seventh grader of eleven, was often detailed to rehearse the lower grades in the following songs with motions.

THE DAISIES

The daisies white are nursery maids
With frills upon their caps
And daisy buds are little babes
They tend upon their laps.

    Sing Heigh-ho while the wind sweeps low
    Wind sweeps low, wind sweeps low
    And nurses and babies are nodding just so.

The daisy babies never cry
The nurses never scold
They never crush the dainty frills
About their cheeks of gold

    Prim and white in the gay sunlight
    Gay sunlight, gay sunlight
    They are nid nodding, Oh beautiful sight.

STARS AND ANGELS

When the little children sleep
Little stars are waking
Angels bright from heaven come
And till morn is breaking
They will watch the live long night
By their beds till morning light
When the little children sleep
Stars and angels watch do keep.

THE BIRDIES BALL which in later years
I learned my husband had sung as a boy in England.

Spring once said to the nightingale
I mean to give you birds a ball
Pray Madam ask the birdies all
All the birdies great and small

(Chorus)

Tral lal lal a lal, tral lal lal a lal.
Tral lal lal a lal, lal la.

The woodpecker came from his hole in a tree
And brought the wren to the company
The cherries ripe and the berries red
A very good spread for the birds, he said.

(Chorus)

Besides these really childish songs, there were the war songs, "Marching through Georgia," "Tramp, Tramp, Tramp, Columbia the Gem of the Ocean," and school always began the day with a full-throated rendering of America.

From my second grade year comes the memory of this sad ballad.

Under the Willow She's Sleeping

Under the willow she's laid with care
Sang a lone mother while weeping
Under the willow with golden hair
My little one's quietly sleeping.

(Chorus)

Fair, fair and golden hair
Sang a lone mother while weeping
Fair, fair and golden hair
Under the willow she's sleeping.

Under the willow no songs are heard
Near where my darling lies dreaming
Naught but the voice of some far off bird
Where life and its pleasures are beaming.

(Chorus)

Under the willow by night and day
Sorrowing ever I ponder
Free from its shadowy, gloomy ray
Oh never again can she wander.

(Chorus)

Under the willow I breathe a prayer
Longing to linger forever
Near to my angel with golden hair
In lands where there is sorrowing never.

(Chorus)

It seemed a strange choice to teach to five-and six-year-olds, but we sang it joyfully quite unaware that it was the story of a mother mourning for her dead child. Our eighteen-year-old teacher must have liked it.

For something more cheerful, here is an echo from the cutting shed introduced by Sally Noyer, designed to keep the cutters awake and their fingers moving. No music, just try to repeat it.

Theophilous Thistle

Theophilous Thistle the successful thistle sifter
While sifting a sieveful of unsifted thistles
Thrust three thousand thistles through the thick
                              of his thumb.

Now if Theophilous Thistle the successful thistle
                              sifter
Thrust three thousand thistles through the thick
                              of his thumb

While sifting a sieveful of unsifted thistles
See that thou the unsuccessful thistle sifter
Thrust not three thousand thistles through the thick
                    of thy thumb
While sifting a sieveful of unsifted thistles.

Here is success to the successful thistle sifter
Who can sift a sieveful of unsifted thistles
Without thrusting three thousand thistles
Through the thick of his thumb.

Then there was this party gimmick of about 1,900 brought to us by
Harriet B. Bailey.

Seat guests in a circle. Leader speaks first line to person at his or her
right. This is passed from one to another around the circle. Leader then
gives first and second sentence. Continue adding one more sentence each
time till all have been attempted, noisy and fun.

One old ox opening oysters
Two toads trying to trot to Tidbury
Three tame tigers taking tea
Four fat friars fanning fainting fleas
Five Frenchmen fricasseeing frogs
Six sorry sinners sobbing softly
Seven Severn salmon slowly swallowing shrimps
Eight educated Englishmen eating eggs
Nine nimble Noblemen nibbling nonparrell
Ten tall tailors twisting thread.

This last one was sent me by John of Gaunt, a friend of Grandmother
S. A. Garrod's, after observing my daily schedule for a week.

A Busy Woman's Wish

I wish I was a rock
A-sitting on a hill
A-doing nothing all day long
But just a sitting still
I wouldn't sleep

I wouldn't eat
I wouldn't even wash
I'd just sit there a thousand years
And rest myself, By gosh.

        (Sometimes I felt like that.)

And this one, which Ed Jones taught Dick when that small boy first learned to talk.

I've got no wife to bother my life
No lover to prove untrue
But all day long with a laugh and a song
I paddle my own canoe.

THINGS

Among my keepsakes is a dull black pendant on a silver colored chain, which was originally a brooch. Whether it was a courtship gift to my mother from Father or whether it was a family treasure that she brought with her when, as a girl of seventeen, she came to America to make her own way in the world, I do not know.

My knowledge of it came because Father sometimes spoke of its fine workmanship and seemed to regret its loss in their first year on the ranch in the Santa Cruz Mountains, so very much.

At that time, there was a narrow pathway along the brush-covered crest of the ridge east of the house. It was on this path that the brooch was lost, probably snatched from her dress by some dry twig as she passed along.

As more of the land was cleared and planted, this ridge too was brought under cultivation being planted to Sauvignon grapes. Year after year, this ground was plowed and cultivated; briars, ferns, and other weeds were hoed out and burned.

This routine continued for almost thirty years. When the place was sold to Henry Pfeffer, he continued the same program, and more years passed. Every spring, this ground was thoroughly stirred up and smoothed down again, until, on one of our frequent Sunday visits, Vince and Henry, farmer fashion, walked out to see how the crops were coming. While strolling along that ridge where years before that path had been, Henry picked up what he thought was a small rock, intending to throw it at a marauding jay. The unusual feel of the thing caused him to give it a second look. He decided it was an ornament off an old-fashioned picture frame.

Later Henry showed it to me, asking what I thought it might be. I recognized it at once from Father's description, and Henry promptly said it was mine to keep.

I scrubbed it with soapy water and an old toothbrush and found that every detail of the dainty ornamentation on its face showing a nesting bird and a second bird perched on a nearby flowering twig was in perfect condition. Its thirty odd years among the sand and rocks of the mountain vineyard had not harmed it in the least.

I had a jeweler attach a small silver loop and wear it occasionally as a necklace. The black substance from which it is fashioned, I was surprised to learn, is hard black rubber such as combs used to be made of.

That narrow path or trail along the ridge, according to a neighbor, Edwin Richardson, who had come into the mountains right after the Civil War, had been made and traveled by the Spanish Padres. In proof of that statement, when I was just a little girl, I found there the rowel of a spur, no doubt hand made by some long-forgotten blacksmith and probably lost by some priest as he passed that way on his slow-going mule.

It had only five points each at least an inch and a half long and badly rusted, of course. My father knew the value of such a find but saw no reason for a little girl to collect such items, so he gave it to a friend who also knew its value.

There was also a soap stone sinker, which grown-ups thought had been shaped by some Indian either going to or coming from the ocean on one of their yearly fishing expeditions. I had found this sinker one day when I was supposed to be picking prunes. It went right along with the rowel from the Spanish spur.

Rain Record

RAINFALL RECORD—JULY 1, 1935, TO JUNE 30, 1969, MT. EDEN ROAD

Year	July	Aug.	Sept.	Oct.	Nov.	Dec.	Jan.	Feb.	Mar.	Apr.	May	June	Total
35-36	.52	.01	1.09	.58	2.12	4.09	10.40	1.42	2.53	.67	.07		23.50
36-37	.25		.88		4.62	5.62	6.80	8.70	.72		.45		28.22
37-38			.62	2.41	8.20	5.59	15.12	7.72	1.13				40.79
38-39			1.53	1.96	.83	3.73	2.88	4.30	.10	.52			15.85
39-40		.44	.25	.58	1.82	11.74	13.37	4.15		.49	.34		33.18
40-41		.46	.09	.40	12.29	8.11	9.35	7.34	4.16				42.20
41-42			.93	.31	9.45	8.29	3.23	3.60	7.15	1.57			34.53
42-43		.15	.55	3.40	2.43	10.41	2.31	2.91	.78				22.94
43-44			.86	1.57	4.36	8.42	2.48	1.95	.81				20.45
44-45			1.92	4.48	1.20	.28	7.97	2.76					18.61
45-46			4.52	2.92	10.86	.31	3.03						21.64
46-47			1.40	3.15	1.05	2.19	4.43	.34	.42		.21		13.19
47-48			2.07	.92	1.84	Gauge Out of Order, P. M. Pike Total							26.09
48-49			.27			6.66	1.18	4.11	10.85		.17		23.24
49-50			.07	2.53	2.34	9.06	3.57	1.50	.25	.25			19.57
50-51			5.63	7.89	7.28		3.34	2.22	2.23	.97	1.86		31.42
51-52			1.35	2.85	11.54	18.61	2.57	9.34	.99				47.25
52-53			3.37	13.78	3.82		4.00	1.82	.49		.07		27.35
53-54		.04	.16	3.28	.81	3.59	4.65	5.84	1.36				19.73
54-55			3.99	5.76	5.44	2.98	.09	2.87	.70				21.83
55-56			2.50	22.60	7.13	5.34	.28	2.67	.85				41.37
56-57		.41	1.43		.77	4.42	6.01	1.57	2.27	2.56	.07		19.51

Year													Total
57-58			.35	1.79	.80	5.86	6.41	13.56	10.80	9.14	.50	.13	49.34
58-59					.31	1.23	8.15	9.95	.60		.03		20.27
59-60			2.87			.95	6.58	5.05	.98	1.90	.46		18.79
60-61				.07	4.59	2.84	1.84	1.17	2.99	1.30	.49	.15	15.44
61-62		.20	.21	.17	4.07	3.70	1.81	12.84	4.79	.14			27.93
62-63				10.79	.35	3.15	6.50	6.71	5.56	4.63	.86		38.55
63-64			.33	1.64	4.80	.18	5.04	.18	2.99	.22	.73	.61	16.72
64-65		.22		1.28	6.89	9.99	6.13	1.11	2.10	5.19			32.91
65-66		.11			7.91	5.51		1.90	2.73	.39	.59	.09	19.23
66-67	.33	.03	.04		6.84	5.37	11.26	.51	9.48	6.86	.15	.41	41.28
67-68				.30	1.61	3.48	9.06	3.51	3.59	1.31	.26		23.12
68-69		.18		.68	1.98	5.60	16.07	13.74	2.13	2.64			43.02
													956.15

Total for thirty-four years: 956.15 inches
Yearly average: 28.122 inches

OUR GOLDEN WEDDING

As the years slipped by, we often did some special thing to mark the anniversary of our wedding day, perhaps a one-day trip somewhere, like up to Mt. Hamilton and over the top to Livermore and home by way of the valley. Once it was a trip to the Pinnacles in San Benito County with a climb to the top of the ridge to have a look at the Salinas Valley from there.

Some years it was just one of the many neighborhood get-togethers that everyone enjoyed, a picnic by day or a dance in the fruit house at night. Sometimes it slipped by completely unnoticed.

Time flowed on—ten, twenty, forty years. The babies grew up, became boys and girls, young adults, married, and established their own homes; and the grandchildren took their places in the family.

Suddenly, we found that we were growing old—a fact we had always managed to ignore. We had, of course, long since found it very satisfactory to let the younger members take over the responsibilities of the ranch and the family. Gradually every task we undertook was bigger and took more time and energy to accomplish than it used to. The hills somehow grew steeper and the pathways longer, but we weren't growing old, Oh no . . .

When the young people began to talk about celebrating Gramp and Gramma's Golden Wedding, we had to admit, "time was catching up."

I was reminded of my old neighbor, Mrs. Van Lone, who for several years before the big day would say, "our Golden Wedding will be on such a day. If we are still alive, I want you to come. My boys are going to give us a party." The dear old lady lived to enjoy her party and a number of years thereafter. I figured we could do it too.

R. V. gave the final go-ahead when he said he would take care of the actual money expense but someone else would have to do all the work.

The right date is April 30. In 1966, it fell on Saturday, so we set Sunday, May 1, for the party.

The first step was to let friends know about it by letter, phone, or word of mouth. A family such as ours can pass out a lot of news when they put their minds to the task; even then there were a few valued friends who were overlooked for which we were all sorry.

There was only one place on the ranch for such an event—the apricot cutting shed and its surroundings. During the last days of April, preparations really took shape. To use an army term, the whole area was thoroughly policed.

Parking lots were put in order, and tables fashioned from fruit boxes and trays were set up in the shed and under the shady oak trees. To be sure of comfortable seating, hundreds of chairs were borrowed from the Masson Winery. For a more festive appearance, a truckload of fir boughs was brought from the Skyline place. These were tied and tacked in place till the old cutting shed looked like a woodland glade.

One spot, where the honored couple were supposed to stand and greet their guests, was especially dressed with golden ribbons and orchids, but the honored couple failed to stay put, so the special spot was given to the wedding cake.

John Maridon, a friend who sometimes catered barbecues for his church or lodge, was persuaded to take over for the day. He and his wife and their helpers came early and stayed late. From two till after five o'clock, steak and beans, salad and french bread were in constant supply, supplemented by punch and coffee dispensed by Mrs. Dorothy Yonge, and of course, wedding cake.

Sunday dawned clear and beautiful. The whole day was perfect, not too hot, not too cold, no wind to blow dust about or upset things, just right.

Our guests began to arrive shortly after midday. It was wonderful to greet so many friends, young and old, from near and far.

Ninety-one-year-old John Felix came from Napa and tiny Andrea Ottaway from next door. Some flew from Los Angeles and many came by auto from San Francisco, Sacramento, and other California cities and towns. There were nearby neighbors and some of my old home neighbors from the mountains. As a conservative estimate of the number present, it set the total at a thousand. It is impossible to name them all, but truly gratifying to know so many wished us well.

A small number of those present on our wedding day were with us, among them my sister, Mrs. Josephine Beatty and her sons Will and Joe, Mrs. Mabel Creffield Klindt, my sister-in-law, Mrs. Mary Garrod Pfeffer and her daughter Rosemary Pfeffer Hogg, Mrs. Rosalie Pfeffer, and Mrs. Maud Pfeffer Morton.

We had asked that no gifts be brought. Nevertheless, some beautiful selections of gold-trimmed glass and lovely silver arrived from friends unable to be with us in person. Flowers, cut, and growing plants came in abundance including fifty cymbidium orchids, one for each year, all in one box.

Due to Vince's many years of acquaintanceship with the members of the state Legislature, we were surprised with congratulatory resolutions from both the Senate and the Assembly, and through the good offices of former Senator Ed Gaffney of San Francisco, a Papal Blessing from the Vatican.

One group of friends decided that since gifts were taboo, they would gather a fund to be donated to my favorite organization. Consequently the sum of four hundred and fifty dollars was added to the treasury of the Saratoga Historical Foundation.

To keep the memory of the day clear, I have an album of photographs of the candid variety which gives a very complete story of the day. This book and the eight by ten prints were put together for us by Ken Wilhelm; the smaller pictures taken by others, I added later. There were many cameras in evidence that day.

The Hoof Printers, a drill team of girls and horses, entertained our guests with a well-executed performance.

Yes, it was a wonderful day. Old friends met who had been out of touch for years and strangers looked about and found they weren't strangers after all.

As one sweet lady, who I am sure could lecture on proper social procedure, remarked, "We went intending to pay our respects, stay the usual fifteen minutes, and be on our way. However, we found everyone else enjoying a pleasant afternoon with congenial company, so we just sat down and did the same."

One wonderful, never-to-be-forgotten day.

1966   *R. V. G.*

That New House

THE END

The third reader of my long-gone school days said something like, "Life is a river, from its small and unimportant beginning it flows steadily onward. It may hesitate, but never stop until early or late its end is reached."

By anyone's calculations, the river of my life has been a long and, on the whole, a very placid one. No treacherous rapids or impassable falls have ever disturbed its steady flow.

I have filled many pages with recollections of what to some may seem a very humdrum and uneventful life. Aren't most lives just that except to the individuals who have lived them?

This self-appointed task has been a very pleasant one. I trust that someone sometime in the future will find pleasure and perhaps a bit of knowledge hidden in these pages.

It is said that "three score years and ten" is one's allotment for life; beyond that, one lives on borrowed time. It has never been clear to me just where and from whom this time is borrowed. I must say, the last decade and a half that I have borrowed from somewhere have been most satisfactory. I most sincerely hope that my credit will hold good awhile longer.

ESG

One Life, Mine

Emma S. Garrod

INDEX

C

California Agriculturist, The (Herring), 125
California Cooperative and Educational Union, 269
California Farmer, 125
California Farmers Inc., 241, 247
California Polytechnic College, 240, 294, 341
California Prune and Apricot Association, 237, 269
Campbell, Mr., 138, 328
Campbell, William, 328
camping trip, 91
"Canadian Boat Song," 65
Canadian Building, 194
canned music. See Edison phonograph
Cardew, Mrs., 84
"Cargo of the Yellow Bus" (Poor), 301
Carl (second son), 9, 29
Carl Emersleben, 29
Carmichael family, 127
Casanova, Jean, 229
Casanova, Kelly, 254
Case, Ethel, 178
Case, Luella, 125
Castle Rock School, 36, 56, 118-19, 125, 130
Cendijos, Pas, 284
Cendijos family, 251
Central School, 36, 44, 66, 81, 110, 295
Charlie (a bird), 317
Charlotte Johanna (sister of Emma Garrod). See Stolte, Charlotte Johanna
Chassler, 41
Chilcote, Bill, 25
Chinaman, The, 54

Chinatown, 49, 145, 155
Chittenden, Mr., 89
Christian Endeavor Society, 80
Christmas, 83
"Christmas Hymn," 351
Civil Defense, 339
Clark, Jean, 279
Cliff House. See Tip Top
Clump, Mr., 186
Cogswell College, 97
College of Notre Dame, 235
Collins, John, 342
Colorado River, 321-22
Columbus Day, 56
"Come All Ye Faithful," 99
Congregational Church, 234, 296
Connolly, Ida, 99
Connolly, Mary, 99
Conway, Frank, 230
Cooper, George, 219, 266, 308, 312, 339, 343
Cooper, James Fennimore, 47
Leatherstocking Tales, 47
Cora (mare), 17
cordwood, 28-29, 32, 58, 74, 77, 99, 182
Corinthian Antique Studio, 235
Cornnet, Mrs., 226
Corpstein, Joe, 233
Costanoans, 327
Cox, Ivan, 226
Crazy Pete. See O'Shaunessey, Peter
Creffield, Ralph, 200, 210, 213
Cunningham, Florence, 177, 324, 326
Saratoga's First One Hundred Years, 326
Cupertino de Oro Club, 315
Cushing, Ed, 73, 131
Cushing, Harry, 110
Cushing, Mrs., 107

Los Gatos Lodge of Odd Fellows, 114
Los Gatos Memorial Park, 131
Los Gatos Primary School, 52
Lotte (child of Eugene), 9
Lotti family, 25
Louis (child of Eugene), 9-10, 12-13,
 193, 230-31, 248, 318
Louis (third son), 9-10, 12-13, 193,
 230-31, 248, 318
"Love Song, A," 351
Lymbery, Bess, 194
Lymbery, Charles, 140
Lyndon Gulch, 84-85, 96, 136
Lyndon Hotel, 52, 68

M

Madrones, 34
mail route, 136
Majors (ran the Ten-mile House),
 86-87
Mallot boys, 75
Mallot family, 25
Mallot girls, 75
Malloy, Mr., 51
Malone, John, 172
Malone family, 231
Manners, Sylman, 284
"Marching Through Georgia," 65
Marcum, Ms. *See* Brown, Mrs.
Maridon, John, 362
Martin, Emma, 107
Martin, Etta, 80
Martin, Isabel, 178
Martin, James, 79-80
Martin, James, Jr., 80
Martin, Mrs., 80
Martin, Tom, 80
Mason, Robert, 324

Matereau, 41
Mattie (mare), 17
"Maude Miller," 98
Mavio, Isabel Priest (Mrs. Richard
 Marquez), 300
May (cow), 59
Maynard, Harry, 324
McAullif, Constance, 173
McCarty, Martin, 328
McConalogue, Billy, 149
McConalogue, Dolly, 149
McConalogue, Fanny, 149
McConalogue, Madeline, 149
McConalogue, Rose, 149
McConologue, Fanny, 188, 190
McDonald, Margret, 153
McElroy and Magner, 49
McGee, Billy, 116
McGillicuddy, Margaret, 172
McGuire family, 231
McHenry, Don, 226, 324
McIntyre, Archie, 85-86
McKinley, William, 211
McLellan, Louise, 225
McLellan, Mrs., 225
McLoughlin, Steve, 194
Merriam, Governor, 239
Methodist Church, 235
Metzger, Artus, 233
Miller, Isidore, 187
Millie Plagemann (Mrs. Fred
 Dohrmann), 161
Miner, Tina, 324
Mini, Joe, 37, 94
Mini, John, 37
Mini, Johnnie, 25, 66
Mini, Joseph, 25, 68
Mini, Mr., 66
Mini family, 25, 42, 66